# *Disability Rights and Law in India*

# *Disability Rights and Law in India*

Maheshwar Singh

Rashtriya Raksha Prakashan
U.P., India

ISBN : 978-81-87393-45-0

First Published in 2016

Reprint 2023



*Published by*
**Rashtriya Raksha Prakashan**
26, G.F. Jaipuria Enclave,
Kaushambi, Ghaziabad-201010
Uttar Pradesh, India
Ph. : 9599720210

*Typesetting—Gaurav Graphices, Delhi-110094*
*E-mail: gauravsingh1908@gmail.com*
*Printed at: Avantika Printers Private Limited.*

# Contents

# Acknowledgements

Towards the completion of this work I am indebted to the direct and indirect support many individuals. I also gratefully acknowledge the Library staff of National Law University, Delhi for their support. Special thanks are also due to Akhil Sharma at Adroit Publishers to have carried out the publication impeccably.

I am indebted to the support, encouragement to work on the issue of disability by my friends. Important among them are Tiken, Bunty, Richa, Amitabh, Yamini, Amrita and Raghwesh. My gratitude is also due to Ranjana jee as a constant source of support. I am thankful to my sister Kumud and brother-in-law, Sri Sunil Kumar Singh as a pillar of strength in my life. Lastly, I remain thankful to my wife, Kadambini, who has been a source of strength at every step of the way.

**Maheshwar Singh**

Delhi Nov. 2016

# Foreword

Disability studies have been an important teaching and research programme in almost noted all the westem universities. They have produced a large volume of knowledge fund on both the theoretical and empirical aspects of disability. ti is one of such research programme which has transcended the disciplinary boundaries in human sciences. In fact, it is at once present everywhere.

Notwithstanding the independent efforts within and beyond the formal academic structure of the universities, disability studies does not get either its share of importance or attention by the Indian academia at large' one firm indicator of this apathy or ignorance is the paucity of literature on the subject. However, in about last two decades disability induced discrimination has drawn the concern of academics, govefilment and NGos. Now, some of the prominent Indian universities have formally begun the teaching and research programme in disability studies. National Law university Delhi has a Research 'Centre for Studies in Disability and Law'.

In recent years, this human rights model of disability has gradually been adopted by the intemational community. This model recognizes the inherent equaiity of all people, regardless of disabilities or differences. It also recognizes society's obligation to support the freedom and equality of all individuals, including those who may need appropriate social supports.

The convention on Rights of People with Disability (CRPD) - the most recent and the most extensive recognition of the human rights of persons with disabilities - outlines the civil, cultural, political, social, and economic rights of persons with disabilities. Its purpose is to "promote, protect, and ensure the full and equal enjoyment of all human rights and fundamental freedoms by people with disabilities and to promote respect for their inherent dignity". India is a signatory to the CRPD but yet to pass conformity legislation. Many attempts have been made but we are yet to get this legislation cleared.

I am pleased to write the foreword for the book titled "Disability Rights and Law in India," by Dr. Maheshwar Singh. The work is very topical and relevant as it is an eamest attempt to analyse the contribution of Indian judiciary (Supreme Court and high courts) and two euasi Judicial bodies namely the Chief commissioner for Persons with Disabilities (CCPD) and National Human Rights commission NHRC) in the development of Equality Rights Jurisprudence for Persons with Disabilities, since these institutions especially the Supreme Court has been very active in upholding the human rights enshrined in the constitution and various human rights treaties. Since its inception, the CCPD has been the most favoured forum for persons with disabilities in case of the violation or non-availability of the rights guaranteed in the Persons with Disabilities (Equal opportunities, protection of Rights and Full Participation) Act (PWD Act), 1995. Although, the powers of CCPD are not as wide as that of the constitutional courts (supreme court and High courts), it has liberally interpreted the provisions of the PWD act and offered relief in favour of persons with disabilities. India has ratified the UN convention on the Rights of Persons with Disabilities (UNCRPD). convention This mandates to ensure all the rights to persons with disabilities on an equal basis with the rest of the society, and the book has looked at judgments, orders etc of the abovementioned bodies in order to have a clear picture as to what extent disability rights have been upheld by the judicial and quasi judicial bodies in India.

This book is an important contribution in the existing source material on disability in India. It will be useful for academics, policy makers and others working in the disability sector.

I extend my best wishes to the author for bringing out such a scholarly publication.

November 9, 2016

**Prof. (Dr.) Ranbir Singh**
Vice Chancellor,
National Law University Delhi

---

(A University of Law Established in 2008 by Act No. I of 2008 of Delhi)
Sector - 14, Dwarka, New Delhi - 110 078, Phone: 011 2803 4253
Email: ranbirsingh2107@gmail.com, vc@nludelhi.ac.in,
Website: http://nludelhi.ac.in

# Acronyms

| | |
|---|---|
| ADL | Activities of Daily Living |
| AIR | All India Reporter |
| ANM | Auxiliary Nurse-midwives |
| AP | Andhra Pradesh |
| CAPART | Council for the Advancement of People's Action in Rural Technology CBR Community Based Rehabilitation |
| CDC | Centers for Disease Control |
| CPWD | Commissioner for Persons with Disabilities |
| CSN | Children with Special Needs |
| CWD | Children with Disabilities |
| DALYs | Disability-adjusted Life Years |
| DC | Defined Contribution |
| DIET | District Institute for Education Training |
| DISE | District Information System for Education |
| DMHP | District Mental Health Programme |
| DPEP | District Primary Education Programme |
| DPO | Disabled Persons Organization |
| DDRC | District Disability Rehabilitation Center |
| EPFO | Employees' Provident Fund Organization |
| EPS | Employees' Pension Scheme |
| FICCI | Federation of Indian Chambers of Commerce and Industry |
| GoI | Government of India |
| IADL | Instrumental Activities of Daily Living |
| IAY | Indira Avaz Yogana ICDS Integrated Child Development Services |
| ICIDH | International Classification of Impairments, Disability and Handicaps |
| IDD | Iodine Deficiency Disorders |
| IED | Integrated Education of the Disabled |
| IEDC | Integrated Education of Disabled Children J&K Jammu and Kashmir |
| LIC | Life Insurance Corporation of India MDG Millennium Development Goal |

| | |
|---|---|
| MDT | Multi Drug Therapy |
| MHRD | Ministry of Human Resource Development |
| MI | Mental Illness |
| MP | Madhya Pradesh MR Mental Retardation |
| MSJE | Ministry of Social Justice and Empowerment |
| MSS | Mahila Swasthya Sanghas |
| MTA | Mother Teacher Association |
| NCPEDP | National Centre for Promotion of Employment for Disabled People NFCP National Filaria Control Program |
| NFHS | National Family Health Survey NGO Non Government Organization |
| NHFDC | National Handicapped Finance and Development Corporation |
| NIACL | New India Assurance Company Limited |
| NLEP | National Leprosy Eradication Programme |
| NPS | New Pension Scheme |
| NREGS | National Rural Employment Guarantee Scheme |
| NSS | National Sample Survey NSSO National Sample Survey Office |
| NTD | Neural Tube Defects OBC Other Backward Class PC Planning Commission |
| PHC | Primary Health Centers |
| POA | Plan of Action |
| PPI | Pulse Polio Immunization campaign |
| PRI | Panchayati Raj Institution |
| PTA | Parent Teacher Association |
| PWD | Persons with Disabilities |
| RCH | Reproductive and Child Health |
| RCI | Rehabilitation Council of India |
| RRTC | Regional Rehabilitation Training Centers |
| SC | Scheduled Caste |
| SCA | State Channelizing Agency |
| SCC | Supreme Court Cases |
| SCERT | State Council of Education Research and Training |
| SGRY | Sampoorna Grameen Rozgar Yojana |
| SGSY | Swaranjayanti Gram Swarozgar Yojana |
| SHG | Self Help Groups SSA Sarva Shiksha Abhiyan |
| ST | Scheduled Tribe |
| TBA | Traditional Birth Attendants |
| TN | Tamil Nadu |
| UP | Uttar Pradesh |
| VEC | Village Education Committee |
| VRC | Vocational Rehabilitation Centre |
| W&CD | Women and Child Development |
| WHO | World Health Organization |
| WWD | Women with Disabilities |

# 1

# Introduction

While estimates vary, there is growing evidence that people with disabilities comprise between 5 and 8 percent of the Indian population (around 55-90 million individuals). This work explores the social and economic situation of this sizeable group. Though, landmark legislation promoting the rights of persons with disabilities to full participation in Indian society has made rapid strides in mainstreaming disability yet, the policy commitments of governments in a number of areas remain in large part unfulfilled. To some extent this was inevitable, given the ambition of commitments made, existing institutional capacity, and entrenched societal attitudes to disabled people in India. However, it also reflects a relative neglect of people with disabilities through weak institutions and poor accountability mechanisms, lack of awareness among providers, communities and PWD of their rights, and failure to involve the non-governmental sector more intensively.

Disability is a complex category as it has been and still is understood and interpreted by different people in very different ways. In almost all societies, individuals with physical or intellectual anomalies have been assumed to be, by the very nature of their condition, inferior. As the term disability carries with it the connotation of a lack or deficiency, whether mental, physical or sensory, it has been defined primarily in terms of medical deficit. However, it has to be acknowledged that the word disability is itself not a homogeneous category, subsuming under it different kinds of bodily variations, physical impairments, sensory deficits and mental or learning inadequacies, which may be either congenital or acquired. Disability has been recognised as a human rights issue in the international arena, with the United Nations Declaration on the Rights of the Disabled Persons focusing attention on the needs of disabled people globally.

## Social Attitudes towards Disability in India

Attitudes of society, families and PWD themselves contribute to converting impairments into disabilities. Research in India has consistently found substantial social marginalization of people with disabilities. The attitudes of specific societies are critical in assessing both the intensity of disability (i.e., how disabling a given type or level of impairment becomes for the individual disabled person) and in assessing areas where collective action is likely to fail the disabled community, and hence public action be desirable. In addition to the attitudes of the general society, the attitudes of persons with disabilities and their families are important, in some ways even more important. At the same time, the different sets of attitudes clearly interact, so that negative views about disabled people in the broader community are likely to be internalized in many cases by people with disabilities and their household members.

Much of the literature on disability in India has pointed to the importance of the concept of karma in attitudes to disability, with disability perceived either as punishment for misdeeds in the past lives of the PWD, or the wrongdoings of their parents. At a more mundane level, people with disabilities are traditionally perceived as somehow inauspicious. Much qualitative research has found considerable social marginalization of people with disabilities in India, though most also acknowledge that the social status of the PWD's family has an impact on their potential acceptance in society. The negative attitude of the able-bodied members of the family and in the community is greatest obstacles towards full participation and equalisation of opportunity.

For a disabled person, segregation, marginalisation and discrimination are norms rather than exception. Faced with barriers put by stereotyped attitudes, they are generally viewed as objects of charity and welfare as the world merrily goes about trampling their most basic human rights. Sadly, this is so despite the United Nations Declaration of Human Rights in 1948 that makes observance of human rights a precondition in 1992, India became a signatory to the Proclamation on Full

Participation and Equality of People with Disabilities in the Asian and Pacific Region. This was adopted at Beijing at a conference convened by the Economic and Social Commission for Asian and Pacific Region. The proclamation brought an obligation upon the country to enact a law as per its solemn affirmations. And so the Persons with Disabilities (Equal Opportunities, Protection of Rights and Full Participation) Act of 1995 got through Parliament. Amongst the four domestic legislations related to disability it is this Act that provides entitlements of rights to persons with disabilities and mandates the government to provide facilities for their full participation. The provisions under the Act are all very empowering but unfortunately, even though the Act was passed almost 19 years ago, its implementation remains woefully inadequate. Those responsible for its implementation and several persons with disabilities often remain unaware of the provisions of the Act.

Most importantly, PWD themselves remain largely outside the policy and implementation framework, at best clients rather than active participants in development. There is also evidence in key areas like employment that disabled people are falling further behind the rest of the population, risking deepening their already significant poverty and social marginalization. The slow progress in expanding opportunities for disabled people in India results in substantial losses to people with disabilities themselves, and to society and the economy at large in terms of under-developed human capital, loss of output from productive disabled people, and impacts on households and communities.

## Disability Rights are Human Rights

In recent years, this human rights model of disability has gradually been adopted by the international community. This model recognizes the inherent equality of all people, regardless of disabilities or differences. It also recognizes society's obligation to support the freedom and equality of all individuals, including those who may need appropriate social supports.

## Disability and Human Rights

### Disability is a Human Rights Issue Because

- People with disabilities experience inequalities – for example, when they are denied equal access to health care, employment, education, or political participation because of their disability.

- People with disabilities are subject to violations of dignity – for example, when they are subjected to violence, abuse, prejudice, or disrespect because of their disability.
- Some people with disability are denied autonomy – for example, when they are subjected to involuntary sterilization, or when they are confined in institutions against their will, or when they are regarded as legally incompetent because of their disability.

A range of international documents have highlighted that disability is a human rights issue, including the World Programme of Action Concerning Disabled People (1982), the Convention on the Rights of the Child (1989), and the Standard Rules on the Equalisation of Opportunities for People with Disabilities (1993). More than 40 nations adopted disability discrimination legislation during the 1990s. The CRPD – the most recent and the most extensive recognition of the human rights of persons with disabilities – outlines the civil, cultural, political, social, and economic rights of persons with disabilities. Its purpose is to "promote, protect, and ensure the full and equal enjoyment of all human rights and fundamental freedom by people with disabilities and to promote respect for their inherent dignity". The CRPD applies human rights to disability, thus making general human rights specific to persons with disabilities, and clarifying existing international law regarding disability. Even if a state does not ratify the CRPD, it helps interpret other human rights conventions to which the state is party. Article 3 of the CRPD outlines the following general principles:

1. respect for inherent dignity, individual autonomy including the freedom to make one's own choices, and independence of persons;
2. non-discrimination;
3. full and effective participation and inclusion in society;
4. respect for difference and acceptance of persons with disabilities as part of human diversity and humanity;
5. equality of opportunity;
6. accessibility;

7. equality between men and women;
8. respect for the evolving capacities of children with disabilities and respect for the right of children with disabilities to preserve their identities.

States ratifying the CRPD have a range of general obligations. Among other things, they undertake to:

- adopt legislation and other appropriate administrative measures where needed;
- modify or repeal laws, customs, or practices that discriminate directly or indirectly;
- include disability in all relevant policies and programmes;
- refrain from any act or practice inconsistent with the CRPD;
- take all appropriate measures to eliminate discrimination against persons with disabilities by any person, organization, or private enterprise.

States must consult with people with disabilities and their representative organizations when developing laws, policies, and programmes to implement the CRPD. The Convention also requires public and private bodies to make "reasonable accommodation" to the situation of people with disabilities. And it is accompanied by an Optional Protocol that, if ratified, provides for a complaints procedure and an inquiry procedure, which can be lodged with the committee monitoring the treaty.

The CRPD advances legal disability reform, directly involving people with disabilities and using a human rights framework. Its core message is that people with disabilities should not be considered "objects" to be managed, but "subjects" deserving of equal respect and enjoyment of human rights. Though, India is a signatory to CRPD but yet to pass a conformity legislation to encompass the scope of the convention of disability. Law and Policy on disability is still in the framework PWD Act of 1995.

## Law and Disability in India

In order to get a complete understanding of the legal framework governing the rights of persons with disabilities, we need to understand the several legislations that cover the field. The Constitution of India is the founding legal document guaranteeing fundamental rights to all persons which includes persons with disabilities. The main legislation on disability rights is the Persons with Disabilities (Equal Opportunities, Protection of Rights and Full Participation) Act, 1995 ("PWD Act") which this introduction will be providing a detailed overview of. Other legislations which also cover some specialized aspects of disability issues are the National Trusts Act, the Rehabilitiation Council of India Act and the Mental Health Act 1987.

The Constitution of India under Chapter III guarantees fundamental human rights to all persons. The right to equality is enshrined in Article 14 of the Constitution and recognizes that all persons are equal before the law. Persons with disabilities are entitled to this guarantee to not be discriminated against in any manner and to be treated equally, which includes the requirement for special treatment where required. Similarly, Article 15 and 16 prohibits discrimination on the grounds of "religion, race, caste, sex, place of birth or any of them and guarantees equal opportunity in matters of public employment. Article 16 (3) & (4) provides that the State can make provision for the reservation of appointments or posts in favour of any backward class of citizens which, in the opinion of the State, is not adequately represented in the services. It is on the basis of Article 16, that the guarantees to reservation and equal opportunity in public employment are made under the PWD Act. The right to equality has been upheld for persons with disabilities not to be discriminated and to be provided equal opportunity in recruitment to the civil services. Article 21 of the Constitution guarantees the right to life to all persons, which has been interpreted by the Supreme Court to include the right to live with dignity, , the right to livelihood, [3] and the right to education. Article 21A guarantees the right to free and compulsory education for all children between the ages of 6-14 years.

Chapter IV of the constitution contains the Directive Principles of State Policy, which are also aims for the State to comply with. The DPSPs provide in Article 38 that the State Policy has to be directed to minimize inequalities, secure right to an adequate means of livelihood and also secure that the operation of legal system promotes justice. Under Article 41, the State shall make provisions for ensuring the right to work, education and public assistance in case of unemployment, old age, sickness and disablement and in other cases of undeserved want. The State shall endeavour to provide for free and compulsory education for all children until they complete the age of 14 years and under Article 46 the State has also the responsibility of promoting with special care the educational and economic interests of the weaker sections of the people. All these provisions are equally applicable to the persons with disabilities.

The denial or violation of any of these rights would entitle any person to approach the High Courts or the Supreme Court in their writ jurisdictions under Articles 226 and 32, respectively, if there is no other alternative or equally efficacious remedy available.

The PWD Act came into force on 1st January 1996, and was enacted in pursuance of India's obligation under the Proclamation on the Full Participation and Equality of People with Disabilities in the Asian and Pacific Region, which it adopted in December 1992. The Act provides for various measures for persons with disabilities to facilitate their access to education, employment, basic infrastructure and social welfare measures.

Under the PWD Act, a 'person with disability' has been defined as any person having 40% or more of any of the following disabilities: (i) Blindness; (ii) Low vision; (iii) Leprosy cured; (iv) Hearing impairment; (v) Locomotor disability; (vi) Mental retardation; and (vii) Mental illness. This is a limited definition, as only persons who fall within this definition as having 40% or more of the above seven disabilities would be categorized as persons with disabilities and would be entitled to get the benefits of the rights and schemes under the PWD Act.

The main rights available to persons with disabilities are in the field of education in public schools, public employment, infrastructure on the roads and in public transport and access to public buildings and a grievance redressal procedure for protection of their rights.

## Education

Under the PWD Act, all children with disabilities below the age of 18 have the right to free and compulsory education that is accessible. This goes even beyond the mandate of the *Right of Children to Free* and *Compulsory Education* Act, 2009 that calls for free education to be provided to children up to the age of 14. The further obligations placed on the government by the PWD Act with respect to formal education are that efforts must be made to see that these children with disabilities are integrated into regular schools that they attend, and that the setting up of special schools with vocational training facilities should be encouraged at the local level in the Government and private sectors, so that children across the country who require special education have access to such schools in their areas. Section 39 of the PWD Act also requires that 3% of all seats in Government and Government-aided educational institutions be earmarked for children or students with disabilities. The PWD Act also requires that the government formulate and implement schemes pertaining to non-formal, functional education, in respect of the following matters:

(a) Conducting part-time classes in respect of children with disabilities who have completed the fifth grade and could not continue full-time studies thereafter;

(b) Conducting special part-time classes to provide functional literacy for children with disabilities in the age group of sixteen and above;

(c) Imparting non-formal education after an appropriate orientation;

(d) Imparting education through open schools or open universities;

(e) Conducting class and discussions through interactive electronic or other media; and

(f) Providing every child with disability the requisite books and equipments, at no cost.

Additionally, to facilitate equal opportunities in education for children with disabilities, the government is obligated to promote research on assistive devices, teaching aids and special teaching materials, and establish and assist special teachers' training institutions. Educational institutions are required to ensure that children with visual disabilities are provided with scribes when required. To further facilitate the mainstreaming of children with disabilities, the government is required to prepare a comprehensive scheme providing for facilities or financial support for transport to and from school, making school supplies available, scholarships, grievance redressal fora, modification of examinations and restructuring of the curriculum.

## Employment

Chapter VI of the PWD Act, containing Sections 32 to 40, addresses the affirmative action measures with respect to the employment of persons with disabilities. It requires that at least three percent of all posts in all jobs under the government are required to be reserved for persons with disabilities, with one percent each being reserved for persons with blindness / low vision, persons with hearing disabilities and persons with locomotor disabilities / cerebral palsy.

To ensure that reservations have meaning, the government is required to identify posts in all public establishments that shall be reserved for persons with disability, based on the suitability of such posts to each category of disability. The list of identified posts so prepared is required to be revised in light of technological developments, at regular intervals of a maximum of 3 years.

Under Section 34, vacancies are required to be advertised, with the details of the reservations for the persons with disabilities, in the Special Employment Exchange and, if not filled, shall be carried forward to the next recruitment year.

There are also many requirements of reasonable accommodations to be provided by the Government under Article 38 of the PWD Act and to formulate schemes for the following:

(a) Relaxations of age limit,

(b) Training,

(c) Creation of an enabling environment and providing incentives to employers.

(d) The government is also required to frame an insurance scheme for its employees with disabilities, and is expressly prohibited from discriminating against employees who acquire disabilities over the course of their employment as well as employees with disabilities in the matter of promotions.

(e) Finally, for those persons with disabilities who are registered with the Special Employment Exchange and have not been able to find gainful employment for over 2 years, the government is required to frame a reasonable scheme for unemployment allowance.

## Accessibility

Accessing public spaces and infrastructure are addressed in Sections 44 to 47 of the PWD Act. Such measures include adapting public transport facilities for easy access to persons with disabilities, installing auditory and tactile indicators on public roads and pavements to aid those with auditory and visual disabilities, and installing ramps, Braille symbols and auditory signals in facilities in public buildings and medical institutions.

## Statutory Authorities and Grievance Redressal

The PWD Act provides for the appointment of a Chief Commissioner for Persons with Disabilities at the central level under section 57 and Commissioners for Persons with Disabilities at the state level under Section 60 of the PWD Act. The Commissioners have the powers to

(i) Co-ordinate with the departments of the State Government for the programmes and schemes for the benefit of persons with disabilities;

(ii) Monitor the utilization of funds disbursed by the State Government;

(iii) Take steps to safeguard the rights and facilities made available to persons with disabilities;

(iv) Submit reports to the State Government on the implementation of the Act at such intervals as that

Government may prescribe and forward a copy thereof to the Chief Commissioner.

In addition to these powers, the Chief Commissioner and Commissioners may of their own motion or on the application of any aggrieved person or otherwise look into complaints relating to deprivation of rights of persons with disabilities or the non-implementation of laws, rules, bye-laws, regulations, executive orders, guidelines or instructions made or issued by the appropriate Governments and the local authorities for the welfare and protection of rights of persons with disabilities, and take up the matter with the appropriate authorities. In order to enquire and adjudicate into these complaints, the Chief Commissioner and the State Commissioners have certain powers of civil court such as summoning of documents, etc.

Thus any matter of discrimination or denial by public authorities in matters of recruitment, promotion, benefits that persons with disabilities are entitled to may be brought before the Commissioners for adjudication and under Section 62 of the PWD Act, , and they can recommend appropriate action to be taken by the offending body.

The central government and many State governments have enacted rules under the PWD Act which include rules on the procedure for filing complaints before the Commissioners. The complainants do not require legal representation during the proceedings, and generally, they may institute a complaint by submitting complete details of their complaint and facts to the relevant Commissioner. In accordance with the Persons with Disabilities (Equal Opportunities, Protection of Rights and Full Participation) Rules, 1996, complaints are ideally to be disposed of within 3 months from the date of notifying the opposite party.

In the event that any party is not satisfied with the decision of the Chief Commissioner or the State Commissioner, the said decision can be challenged in a writ petition in the respective state High Court by the aggrieved party.

## Education, Employment and Disability in India

Like any other group, education is critical to expanding the life prospects of people with disabilities. In addition, the socialization of children with disabilities (CWD) through education assumes an unusually important role in societies such as India where social exclusion of PWD is significant. Despite its importance and notable progress in recent years, educational outcomes for children and adults with disabilities remain very poor. Illiteracy rates both for all PWD and for school-age disabled children remain much higher than the general population, and school attendance among school age CWD continues to lag that of non-disabled children by wide margins in the face of limited institutional capacity, and often constrained resources. Equally, it raises difficult trade-offs for those responsible for allocation of public resources for education. While Indian law and policy are clear in the commitment to the right of all children to basic education, in practice difficult issues arise. For example, if a given fiscal allocation aims to maximize enrolment, minimize drop-out and improve quality of education for all children, there may be tough choices in cases where the resource requirements for CWD are higher than for other children and bringing CWD into the system implies that greater numbers of non-disabled children do not enroll or drop out as a result. This is an area where a rights-based approach and that of economists and utilitarian can conflict. Weak institutional coordination, poor expenditure performance, and a range of issues in delivery of education limit the inclusion of children with disabilities in education, though there has been marked progress in recent years at the primary level under SSA. Several institutional divisions hinder coordinated and inclusive education. They include split management of education of CWD between MHRD (responsible for education of CWD within the general system, which accounts for the large majority of CWD who are attending school) and MSJE (which is responsible for most special education facilities), weak coordination on teacher training between Rehabilitation Council of India and the general teacher training system with respect to special needs, lack of coordination in early identification of children with special needs, and belated (though growing) efforts towards convergence between government and NGOs/communities.

India's implementation capacity is generally weak in a number of areas of service delivery which are most critical to improving the situation of disabled people, and it is not realistic to expect that all the actions needed by many public and non public actors can be taken all at once. It is important therefore to decide the most critical interventions and "get the basics right" first. Obvious priorities include:

(i) preventive care, both for mothers through nutritional interventions, and infants through both nutrition and basic immunization coverage;

(ii) Identifying people with disabilities as soon as possible after onset. The system needs major improvements in this most basic function;

(iii) major improvements in early intervention, which can cost effectively transform the lives of disabled people and their families, and their communities; and

(iv) expanding the under-developed efforts to improve societal attitudes to people with disabilities, relying on public-private partnerships that build on successful models already operating in India.

Qualitative research into attitudes to PWD in India finds that households generally believe that disability is due to the "sins" of disabled people or their parents and hence deserved in large measure. Equally, communities have poor assessments of the capacities of disabled people to participate in key aspects of life, with negative opinions on the capacity of disabled children to participate in regular school and for disabled adults to be effective members of the workforce. While general opinions on participation of persons with disabilities in community life are more open, they often do not appear to be realized in practice. Negative attitudes towards some disabilities are much more pronounced than others, with those with mental illness and mental retardation the most marginalized. Most worrisome, both families of disabled people and people with disabilities themselves often share the low opinions of their communities of the capacities of disabled people to be independent and productive members of society. This internalization of negative attitudes reinforces social marginalization. Changing societal attitudes – in families, service providers, and disabled individuals, and the community at large – will be critical if disabled people are to realize their full social and economic potential.

There are a range of public programs to promote PWD employment, but their impact has been negligible and largely confined to urban areas. This is in part due to weaknesses in design and implementation. Broader impacts on employment outcomes for people with disabilities will be dependent firstly on efforts to change perceptions on the productive contribution that disabled people can make, an effort that will require engagement of the public, private and NGO sectors.

Public sector employment reservations exhibit poor outcomes due to design and implementation problems. Despite a 3 percent reservation in public employment, as of 2003, only 10 percent of posts in public employment had been identified as "suitable" for PWD. As a result, the share of PWD in all posts thus remains negligible, at 0.44 percent. A second feature of the quota policy is that it applies only to three disability types – loco motor, visual and hearing – which limit many other disabled people from accessing jobs. A final and broader question on the policy is consistency with good international practice, which in the area of disability is moving away from quota-based approaches. Even if the quota system is retained, there is significant scope to improve it.

Private sector employment incentives for hiring disabled people are few and piecemeal. The PWD Act makes provision for a private sector incentives policy, with a target of 5 percent of the private sector workforce being people with disabilities. However, neither Government of India (GoI) nor states have introduced a general incentives policy (though there is a specific new incentive provided for formal sector workers in the 2007/08 budget). In the late 1990s, employment of PWD among large private firms was only 0.3 percent of their workforce. Among multinational companies, the situation was far worse, with only 0.05 percent being PWD. However, there are a number of private and public sector firms which have far better performance on PWD hiring, and offer good practice examples of more inclusive workplaces.

A national network of special employment exchanges for disabled people exists, but plays a negligible role in promoting their employment. Employment exchanges exist in state capitals, but overall, the link between employment exchanges and establishments in the private sector is weak. As a result, the job placement ratio is very low for both special and other exchanges, 0.9 percent and 0.7 percent of registered PWD respectively in 2003, and has roughly halved over the past decade. The downward trend reflects shrinking job opportunities in the public sector, and a general failure of exchanges to reach out to private employers.

### Disability and Access to Justice:

The United Nations Convention on the Rights of Persons with Disabilities (CRPD) and its accompanying Optional Protocol represent an extremely important effort to provide consistent, fundamental protections for persons with disabilities. The CRPD consists of 50 articles relating to the rights and treatment of persons with disabilities, and the Optional Protocol contains an additional 18 articles that allow persons with disabilities to vindicate their rights through the UN Committee on the Rights of Persons with Disabilities. The CRPD and the Optional Protocol truly are human rights documents. In its very first Article the Convention declares that, "the purpose of the present Convention is to promote, protect and ensure the full and equal enjoyment of all human rights and fundamental freedoms by all persons with disabilities, and to promote respect for their inherent dignity . The Convention is quite ambitious, attempting to address most aspects of civilized life, including, among other topics, accessibility, awareness raising, discrimination, liberty and security of person, independent living, personal mobility, education, employment, and recreation. Article 13, titled "Access to justice" states:

(1) States Parties shall ensure effective access to justice for persons with disabilities on an equal basis with others, including through the provision of procedural and age-appropriate accommodations, in order to facilitate their effective role as direct and indirect participants, including as witnesses, in all legal proceedings, including at investigative and other preliminary stages.

(2) In order to help to ensure effective access to justice for persons with disabilities, States Parties shall promote appropriate training for those working in the field of administration of justice, including police and prison staff.

Given the nature of any international Convention, much of the language is general and aspirational. But there are significant reporting and monitoring requirements that attempt to ensure that the Convention moves beyond aspirational language into implementation at the national and local level. In essence, the CRPD attempts to address the gaps in other human rights agreements that do not directly consider the rights of persons with disabilities. Although the CRPD has substantial support around the world, not all nations have embraced it in its entirety. India is one of the first signatories of CPRD and ratified it too yet it has not amended the exiting legislation or made new law for people with disabilities in conformity with the convention.

The access to justice provision in the Convention, Article 13, both reminds us and confirms that persons with disabilities face problems with legal representation and protection. Some of the challenges involve access to resources and thus are similar to those faced by individuals who are economically disadvantaged. Disability stereotyping and the multiple identities of persons with disabilities, however, can exacerbate these disadvantages. For example, women with disabilities may fail to fit comfortably into society's expectations and perceptions regarding women's roles generally, leading to invisibility and exclusion from meaningful participation in society. Persons with disabilities often must rely on increasingly scarce free or low-cost legal services and therefore have less choice in who represents them, and generally have less understanding and access to the legal system. It is critically important to recognize the problems involving cost and availability of competent legal services. I have discussed some of these challenges in chapters of the book through case laws.

## Bridging the Gaps: Training Advocates and Civil Society Organisations

Law schools in India can offer opportunities related to disability law that provide representation and resources to persons with disabilities, advocate for policy change, and train advocates to represent persons with disabilities. These offerings may range from degree or certification programs to clinical experiences dedicated to serving clients with disabilities.

Likewise, society organisation and legal research centres outside the academia can be an important resource to provide free legal support to disabled people in Chief Commissioner of disabilities court of the High Courts and the apex courts. Legal services authority could be another important nodal agency to help the disabled in realised justice.

Keeping all the above issues in mind this book is an attempt to look at the disability issues in India thorough decided case laws. It will be useful reference guide to the policy-makers, practitioners, researchers, academics, development agencies, and civil society.

## Aims and Objectives of the Book

This work is an attempt to analyse the contribution of Indian judiciary (Supreme Court and high courts) and two Quasi Judicial bodies namely the Chief Commissioner for Persons with Disabilities (CCPD) and National Human Rights Commission (NHRC) in the development of Equality Rights Jurisprudence for Persons with Disabilities, these institutions especially the Supreme Court has been very active in upholding the human rights enshrined in the constitution and various human rights treaties. Since its inception, the CCPD has been the most favoured forum for persons with disabilities in case of the violation or non-availability of the rights guaranteed in the Persons with Disabilities (Equal Opportunities, Protection of Rights and Full Participation) Act (PWD Act), 1995. Although, the powers of CCPD are not as wide as that of the constitutional courts (Supreme Court and high courts), it has liberally interpreted the provisions of the PWD act and offered relief in favour of persons with disabilities. India has ratified the UN Convention on the Rights of Persons with Disabilities (UNCRPD). This convention mandates to ensure all the rights to persons with disabilities on an equal basis with the rest of the society, this is a high time to study the judgments, orders etc of the abovementioned bodies in order to have a clear picture as to what extent the right to Equality is developed vis-a-vis persons with disabilities.

Following the above objectives the book is divided in Six chapters. Each chapter covers a major theme in identified in the PWD Act of 1995

## Equality and Disability Rights Jurisprudence in India

Chapter one offers introduction of the evaluation of disability rights jurisprudence till date. In India the courts and commissions (CCPD and NHRC) have played a significant role in the equality rights jurisprudence for persons with disabilities. Since India has ratified the disability rights convention, it is obligatory upon India to suitably modified laws in order to harmonise with the convention principles. Therefore this is the high time to look at the judgements, orders etc. of the courts and commissions in the light of the convention provisions and appreciate to what extent the principles derived from these judgements , orders etc. are in conformity with the convention principles.

This chapter also presents a comparative analysis of the various approaches to define disability. The chapter also gives a brief overview of the important international and national laws mainly the United Nations Convention on the Rights of Persons with Disabilities, 2006 (UNCRPD) and Persons with Disabilities (Equal Opportunities, Protection of Rights and Full Participation) Act, 1995 (PWD Act) policies etc. dealing with disability.

This chapter also discusses the concept of equality as enshrined in the constitution of India and developed by the Supreme Court. The chapter also presents and analysis of the two principles of equality applied in the disability rights jurisprudence namely Non-discrimination and Reasonable Accommodation. The chanter also discusses the role of the commissions (CCPD and NHRC) in the area of equality rights jurisprudence for persons with disabilities.

## Disability Law, Education and Policy in India

Chapter II starts with the discussion of various issues involved in the education of persons with disabilities and how they have been addressed in international law as well as national law mainly the UNCRPD and PWD Act.. After discussing the issues the judgements, orders etc. of the courts and commission are analysed. The chapter ends with the summary of important points emerging from the above judgements, orders etc.

## Disability and Employment in India

Chapter III starts with the main issues involved in the employment of persons with disabilities and how these issues are addressed in international as well as national law mainly the UNCRPD and PWD Act.. After this, the chapter analyses some of the important judgements, orders of the courts and commission (CCPD) on these issues. The chapter ends with a summary of the important points emerging from the above analyses.

## Accessibility and Disability Law In India

Chapter IV starts with the analysis of the concept of accessibility vis a vis persons with disabilities and various issues involved with it. It also discusses the provisions of international and national law mainly the UNCRPD and PWD Act addressing these issues. Subsequently the chapter presents and analysis of some of the important judgements, orders of the courts and commission (CCPD). The chapter ends with a summary of important points emerging from the above analysis.

## Disability and Social Security in India

Chapter V starts with the analyses of the concept of social security and its special relevance to the persons with disabilities. It also discusses how it has been incorporated in international and national law mainly the UNCRPD and PWD Act. Subsequently it presents and analyses of the important judgements and orders of the courts and commission (CCPD). The chapter ends with the summary of important points emerging from the above analysis.

## The Way Ahead: In Lieu of Conclusion

Chapter VI starts with the critical analysis of the main findings or the important points emerging from the research. The chapter ends with some suggestions to improve the scenario in India.

# 2

# Equality and Disability Rights Jurisprudence in India

## Introduction

Persons with disabilities remain amongst the most marginalized in every Society. While the international and national human rights framework has changed lives everywhere, persons with disabilities have not reaped the same benefits. Regardless of a country's human rights or economic situation, they are generally. The last in line to have their human rights respected

The World Report on Disability[1] published by the World Health Organisation *[WHO]* estimates that the number of persons with disabilities in the world has increased and that the previous estimate of ten per cent was revised upwards to fifteen per cent, yielding a global figure of more than one billion persons with disabilities.

The combined population of the least developed countries is 800 million, which makes the number of persons with disabilities hard to ignore. The increased emphasis on inclusive development by all stakeholders makes it imperative that decision makers at all levels include persons with disabilities in their development initiatives. Studies have shown that investing in the education, rehabilitation, and accessible environment requires fewer resources as compared to the resources invested in building separate instructions for them and keep them in these institutions and thus compelling them to a life of dependency and charity. This kind of institutionalised life leads to various kinds of psychological problems in them as they are deprived of leading a life of freedom and dignity.

Historically, the condition of having a disability has been viewed as tragic. Through ignorance and fear, people with disabilities were typically disabled beggars or indigents. The word "handicap" itself is said to derive from "cap in hand," an activity familiarly associated with panhandling.

In USA, by the 19th century, it was common for people with disabilities to be institutionalized, and they were looked upon as patients or clients who needed curing. This practice had the effect of excluding people with disabilities from the rest of the society and implied that something was inherently and permanently wrong with them. It provided no room for integration, and perpetuated myths of inequality.

Disability has been made visible in American life primarily as an outcome of military engagement and, therefore, was managed by the federal government in the War Department and, later, at the Veterans Administration. Civilians with disabilities were largely invisible and unaccounted for by the government until the latter half of the twentieth century when the social and physical isolation of people with physical and mental disability became the focus of civil rights legislation. Until that time, society managed to keep people who were different out of sight by building institutions such as nursing homes, asylums, and homeless shelters and using statutes such as ugly laws to prohibit from public places, people whose different appearance might offend the citizenry.

### NHRC (India) in one of its annual reports[2] 2003-2004 states

"Long held beliefs, attitudes and perception of disability sometimes conflict with the human rights values and principles, which recognize that all persons not only possess

inherent self-worth but are also inherently equal, regardless of their differences. The Commission, therefore, finds it impossible to accept the plea that because certain forms of human rights abuses or violations had long persisted in the country whether for societal, behavioural or any other reason, these should continue to be acquiesced in, or tolerated in the future. A 'wrong' does not become 'right' even if it has continued for long in the past.

In the recent years, there have been vast and positive changes in the perception of the society towards persons with disabilities. It has been realized that a majority of persons with disabilities can lead a better quality of life if they have equal opportunities and effective access.

A number of non-binding and binding instruments in the form of declarations, resolutions, conventions, enactments, policies etc have been adopted during the last sixty years which reiterate the commitment of the society to ensure the realisation of all the human rights to each and every section of the society including the persons with disabilities. The most significant of them is the Convention on the Rights of Persons with Disabilities (UNCRPD) 2006. "What the Convention endeavours to do," said Don MacKay, Chairman of the committee that negotiated the treaty, "is to elaborate in detail the rights of persons with disabilities and set out a code of implementation".

Countries that join in the Convention engage themselves to develop and carry out policies, laws and administrative measures for securing the rights recognized in the Convention and abolish laws, regulations, customs and practices that constitute discrimination (Article 4).

This convention deals with the wide variety of rights which must be available to the persons with disabilities on an equal basis with others. In fact the most of the rights enumerated in the convention are not new. These rights have been mentioned in the earlier human rights conventions. This convention seeks to tailor them according to the special needs of the persons with disabilities. These rights include inter alia the rights in respect of life, education, employment, political and cultural life, accessibility, personal mobility and so on.

The Constitution of India ensures equality, freedom, justice and dignity of all individuals and implicitly mandates an inclusive society for all including persons with disabilities. Supreme Court and various high courts have very liberally interpreted the fundamental rights enshrined in the constitution and read the international treaties and conventions on human rights into them. Apart from this, two commissions namely—the NHRC and CCPD came into existence in the last decade of 20$^{th}$ century which played a significant role in upholding the right to equality and dignity of persons with disabilities through their various orders, instructions etc. it is the need of the hour to conduct studies on the impact of these development on the disability rights jurisprudence. The work research is a humble attempt in this direction.

## Definition of Disability

The definition of disability is a reflection of approaches prevalent in the society. There have been two main approaches to define disability: Disability is treated as "individual pathology"[3].

According to this approach, disability results from the defect or impairment present in the person. This approach treats disability as a medical issue and believes that disability requires medical solution.

According to this approach, persons with disabilities are incapable of holding rights[4] because of their impairments. They are the Objects of rights and it is the pious duty of the society to provide them with the basic needs such as food, housing, clothing, health care facility, etc. as a result, till very recently, they were being provided with very little education including the vocational education and training. They were not considered to be capable of participating in economic, political, social, and cultural life of the society. This approach is generally referred to as the Individual Model of disability[5].

The second approach treats disability as a "Social Pathology"[6]. According to this approach, disability results not from the defect or impairment in the person but the environmental and situational factors. For example a person with loco motor disability cannot access public transport, services, buildings etc not because of his/her impairment etc but due to the fact that they have not been designed taking in to considerations his/her needs.

The *World Report*[7] *on Disability released by the World Bank on* In June 2011 highlights some of the most common barriers to the inclusion of persons with disabilities, such as:

1. Inadequate policies and standards for disability-inclusive society and development;

2. Negative attitudes towards disability;
3. Lack of provision of services and service delivery for persons with disabilities;
4. Inadequate funding for disability-inclusive development;
5. Lack of accessibility to the physical environment and information and communications technologies;
6. Lack of consultation and involvement of persons with disabilities;
7. Lack of statistical data and evidence-based research on disability.

According to this approach, persons with disabilities are the Subjects not Objects of all the human rights on an equal basis with others in the society[8], disability is one of the human diversities. There needs to be Main-streaming of disability in law, policy, architectural design of the buildings, roads, modes of transports etc, education system, workplaces etc. Main-streaming here means that while formulating or designing the above, the special needs of persons with various types of disabilities should be taken into consideration. This approach is generally referred to as the Social Model of disability[9].

Although the second approach finds favour in the contemporary International as well as National law, both the approaches are prevalent.

Disability is defined in two ways. Some countries enumerate the types of disabilities which they cover in there laws and define each of them. With regard to the provisions of rights, these countries adopt the social model, for example, Disability Discrimination Act, 1995 (DDA) [UK] and Persons with Disabilities (Equal opportunities, protection of rights and full participation) act 1995 (PWD Act) [India] adopt the Medical model while defining disability and adopt the Social model while dealing with various rights guaranteed for persons with disabilities. Indian law under section 2 (I) recognizes seven types of disabilities namely:

1. Blindness
3. Low vision

4. Leprosy-cured
5. Hearing impairment
6. Loco motor disability
7. Mental retardation
8. Mental illness
9. Autism
10. Multiple disabilities

The PWD Act provides for various rights to persons with disabilities, these rights are mainly related to education, employment, access, non-discrimination, social security etc. Another approach to defined disability is to set out the criteria and cover every one who satisfies the criteria. This approach unlike the previous one, does not specifically enumerate the types of disabilities. The Convention on the Rights of persons with Disabilities follows this approach.

Article 1 of the convention inter alia defines the term persons with disabilities as: "Persons with disabilities include those who have long-term physical, mental, intellectual or sensory impairments which in interaction with various barriers may hinder their full and effective participation in society on an equal basis with others". Clause (e) of the preamble to the convention recognises the significance of social factors in defining disability. It reads: (e) Recognizing that disability is an evolving concept and that disability results from the interaction between persons with impairments and attitudinal and environmental barriers that hinders their full and effective participation in society on an equal basis with others. The Equality Act, 2010 [UK] and Americans with Disabilities Act, 1990 (ADA) [USA] and other developed legal systems also follow this approach.

## Definition under Americans with Disabilities Act, 1991 (ADA)

The Americans with Disabilities Act, 1991 (ADA) does not provide a specific list of covered disabilities; rather it broadly defines "disability" as "a physical or mental impairment that substantially limits one or more of the major life activities of

[an] individual ... a record of such impairment ... or being regarded as having such an impairment.

There is no clear definition of "impairment". Regulations promulgated pursuant to the ADA suggest that an impairment may be "any physiological disorder, or condition, cosmetic disfigurement, or anatomical loss affecting one or more of the following body systems: neurological, musculoskeletal, special sense organs, respiratory (including speech organs), cardiovascular, reproductive, digestive, genito-urinary, hemic, and lymphatic, skin, and endocrine" and "any mental or psychological disorder, such as mental retardation, organic brain syndrome, emotional or mental illness, and specific learning disabilities.

The Equal Employment Opportunity Commission (EEOC) has defined "major life activities" as "functions such as caring for oneself, performing manual tasks, walking, seeing, hearing, speaking, breathing, learning and working. This list is not exclusive. The EEOC regulations require that when the major life activity is "working", the individual must show "significant restriction" in the ability to perform either a class of jobs or a broad range of jobs in various classes as compared to the average person having comparable training, skills and abilities.

## Per se Disabilities

It has been suggested that certain impairments may qualify has per se disabilities - i.e., they may always be considered disabilities, regardless of the specific circumstances of the case. Potential per se disabilities include HIV infection, paraplegia, and deafness, hardness of hearing, lung disease, blindness, mental retardation, alcoholism, epilepsy, diabetes and manic depression.

The definition of 'disability' under the Equality Act, 2010 (UK)

## According to the Equality Act, 2010 (UK) Act, a person has a disability if

- they have a physical or mental impairment
- the impairment has a substantial and long-term adverse effect on their ability to perform normal day-to-day activities

**For the Purposes of the Act, these words have the following meanings**

- 'substantial' means more than minor or trivial
- 'long-term' means that the effect of the impairment has lasted or is likely to last for at least twelve months (there are special rules covering recurring or fluctuating conditions)
- 'normal day-to-day activities' include everyday things like eating, washing, walking and going shopping

People who have had a disability in the past that meets this definition are also protected by the Act. There are additional provisions relating to people with progressive conditions. People with HIV, cancer or multiple sclerosis are protected by the Act from the point of diagnosis. People with some visual impairment are automatically deemed to be disabled.

There is a difference of opinion amongst experts as to whether the broad based approach adopted in the convention is preferable over the restrictive definition as preferred in the Indian enactments dealing with disability.

The supporters of the former argue that it adopted the functional approach. A number of disabilities which may be difficult to be defined with precision, can be covered under this broad definitions.

The supporters of the latter approach which defines and enumerates the types of disabilities argue that if the former approach is adopted, it will enlarge the definition in such a way that it will become unmanageable. There are many border line cases on which there will be dispute as to whether or not they can be covered under the definition of disability. If there exist certain disabilities which deserve to be included in the definition, it would be a better approach to incorporate them specifically in to the definition rather than broadening the definition in such a manner as defined in the convention.

It is submitted that in India, there has been a slight tilt towards the UNCRPD approach to define disability. Courts have given relief in various types of cases which are not covered under the definition of disability as defined under Indian law.

- heart ailments being considered within the scope of disability;
- tinnitus being recognised as a hearing impairment[10];
- dwarf persons being considered for inclusion in the term locomotor disabilities[11];
- dyslexia included within the ambit of disabilities[12];

Similarly in Union of India v. Devender Kumar Pant[13] the Supreme Court applied the principles of non discrimination in employment stated in sections 47 of the PWD act to a person with colour blindness.

## Disability Rights Jurisprudence

The entire disability rights jurisprudence revolves around the two concepts namely

1. Egalitarianism or essential equality of all men
2. Reasonable accommodation

Non discrimination signifies that the persons with disabilities should not be made subject to restriction impediments etc in enjoyments of the various rights available to other human being. These rights include inter alia the rights concerning employment, education, public services, political and cultural rights.

Reasonable accommodation or inclusion means that the special needs arising out of the physical impairments of the persons with disabilities should be taken care of by the society so that they can enjoy the rights on the equal basis with others. This will come under non-discrimination measures. Without reasonable accommodation the right to equality or non discrimination is meaningless.

For example if the study material is not available in formats accessible to the persons with visual or hearing impairments, they will not be able to received education. Similarly, the school building should be design in such a manner that the persons with loco motor impairments can access it without much difficulty.

This work attempts to examine the present status of the Right to Equality in the context of the disability rights jurisprudence in the light of the judgments, orders, and instructions etc of— the CCPD, NHRC and Supreme Court.

In early days, the trend was to define the human rights in terms of their application to every human being. The Universal Declaration of Human Rights (UNDHR) 1948 and two binding treaties which incorporated in themselves the rights contained in the UDHR namely—International Covenant on Civil and Political Rights 1966 and International Covenant on Economic, Social and Cultural rights 1966 are the example of this trend. Persons with disabilities are also (Persons) therefore these conventions are equally applicable to them like others.

Later, it was realised that despite these instruments, certain disadvantaged groups have not been able to avail these rights on the equal basis with the rest of the society. It was felt that these groups require special protection. As a result a number of treaties were adopted which defined human rights specifically in their context. Convention for Elimination of all Forms of Discrimination against Women 1979 (CEDAW), Convention on the Rights of Child (CRC) and recently concluded Convention on the Rights of Persons with Disabilities (UNCRPD) are the example of this trend. It is significant to note here that the CEDAW and CRC are also applicable to persons with disabilities who are women and children respectively. For purposes of this work, the Convention on the Rights of Persons with Disabilities (UNCRPD) is of special significance.

Apart from this, the various specialized agencies of the UN have also played a significant role in the promotion of protection of the Human Rights of persons with disabilities, various conventions, resolutions etc. of the International Labour Organization (ILO), World Health Organization (WHO), United Nations Educational Scientific and Cultural Organization (UNESCO), United Nations Children Fund (UNICEF), etc. have contributed significantly in this area.

## United Nations and Persons with Disabilities

The United Nations was founded on the principle of equality for all. The Preamble to the United Nations Charter affirms the dignity and worth of every human being and gives primary importance to the promotion of social justice. Persons with disabilities are, de facto, entitled to all the fundamental human rights upheld by the Charter and other human rights instruments.

The General Assembly established the foundation for the promotion and protection of human rights in 1948, when it proclaimed the Universal Declaration of Human Rights. Article 25 of the Declaration states that each person has "the right to security in the event of unemployment, sickness, disability, widowed, old age or other lack of livelihood in circumstances beyond his control". Further anti-discrimination principles were established by such human rights instruments as the International Covenant on Civil and Political Rights and the International Covenant on Economic, Social and Cultural Rights, which came into force in 1966. Together they form the most comprehensive international code of legally binding provisions in the area of human rights. The two Covenants develop and supplement the provisions of the Universal Declaration, and the three instruments together make up what has come to be known as the International Bill of Human Rights.

The 1970s marked a new approach to disability. The concept of human rights for persons with disabilities began to be accepted internationally. In 1971 On 20 December the General Assembly proclaimed the Declaration on the Rights of Mentally Retarded Persons and called for national and international action to embrace it as the accepted basis and frame of reference for protecting the rights of the persons with disabilities. In 1975 In December the General Assembly adopted the Declaration on the Rights of Disabled Persons, which states that all persons with disabilities are entitled to the rights stipulated, without respect to race, colour, sex, language, religion, political or other opinions, national or social origin, state of wealth, birth or any other situation.

In 1982 the General Assembly adopted the World Programme of Action concerning Disabled Persons. Disability policy was now structured in three main areas: prevention, rehabilitation, and equalization of opportunities.

With the proclamation of the United Nations Decade of Disabled Persons, 1983-1992, the General Assembly encouraged Member States to use the Decade to implement the World Programme of Action.

In 1991 the General Assembly adopted the Principles for the Protection of Persons with Mental Illness and for the Improvement of Mental Health Care. Twenty-five principles defined the fundamental freedoms and basic rights of persons with intellectual disabilities.

In 1992 the end of the Decade of Disabled Persons was marked by the General Assembly with the establishment of the International Day of Disabled Persons on 3 December. The General Assembly also summarized the United Nations' goals in the field of disability, again emphasizing the importance of the full integration of persons with disabilities into society and encouraging future United Nations conferences to include discussion of disability issues.

In 1993 the Standard Rules on the Equalization of Opportunities for Persons with Disabilities were adopted by the General Assembly. The Rules summarized the message of the World Programme of Action and state preconditions for equal opportunity. They also targeted areas of equal participation and promote implementation measures and monitoring mechanisms.

In December 2001, Mexico proposed in the General Assembly to establish an Ad Hoc Committee to consider proposals for a comprehensive and integral international convention to protect and protect the rights and dignity of persons with disabilities.

In August 2002, December 2006, the Ad Hoc Committee meets eight times to draft the Convention on the Rights of Persons with Disabilities and its Optional Protocol.

On 13th December 2006, the Convention on the Rights of Persons with Disabilities was adopted by the General Assembly.

On 30th March 2007, the Convention and Optional Protocol opened for signature at UN Headquarters in New York. States or regional and international organizations may now sign the Convention and Optional Protocol at any time at UN Headquarters in New York.

Unite Nations Convention on the Rights of Persons with Disabilities (UNCRPD)

In December 2006 the UN General Assembly adopted a convention namely the Convention on the Rights of Persons with Disabilities (UNCRPD). India ratified the convention on 1st October 2007.

**The Principles of the Present Convention are:**

(a) Respect for inherent dignity, individual autonomy including the freedom to make one's own choices, and independence of persons;

(b) Non-discrimination;

(c) Full and effective participation and inclusion in society;

(d) Respect for difference and acceptance of persons with disabilities as part of human diversity and humanity;

(e) Equality of opportunity;

(f) Accessibility;

(g) Equality between men and women;

(h) Respect for the evolving capacities of children with disabilities and respect for the right of children with disabilities to preserve their identities[14].

Countries that join in the Convention engage themselves to develop and carry out policies, laws and administrative measures for securing the rights recognized in the Convention and abolish laws, regulations, customs and practices that constitute discrimination[15].

As a change of perceptions is essential to improve the situation of persons with disabilities, ratifying countries are to combat stereotypes and prejudices and promote awareness of the capabilities of persons with disabilities[16]. Countries are to guarantee that persons with disabilities enjoy their inherent right to life on an equal basis with others[17] ensure the equal rights and advancement of women and girls with disabilities[18] and protect children with disabilities[19].

Countries are to ensure the equal right to own and inherit property, to control financial affairs and to have equal access to bank loans, credit and mortgages[20]. They are to ensure access to justice on an equal basis with others[21], and make sure that persons with disabilities enjoy the right to liberty and security and are not deprived of their liberty unlawfully or arbitrarily[22]. Countries must protect the physical and mental integrity of persons with disabilities, just as for everyone else[23], guarantee freedom from torture and from cruel, inhuman or degrading treatment or punishment, and prohibit medical or scientific experiments without the consent of the person concerned. Laws and administrative measures must guarantee freedom from exploitation, violence and abuse. In case of abuse, States shall promote the recovery, rehabilitation and reintegration of the victim and investigate the abuse. Persons with disabilities are not to be subjected to arbitrary or illegal interference with their privacy, family, home, correspondence or communication. The privacy of their personal, health and rehabilitation information is to be protected like that of others.

On the fundamental issue of accessibility, the Convention requires countries to identify and eliminate obstacles and barriers and ensure that persons with disabilities can access their environment, transportation, public facilities and services, and information and communications technologies. Persons with disabilities must be able to live independently, to be included in the community, to choose where and with whom to live and to have access to in-home, residential and community support services. Personal mobility and independence are to be fostered by facilitating affordable personal mobility, training in mobility skills and access to mobility aids, devices, assistive technologies and live assistance.

Countries recognize the right to an adequate standard of living and social protection; this includes public housing, services and assistance for disability-related needs, as well as assistance with disability-related expenses in case of poverty. Countries are to promote access to information by providing information intended for the general public in accessible formats and technologies, by facilitating the use of Braille, sign language and other forms of communication and by encouraging the media and internet providers to make on-line information available in accessible formats. Discrimination relating to marriage, family and personal relations shall be eliminated.

Persons with disabilities shall have the equal opportunity to experience parenthood, to marry and to found a family, to decide on the number and spacing of children, to have access to reproductive and family planning education and means, and to enjoy equal rights and responsibilities regarding guardianship, ward ship, trusteeship and adoption of children. States are to ensure equal access to primary and secondary education, vocational training, adult education and lifelong learning. Education is to employ the appropriate materials, techniques and forms of communication. Pupils with support needs are to receive support measures, and pupils who are blind, deaf and deaf-blind are to receive their education in the most appropriate modes of communication from teachers who are fluent in sign language and Braille. Education of persons with disabilities must foster their participation in society, their sense of dignity and self worth and the development of their personality, abilities and creativity. Persons with disabilities have the right to the highest attainable standard of health without discrimination on the basis of disability. They are to receive the same range, quality and standard of free or affordable health services as provided other persons, receive those health services needed because of their disabilities, and not to be discriminated against in the provision of health insurance. To enable persons with disabilities to attain maximum independence and ability, countries are to provide comprehensive Habilitation and rehabilitation services in the areas of health, employment and education. Persons with disabilities have equal rights to work and gain a living. Countries are to prohibit discrimination in job-related matters, promote self-employment, entrepreneurship and starting one's own business, employ persons with disabilities in the public sector, promote their employment in the private sector, and ensure that they are provided with reasonable accommodation at work. Countries are to ensure equal participation in political and public life, including the right to vote, to stand for elections and to hold office. Countries are to promote participation in cultural life, recreation, leisure and sport by ensuring provision of television programmes, films, theatre and cultural material in accessible formats, by making theatres, museums, cinemas and libraries accessible, and by guaranteeing that persons with disabilities have the opportunity to develop and utilize their creative potential not only for their own benefit, but also for the enrichment of society. Countries are to ensure their participation in mainstream and disability-specific sports. Countries are to provide development assistance in efforts by developing countries to put into practice the Convention. To ensure implementation and monitoring of the Convention, countries are to designate a focal point in the government and create a national mechanism to promote and monitor implementation. The Convention and Optional Protocol entered into force on 3 May 2008, after the Convention received its 20th ratification, and the Optional Protocol 10 ratifications. Fourth session of the Conference of States Parties was held between 7 to 9 September 2011. The theme of the session was "Enabling Development, Realizing the Convention on the Rights of Persons with Disabilities". The following were the sub-themes of the Conference: "Realizing the Convention through International Cooperation", "Political and Civil Participation" and "Work and Employment".

## National Framework Constitution

Article 14 of the constitution ensures that the State shall not deny to any person equality before the law or the equal protection of the laws within the territory of India.

The Supreme Court of India has very liberally interpreted the fundamental rights enshrined in the constitution. Rights contained in International treaties and conventions on human rights which are not inconsistent with the constitutional provisions or the laws have been read into the fundamental rights. In a number of judgments the court has made these rights available to the traditionally disadvantaged classes of people including the persons with disabilities.

According to Article 21, no person shall be denied the right to life and personal liberty accept according to the procedure established by law. It is well settled through several judgments of the Supreme Court of India that the Fundamental Right to Life guaranteed under Article 21 of the Constitution is an overarching right under which several other rights are subsumed as necessary components of life. For instance, in Chameli Singh v. State of U.P, The Supreme Court observed, "Right to life guaranteed in any civilized society implies the right to food, water, decent environment, education, medical care and shelter.. .All civil, political, social and cultural rights enshrined in the Universal Declaration of Human Rights or under the Constitution of India cannot be exercised without these basic human rights."

The Directive Principles of State Policy contained in part 4 of the Constitution also lend support to the rights of persons with disabilities. Directive Principles have often been used by the courts to adjust and expand the ambit of fundamental rights, and also to interpret other Constitutional provisions. Recently, the courts have even been issuing directions to the government and various administrative authorities to take positive action to remove grievances caused by non-implementation of the directive principles. It helps that some directive principles specifically mention rights of persons with disabilities. For instance, Article 41 specifically provides for effective provision to be made by the state for securing the right to work, to education and to public assistance in cases of "disablement". Article 39A envisages equal justice and free legal aid to all citizens and that opportunities for securing justice are not denied to any citizen by reason of economic or "other disabilities." Articles 46 and 47 also have the potential for raising the standards of living, education and development of persons with disabilities.

## Other Legislations

The parliament of India has enacted four legislations for Persons with disabilities viz.

(i) Persons with Disability. (Equal Opportunities, Protection of Rights and Full Participation) Act, 1995, which provides for education, employment, creation of barrier free environment, social security, etc.

(ii) National Trust for Welfare of Persons with Autism, Cerebral Palsy, Mental Retardation and Multiple Disability Act, 1999 has provisions for legal guardianship of the four categories and creation of enabling environment for as much independent living as possible,

(iii) Rehabilitation Council of India Act, 1992 deals with the development of manpower for providing rehabilitation services.

(iv) The mental health act 1987 deals with Mental health authorities psychiatric hospital and nursing homes admission and detention in psychiatric hospital or nursing homes inspection, discharge, leave of absence and removal of mentally ill person.

The most significant enactment for our purpose is the Persons with Disability. (Equal Opportunities, Protection of Rights and Full Participation) Act, 1995.

This act provides for education, employment, creation of barrier free environment, social security, etc. this act adopts the approach that the persons with disabilities be provided equal opportunity in these areas by removing barriers of various kinds such as making available the educational material in Braille and other accessible formats, recognition of sign language, removing architectural barriers, providing assistive/accessibility appliances etc. the act also provides for special measures where necessary for this purpose. The act provides for a number of bodies at the national and state level for making policies and monitoring their implementation. These bodies include—national and state co-ordination committees and executive committees and chief commissioner at the national level and state commissioners at state level. The chief commissioner and state commissioners also perform the quasi judicial functions by adjudicating complaints of deprivation of the rights.

## Disability Rights and Equality

The struggle of the disability rights movement has been to ensure for persons with disabilities the enjoyment of all the rights on an equal basis with the rest of the society. Although the rights guaranteed under the constitution of various countries and international treaties, conventions etc. of human rights are equally applicable to persons with disability, they have not reaped the benefits of these rights to the fullest extent. It was realised later that the rights need to be contextualised considering the special needs of persons with disabilities. In other words, the rights need to be defined in such a manner that they take into account the needs and circumstances peculiar to the various types of disabilities. For example persons with visual disability will not be able to enjoy the right to education to the fullest extent unless the right is defined in such a manner that it guarantees the availability of educational material in braille, large print, audio books or e-text.

The guaranty of equal enjoyment of rights requires the application of two guiding principles while contextualising the rights to persons with disabilities. These principles are complementary to each other. They are:

1. Non-discrimination
2. Reasonable Accommodation

These two principles are the crux of the entire disability rights jurisprudence. The international and national binding and non-binding instruments which provide for the rights of persons with disability are mainly based on these principles.

## Non-Discrimination

Equality or non discrimination signifies that the persons with disabilities should not be made subject to restrictions impediments etc in enjoyment of the various rights available to the rest of the society. These rights include inter alia the rights concerning employment, education, public services, political and cultural rights. The Convention on the Rights of Persons with Disabilities [UNCRPD] in its various articles recognises this right[24]. Para 3 of Article 2 of the convention defines discrimination as:

> "Discrimination on the basis of disability" means any distinction, exclusion or restriction on the basis of disability which has the purpose or effect of impairing or nullifying the recognition, enjoyment or exercise, on an equal basis with others, of all human rights and fundamental freedoms in the political, economic, social, cultural, civil or any other field. It includes all forms of discrimination, including denial of reasonable accommodation."

Article 3[25] enumerates the General Principles of the convention. Clause (b) of the said Article enumerates "Non-discrimination" as one of the guiding principles of the convention.

Article 12[26] (guarantees for persons with disabilities the Equal recognition before the law.

NHRC in its 2000-2001[27] annual report recommends to include non-discrimination clauses in all chapters dealing with positive rights i.e. education, employment, access etc. It also recommend to include a new section to provide that no person shall be discriminated against only by reason of mental, physical or sensory impairments, whether or not such impairments have been expressly included in the statute.

## Reasonable Accommodation

Reasonable accommodation or inclusion means that the special needs arising out of the physical impairments of the persons with disabilities needs to be taken care of by the society so that they can enjoy the rights on the equal basis with others. This will come under non-discrimination measures. Without reasonable accommodation the right to equality or non discrimination is meaningless.

For example if the study material is not available in formats accessible to the persons with visual or hearing impairments, they will not be able to received education. Similarly, the school building should be design in such a manner that the persons with locomotor impairments can access it without much difficulty.

The convention[28] in para 4 of Article 2 defines reasonable accommodation as under: "Reasonable accommodation" means necessary and appropriate modification and adjustments not imposing a disproportionate or undue burden, where needed in a particular case, to ensure to persons with disabilities the enjoyment or exercise on an equal basis with others of all human rights and fundamental freedoms". Clause (d)[29] of Article 3 recognises it as one of the guiding principles of the convention. It reads: "(d) Respect for difference and acceptance of persons with disabilities as part of human diversity and humanity;" Various Articles of the convention guaranty this right. Article 9[30] deals with the accessibility of physical environment as well as of information and communication.

- The study material and the medium of instruction need to be in accessible format[31].
- Equal opportunity of work and employment suitable modification of the work environment so that the persons

with disabilities can enjoy this right on an equal basis with others[32].

- Suitable modification of Public and Political and Cultural recreation, leisure and sport environment so that persons with disabilities can enjoy these right on an equal basis with others[33].

According to the Americans with Disabilities Act, 1990 (ADA), Reasonable accommodation may include, but is not limited to

- Making existing facilities used by employees readily accessible to and usable by persons with disabilities.
- Job restructuring, modifying work schedules, reassignment to a vacant position;
- Acquiring or modifying equipment or devices, adjusting or modifying examinations, training materials, or policies, and providing qualified readers or interpreters.

In subsequent chapters, this work will look at the judgment, orders, instructions, etc. of three important institutions namely the Indian Judiciary (Supreme Court and High Courts), Office of the Chief Commissioner for Persons with Disability (CCPD) and National Human Rights Commission ( NHRC) on the right to equality and persons with disabilities. The reason for selecting these institutions is that the persons with disabilities and there organisations have resorted to these institutions for the redressal of their grievances.

## Constitution of India

Article 14, 15 and 16 are the most relevant provisions for the present purpose. Article 14 deals with the general principles of equality whereas Article 15 and 16 deal with specific issues of equality. The Supreme Court has stressed upon the conjoint reading of these articles.

Article 14 of the constitution provides that The State shall not deny to any person equality before the law or the equal protection of the laws within the territory of India.

The first expression 'equality before the law' which is taken from the English common law, is a declaration of equality of all persons within the territory of India, implying thereby the absence of any special privilege in favour of any individual. Every person, whatever be his rank or position, is subject to the jurisdiction of the ordinary courts. Prof. Dicey in explaining the concept of legal equality, as operating in England, said: "With us every official, from the Prime Minister down to a constable or a collector of taxes, is under the same responsibility for every act done without any legal justification as any other citizen."[34] The second expression, 'the equal protection of the *laws'*, which is rather a corollary of the first expression, and is based on the last clause of the first section of the Fourteenth Amendment to the American Constitution, directs that equal protection shall be secured to all persons within the territorial jurisdiction of the Union in the enjoyment of their rights and privileges without favoritism or discrimination. It has been said that 'the equal protection of the laws' is a pledge of protection or guarantee of equal laws.

Thus Article 14 uses two expressions to make the concept of equal treatment a binding principle of State action. The nature and the extent of the guarantee is the same under both the expressions. Patanjali Sastri, C.J. has rightly observed that the second expression is a corollary of the first.[35] Indeed, it will be difficult to imagine any violation of 'the equal protection of the laws', which would not also be a violation of 'equality before the law'. However, the Court has clarified that even if there is much in common between the two expressions in Article 14 they do not mean the same thing. "The word 'law' in the former expression is used in a generic sense a philosophical sense whereas the word 'laws' in the latter expression denotes specific laws."

The guiding principle of the Article is that all persons and things similarly circumstances shall be treated alike both in privileges conferred and liabilities imposed. 'Equality before the law' means that amongst equals the law should be equal and should be equally administered and that like should be treated alike. Hence, what it forbids is discrimination between persons who are substantially in similar circumstances or conditions. It does not forbid different treatment of unequals. The rule rather is that like should be treated alike and that unlike should be treated differently. Equal treatment of unequals is as bad as unequal treatment of equals. As a matter of fact all persons are not alike or equal in all respects. Application of the same laws uniformly to all of them will therefore be inconsistent with the principle of equality. It is accepted that persons may be classified into groups and such groups may differently be treated if there is a reasonable basis for such difference. Article 14 forbids class legislation, but does not forbid classification or differentiation which rests upon reasonable grounds of distinction. The rule of differentiation is that in enacting laws differentiating between different persons or things in different circumstances which govern one set of persons or objects such laws may not necessarily be the same as those governing another set of persons, or objects so that the question of unequal treatment does not really arise between persons governed by different conditions and different set of circumstances. The principle of equality does not mean that every law .must have universal application for all persons who are not by nature, attainment or circumstances in the same position. The varying needs of different classes of persons require different treatment.

The Constitution of India applies uniformly to all citizens of India whether or not they are healthy and normal or disabled (physically or mentally) and irrespective of their religion, caste, gender, creed etc. The only requirement is that the people to whom the Constitution will apply have Indian citizenship. Part three of the constitution enumerates various Fundamental Rights and part four deals with the Directive Principles of State Policy. The Supreme Court of India has interpreted the Fundamental Rights in such a manner that the scopes of these rights have been broadened to such an extent that a number of Directive Principles and various, rights enshrined in International Treaties and Conventions have become the part of Fundamental Rights. The constitution is the reservoir of rights. Persons with Disabilities and approach the Supreme Court and High Courts for the enforcement of even those rights which do not find place in disability legislations.

It is worth mentioning that unlike the Canadian Charter of Rights and Freedoms, the German Constitution and other modern constitutions, there is no provision which explicitly bars discrimination on grounds of disability. The constitution also does not employ an open textured term such as 'other status' as is the case with Article 26 of ICCPR which can be construed to include 'disability'.

Formal recognition of discrimination on the ground of disability is a recent phenomenon and is not reflected in the laws in India. For instance, the Constitution of India in Articles 15 and 16 prohibit discrimination in the matter of employment and access to public facilities on grounds of religion, race, caste, sex and place of birth, but is silent on disability. However, when the special provisions benefiting persons with disability are particularly aimed at their participation whether in employment or otherwise, the Constitution and judicial interpretation take a more unequivocal position. A positive legislative regime on disability has evolved since Article 6(3) & (4) of the Constitution encourages affirmative action and legislative measures in favour of any backward class of citizens, which in the opinion of the State, are not adequately represented in the services. Judicial pronouncements from the Supreme Court as well as the High Courts of the country, have left no doubt that the Constitution does not merely guarantee "formal" equality. Mere formal equality would mean that the society would simply reflect its extant hierarchy and order in the distribution of rewards and would oblige the state to only be responsible for treating all persons in the same manner, based on objective standards. However, it is the model of "substantive" equality that the Indian Constitution has espoused under Article 14, as opposed *to* "formal" equality This implies that only equals must be treated as equals and unequals may not be treated as equals, which makes it the constitutional responsibility of the State to ensure that the systemic and historical conditions of disadvantaged classes *of* persons are taken into account in providing equal status and equal opportunities.

Article 15(1) enjoins on the Government not to discriminate against any citizen of India (including the disabled) on the ground of religion, race, caste, sex, place of birth or any of them.

Article 15(2) States that no citizen (including the disabled) shall be subjected *to* any disability, liability, restriction or condition on any of the above *grounds* in the matter of their access to shops, public restaurants, hotels and places *of* public entertainment or in the use of wells, tanks, bathing ghats, maintained wholly or partly out of government funds or dedicated *to* the *use* of the general public. Women and children and those belonging to any socially and educational backward classes or the Scheduled Castes & Tribes can be given the benefit of special laws or special provisions made by the State. There shall be equality of opportunity for all citizens (including the disabled) in matters relating to employment or appointment to any office under the State

These Articles, particularly the meaning of the phrase "backward class (es) of citizens" and whether they include persons with disabilities, came up for interpretation in *Indra Sawheny & Ors. v. Union of India & Ors*, The Apex Court has pointed *out* "Mere formal declaration of the right would not make unequals equal. To *enable* all to compete with each other on an equal plane, it is necessary to take positive measures to equip the disadvantage and the handicapped to bring them to the *level of* fortunate advantaged... Article 14 and Article 16(1) no doubt would *by* themselves permit such positive measures in favour of the disadvantage to make real the equality guaranteed by them." It was held by a majority judgment that even Though "backward class (es) of citizens" as used in clauses (4) of Articles 15 and 16 did not cover persons with disabilities, the constitutional scheme and spirit of Articles 14, and clauses (1) of Articles 15 and 16 allowed for reservation and Other kinds of affirmative action, in favour of persons with disabilities.

Article 41 states that the state/shall, within the limits *of* its economic capacity and development, make effective provisions for securing the *right* to *work, to education* and to public assistance in cases of unemployment, old age, sickness and *disablement.*

Persons with Disabilities (Equal Opportunities, Protection of Rights *arid* Full Participation) Act, 1995, ensures the right to equality in its various *provisions* The chapters dealing with education, employment, *non-discrimination* etc. *ensure* these rights on the basis of equality. These chapters also provide *for the accommodation* of the special needs of persons with disabilities, for example, the *chapter dealing* with education provide for the facility of scribe to the visually *disabled students*

The chapter dealing with employment provide for the identification and reservation of employment for persons with disabilities. Similarly the chapter dealing with non-discrimination provide for the modification of roads, transport system etc so that the persons with disabilities can negotiate with them on an equal basis with others.

## CCPD Contribution to the Right to Equality for Persons with Disabilities

Office of the Chief Commissioner for Persons with Disabilities (CCPD) is established under section 57 of the Persons with Disabilities (Equal Opportunities, Protection of Rights and Full Participation) Act, 1995. This act under section 60 provides for the appointment of commissioners in states on almost the similar lines as CCPD at the centre. It may be mentioned here that in UK and USA the trend is to establish one single body to deal with all types of discrimination. For such as disability, gender, age, race etc. UK has established the Equality and Human Rights commission in 2007. Similarly USA has established the Equal Opportunity Commission to deal with the discrimination in workplace. In India, the NHRC is empowered to take cognisance of complaints on any type of discrimination including disability. As compared to CCPD, it has more powers to implement it[s] orders. In spite of this, the CCPD has been the main forum for disability related complaints. There are various reasons for this.

Firstly, this forum is cheaper as compared to the regular courts; no court fee is prescribed to approach this forum. Similarly there is no requirement of lawyer to present the case before it. The complainant himself or any other person or organisation on his/her behalf can appear to argue the matter.

Secondly, this forum is devoid of any procedural technicalities. Law of procedure and evidence is not applicable in this forum.

Thirdly, the people who have been appointed as Chief Commissioners and Deputy Commissioners have been either from the disability sector or have acquired reasonably good understanding about disability issues. As a result, persons with disabilities feel more comfortable before this forum as compared to regular courts and other quasi judicial bodies.

Fourthly, in most of the states, the commission have either not been established or have not been very affective forum for the redressal of complaints. As a result, persons with disabilities and there organisations have approached this forum.

Fifthly, in majority of cases, CCPD has adopted the procedure of conciliation rather than the adversarial procedure. This procedure has been acceptable to complainants as well as the authorities against whom the complaint has been made. Researcher has found that majority of cases in which this procedure has been followed, parties have agreed to the solutions acceptable to both of them. The fact that CCPD does not have the power to execute its decisions nor it can initiate contempt proceedings is case of non-compliance of its decisions, the conciliation procedure has been very affected in giving relief to complainants against the authorities.

Despite all this, the CCPD has not been as affective as it should be. There are number of reasons for this.

Firstly, as mentioned earlier, CCPD does not have the machinery to enforce its decisions.

The position is slightly different with respect to such bodies in UK and USA. The Equality and Human Rights Commission [UK] and the Equal Opportunity Commission [USA] are different from CCPD in this respect. These commissions can initiate legal proceedings against the parties if the matter is not settled through mediation. In India, the NHRC has similar powers. Section 18 of the Protection of Human Rights Act, 1993 provides for the steps which the NHRC can take after enquiry.

## National Human Rights Commission (NHRC)

NHRC is established under the Protection of Human Rights Act, 1993. It has been very active in the field of disability rights. It organises workshops, training programmes etc from time to time to sensitise the people about disability rights. It has come up with various publications. NHRC as passed various instructions to uphold the rights of persons with disabilities however the CCPD has remained the most favoured forum for persons with disabilities. NHRC has recommended from time to time various amendments to strengthen the disability legislations. It has written letters to state governments and other authorities stressing upon the proper implementation of disability legislation.

## International Position

### United Nation Convention on the Rights of Persons with Disabilities (UNCRPD)

The Convention on the Rights of Persons with Disabilities (UNCRPD) guarantees the right to equality in its various provisions. Infact the Right to Equality is the guiding theme of the convention. The convention guarantees various rights persons with disabilities on an equal basis with others. These rights include inter alia right to education, employment, Participation in political and public life, Participation in political and public life and Access to Justice. It recognises both the principles of disability rights jurisprudence i.e. Non-discrimination and Reasonable Accommodation.

Article 3 enumerates the guiding principles of the convention. The principle of non-discrimination is enumerated in clause (b) of this Article. Likewise clause (c) of the Article enumerates the principles of Full and effective participation and inclusion in society. Clause (e) recognises the principles of Equality .The principles of Reasonable Accommodation is enumerated in clause (a) (d) and (f) of Article 3 clause (a) recognises the principles of respect for inherent dignity, individual autonomy including the freedom to make one's own choices, and independence of persons. Article 5 guarantees equality and non-discrimination. Similarly Article 12 guarantees the Persons with Disabilities Equal recognition before the law.

Clause d gives reorganisation to the principles of Respect for difference and acceptance of persons with disabilities as part of human diversity and humanity. Clause (f) recognises the principles of Accessibility.

Article 9 provides for the Accessibility of physical environment as well as of information and communication. The provisions relating to education, employment, participation in various activities etc. provide inter alia for the modification of the environment considering the special needs of various types of disability so that the persons with disabilities can participate in them effectively on the basis of equality.

## International Covenant on Civil and Political Rights (ICCPR)

Leading commentators to describe equality and non-discrimination as 'the dominant single theme of the Covenant' which 'runs like a red thread throughout the Covenant.'

The provisions that guarantee equality or prohibit discrimination include

- The obligation of States parties to respect and ensure the enjoyment of the rights and freedoms recognised in the Covenant without distinction of any kind (Article 2(1));
- The equal right of men and women to the enjoyment of the rights set forth in the Covenant (Article 3);
- The right to equality before the courts and tribunals (Article 14);
- The right to equality of rights and obligations of spouses in relation to marriage (Article 23(4));
- The right of children to protection without discrimination (Article *7);*
- The right to take part in the political and public life of one's country without discrimination (Article 25);
- The right to equality before the law and equal protection of the law (Article 26); the rights of minorities (Article 27).

## These Provisions in Themselves Are no Guarantee for the Respect of Disabled and Disability Rights.

It requires much more than just legal provisions to ensure justice for the disabled yet the provisions of international law and following municipal legislations on disability in India provides very strong legal protection to the disabled community.

## Endnotes

1. Quoted in the report of Special Rapporteur on Disability presented at the 50th session of the Commission for Social Development
2. NHRC annual report 2003-2004 See generally National Human Rights Commission Disability Manual, 2005 PP 18 -19

3. See Ibid. PP 17-18
4. The Individual and Social Models of Disability By Mike Oliver Reader in Disability Studies Thames Polytechnic Paper presented at Joint Workshop of the Living Options Group and the Research Unit of the Royal College of Physicians on People with Established Locomotor Disabilities in hospitals on Monday 23rd July 1990
5. See Ibid. PP 19-20
6. Quoted in the report of Special Rapporteur on Disability presented at the 50th session of the Commission for Social Development
7. See Ibid. PP 21-25
8. The Individual and Social Models of Disability By Mike Oliver Reader in Disability Studies Thames Polytechnic Paper presented at Joint Workshop of the Living Options Group and the Research Unit of the Royal College of Physicians on People with Established Locomotor Disabilities in hospitals on Monday 23rd July 1990

0. M.V. Ramana Rao v. A.P.S.R.T.C., 2003 (3) ALD 550: 2003 (4) ALT 150 (AP HC)

10. Bogga Mallesh v. The Commissioner, Disabled Welfare Department, W.P. No. 22440 of 2004 (AP HC)
11. Disabled Rights Group v. Delhi University, CWP No. 10055/ 2004 (Del HC)
12. Manu/SC/1167/2009, AIR 201OSC1253
13. (Article 3).
14. (Article 4)
15. (Article 8)
16. (Article 10)
17. (Article 6)
18. (Article 7)
19. (Article 12)
20. (Article 13)
21. (Article 14)
22. (Article 17)
23. UNCRPD Art 2 para 3, "Discrimination on the basis of disability" means any distinction, exclusion or restriction on the basis of disability which has the purpose or effect of impairing or nullifying the recognition, enjoyment or exercise, on an equal basis with others, of all human rights and fundamental freedoms in the political, economic, social, cultural, civil or any other field. It includes all forms of discrimination, including denial of reasonable accommodation.

24. Ibid. Art 3 CL (b) Non-discrimination

25. Ibid. Art 12 Equal recognition before the law

    1. States Parties reaffirm that persons with disabilities have the right to recognition everywhere as persons before the law.

    2. States Parties shall recognize that persons with disabilities enjoy legal capacity on an equal basis with others in all aspects of life.

    3. States Parties shall take appropriate measures to provide access by persons with disabilities to the support they may require in exercising their legal capacity.

    4. States Parties shall ensure that all measures that relate to the exercise of illegal capacity provide for appropriate and effective safeguards to prevent abuse in accordance with international human rights law. Such safeguards shall ensure that measures relating to the exercise of legal capacity respect the rights, will and preferences of the person, are free of conflict of interest and undue influence, are proportional and tailored to the person's circumstances, apply for the shortest time possible and are subject to regular review by a competent, independent and impartial authority or judicial body. The safeguards shall be proportional to the degree to which such measures affect the person's rights and interests.

    5. Subject to the provisions of this article, States Parties shall take all appropriate and effective measures to ensure the equal right of persons with disabilities to own or inherit property, to control their own financial affairs and to have equal access to bank loans, mortgages and other forms of financial credit, and shall ensure that persons with disabilities are not arbitrarily deprived of their property.

26. NHRC annual report 2000-2001

27. UNCRPD 2006

28. Ibid. Art 3 (d)

29. Ibid. Art 9

30. Ibid. Art 24

31. Ibid. Art 27

32. Ibid. Art 29 and 30

33. Dicey: *Law of the Constitution,* 10th Ed., p. 193.

34. State of W.B. v. Anwar Ali Sarkar, AIR 1952 SC 75,79.

# 3

# Disability Law, Education and Policy in India

## Introduction

It is said that Knowledge is Power. Education is the most effective vehicle of social and economic empowerment. There is a need for mainstreaming of the persons with disabilities in the general education system through Inclusive education.

Education is a social right that is intimately connected to the exercise of many other human rights. For example, education is important for the enjoyment of the right to work, right to participation into the political life etc. Education supports greater autonomy and freedom of participation in all aspects of society.

The two principles of disability rights jurisprudence instead of discussed in chapter 2 of this thesis are applicable to the right of education of persons with disabilities. On one hand the right to receive education of every kind whether it is primary, secondary or tertiary or professional/vocational should be available to them without discrimination and on the equal basis with others, on the other hand, reasonable accommodation needs to be made with regard to accessibility of study material and mode of instructions, examination pattern, build environment of the institutions etc.

## Disability and Indian Constitution

The Constitution of India not only recognizes right to education but also emphasises its importance for the vulnerable and weaker sections. Constitution of India Article 41[1]

Article 46 commands that the State shall promote with special care of the educational and economic interests of the weaker sections of the people, and, in particular, of the Scheduled Castes and Scheduled Tribes.

With the Eighty-Sixth Amendment, the right to free and compulsory education has become a fundamental right. Originally, this right was a part of the Directive Principles under Article 45. Other noteworthy aspect of this amendment is that the fundamental right to education has been arranged as an extension of the right to life, as Article 21 A[2]

The Eighty Sixth Amendment has brought another important facet of education, i.e. early or pre-school education under the constitutional framework. Article 45[3]

This provision is of particular relevance for children with disabilities. These amendments are not only important from the perspective of an individual right but they have enlarged the scope of duties both for the State and citizens. The duties of citizens outlined in Article 51A of the Constitution[4]. The Right to Free and Compulsory Education Act, 2009 under Section 3 puts the persons with disabilities as one of the Disadvantaged sections of the society, the act mandates 25 percent reservation of seats for the disadvantaged groups including persons with disabilities in government and private educational institutions.

## Issues Relevant to the Education of Persons with Disabilities

The ICESCR in General Comment No. 13[5] (para.6) elaborates on the four main elements of the right to education: availability, accessibility, acceptability and adaptability. These parameters are useful in assessing whether the education has acquired capacity to respond to the needs of learners with disability. For an inclusive society it is important that all systems, services and procedures remain within the reach of all members.

With regard to the education of persons with disabilities, a number of issues needs to be addressed.

Firstly, in a country like India where a large number of people live below poverty line, the education of persons with disabilities becomes a challenging task. In majority of cases, persons with disabilities do not enjoy the same status in the family as compared to the others. They are considered as burden on society. There is stigma attached to them that they cannot lead a productive life in the society. As a result, society does not think it beneficial to invest its valuable resources on their education.

The Committee on the Rights of the Child in General Comment No. 1[6] (para 10) notes that 'discrimination against children with disabilities is also pervasive in many formal educational systems and in a great many informal educational settings, including in the home.' Prohibiting such discrimination the Committee states, in the same comment 'all such discriminatory practices are in direct contradiction with the requirements in Article 29(1)(a) that education be directed to the development of child's personality, talents and mental and physical abilities to their fullest potential.

The Convention on the Rights of Persons with Disabilities (UNCRPD), 2006 deals with this issue[7]. It provides inter alia that:

a) Persons with disabilities are not excluded from the general education system on the basis of disability, and that children with disabilities are not excluded from free and compulsory primary education, or from secondary education, on the basis of disability;

b) Persons with disabilities can access an inclusive, quality and free primary education and secondary education on an equal basis with others in the communities in which they live;

The PWD Act, 1995[8] also makes provision in this matter it provides inter alia that:

a) Every child with a disability has access to free education in an appropriate environment till he attains the age of eighteen years;

b) State shall endeavour to promote their integration in the normal schools;

c) promote setting up of special schools in Government and private sector for those in need of special education, in such a manner that children with disabilities living in any part of the country have access to such schools; and

d) State shall endeavour to equip the special schools for children with disabilities with vocational training facilities.

Similarly, Section 30 of the act amongst other things, provides for the formulation of schemes with regard to the financial support to the students with disabilities these include:

a) The supply of books, uniforms and other materials to children with disabilities attending school.

b) The grant of scholarship to students with disabilities.

National Policy[9] for Persons with Disability 2006 also deals extensively with the education of persons with disabilities.

Secondly, the premises of educational institutions need to be made accessible for persons with disabilities. For example, persons with orthopedic disability cannot move freely within the premises of these institutions. Persons with visual disability also face various problems while negotiating with the physical environment of these institutions. Apart from this, the public roads, buses, railways, etc are also highly inaccessible for persons with disabilities.

The PWD act[10] deals with makes provisions in this matter. It mandates the governments and their instrumentalist to prepare a comprehensive scheme with respect to:

1) Transport facilities to the children with disabilities or in the alternative financial assistance to the parents or guardians to enable their children with disabilities to attend schools.

2) The removal of architectural barriers from schools, colleges or other institution, imparting vocational and professional training;

Thirdly, the study material and the medium of instruction needs to be made available in format and manner suitable to the needs of the various types of disabilities. For example, the persons with visual disability face various problems in accessing the study material because it is not available in Braille, Audio-books, Large Print, etc. Apart from this, the curriculum needs to be adapted to the special needs of persons with disabilities. e.g. for pupil with visual disabilities, graphs and diagrams needs to be supplemented by descriptive explanation. Similarly pupil with hearing disability faces difficulty in following instructions because of the non-availability of Sign Language Interpreter in educational institutions.

**UNCRPD[11] deals with these issues also. It mandates:**

1) Reasonable accommodation of the individual's requirements should be provided;
2) Persons with disabilities receive the support required, within the general education system, to facilitate their effective education;
3) Effective individualized support measures are provided in environments that maximize academic and social development, consistent with the goal of lull inclusion.

The PWD Act also provides for the formulation of schemes with regard to:

4) Suitable modification in the examination system to eliminate purely mathematical questions for the benefit of blind students and students with low vision;
5) Restructuring of curriculum for the benefit of children with disabilities;
6) Restructuring the curriculum for benefit of students with hearing impairment to facilitate them to take only one language as part of their curriculum.

Fourthly, persons with disabilities who have difficulty in writing such as visually disabled and various types of orthopaedically disabled students needs to be provided with the facility of scribe during exams. The norms for availling scribe should be reasonable so that persons with disability do not face undue hardship. At the same time steps need to be taken so that the facility of scribe is not abused. Since writing exams through scribe requires more time, extra time needs to be given to write the examinations.

While formulating policy in this matter the technological development needs to be taken into consideration. e.g. persons with visual disability should be allowed to use computer in place of scribe during exam.

According to PWD Act[12] all educational institutions are mandated to provide amanuensis to blind students and students with low vision.

Although this section covers the case of blind and low vision students, the courts and commission have directed. To provide this service to other disabled candidates who have difficulty in writing.

Fifthly, similarly the curriculum needs to incorporate learning Braille, mobility skills etc. Persons with hearing disability are required to be trained in sign language. For this purpose adequate number of teachers needs to be trained in these skills.

The convention[13] deals with these issues. These include:

1) Facilitating the learning of Braille, alternative script, augmentative and alternative modes, means and formats of communication and orientation and mobility skills, and facilitating peer support and mentoring;
2) Facilitating the learning of sign language and the promotion of the linguistic identity of the deaf community;
3) Ensuring that the education of persons, and in particular children, who are blind, deaf or deaf blind, is delivered in the most appropriate languages and modes and means of communication for the individual, and in environments which maximize academic and social development.

Sixthly, to provide persons with disability level playing field, seats need to be reserved and filled in the all types of educational institutions and courses which persons with disabilities can pursue with suitable adaptation and accommodations. PWD act[14] mandates that all Government educational institutions and other educational institutions receiving aid from the Government shall reserve not less than three percent seat for persons with disabilities.

In view of the above an analysis of the judgments, orders etc. on educational matters given by the courts, CCPD and NHRC is analysed in the following section.

## Access to Free Education

### Cases

Right of a disabled child to be admitted in school even if he/ she is overage

*In Shri Umesh Kumar v. The Secretary Department of Elementary Education & Literacy, Department of Ministry of Human Resource Development, New Delhi*[15] Complainant, the father of a hearing impaired child filed a complaint regarding denial of admission to his son in class first due to overage. He submitted that his son was attending aural rehabilitation programme and has started communicating verbally in short sentences and writing in complete sentences which would qualify him to enter mainstream education.

Upon considering the reply of the Kendriya Vidyalaya Sangathan, the court in a letter to the Secretary, Department of Elementary Education & literacy, Ministry of Human Resource Development, mentioned that the stand taken by Kendriya Vidyalaya Sangathan was not in line with the Principles of Sarv Shiksha Abhiyan which encourages grade appropriate mainstreaming as well as it was also not in tandem with the disabilities Act and national education policy which mandate appropriate government and local authorities to provide appropriate intervention for education and mainstreaming of children with disabilities.

In the mean time, the complainant submitted that his son was admitted in class two on the basis of the recommendation/ instructions letter issued by the court.

The respondent submitted that the issue of overage with respect to the children with disabilities might be examined in the light of the letter of the court and the policy and inclusive education and the provisions of the Right to education Act 2009 and a decision might be taken by the ministry within three months.

Right of child with hearing disability to be admitted in the fourth year of the course despite the fact that the institution did not has the requisite facility for special education

*In Shri Kishan Lai v. Kathak Kendra*[16] The complainant submitted inter alia that his son had passed three years course successfully. The respondent was denying him admission in the 4th year due to his disability.

The respondent submitted that after completion of three years foundation course, the then Director of the respondent institute allowed the complainant's son to come to the dance classes without paying any fee as a special case, the complainant was also told that no exams would be taken in case of his son as he was unable to follow the syllabus along with other children. Since his son admitted in three years foundation course which he had already completed, respondent institution could grant him certificate for completion for three year foundation course. During hearing the complainant stated inter alia that his child's hearing disability can be corrected with the use of hearing AID. The respondent also reiterated that the complainant's child needed special attention and the respondent institution had no resource and infrastructure for imparting training to persons with disability. However if complainant insists to continue his child dance training at the respondent institution for another two years, the respondent had no objection to her readmission in 4th year of the course.

Since the respondent had agreed to admit complainant's child in the next session, the court advised the complainant to approach the respondent in the next session for admission. The respondent was also advised by the court to help the complainant's child and facilitate teaching and learning process so that he could complete five year foundation course.

Instructions should be issued to Head Master for not refusing admission to persons with disabilities with because they are bound to admit them in view of the mandate of the constitution.

*In Parvathi Ramakrishnan* v. *The Chief Secretary, Govt, of NCT of Delhi and Ors*[17] In this case, the complainant affirmed that the act provides for three percent reservation for persons with disabilities in government educational and other educational institutions receiving aid from the government. She alleged that the schools run by the respondents are not giving reservation as per the act.

Respondent no. 2 submitted inter alia that the enforceability of section 39 of the act for the purpose of seeking admission has no meaning as the respondent is liable to provide education to each and every ward including ward of disabled category and is doing so in compliance of the provision in article 39 of the Constitution of India read with article 275 and relevant provisions of Delhi Municipal Corporation Act, 1957.

During the conciliation meeting the respondent no. 2 agreed to issue instructions to all the Headmasters within one week for not refusing admission to students merely on the grounds of disability.

The court closed the proceeding with the advised to the respondent no. 2 to appoint the special educational teacher if the number of disable students was eight or more. The court also said that the schools should establish a resource centre for persons with disabilities.

Instructions should be issued to Head Masters for not denying admission to students with disabilities specially the students with mild and moderate level of disability

*In Mahesh Sharma v. Commissioner Municipal Corporation of Delhi*[18] The complainant affirmed that the Municipal Corporation of Delhi had decided to close the schools meant for mentally retarded children because of the low enrolment of children. The Complainant brought to the notice to the commission that a substantial number of children are getting training in the institutes run by NGOs because schools run by the government are been closed. The act imposes responsibility on the government to make provisions of education and training for mentally retarded children.

During conciliation meeting, the complainant further emphasized that already less than three percent children with disability have access to education. Closing down the centers would further aggravate the situation and deprived then with from their right to education.

After hearing both the parties, the court proposed that the parties might consider to settle the case on certain terms and conditions suggested by this court. The important amongst them were:

- That the Respondent will issue instructions to Head Master and Head Mistresses of the schools under their administrative control for not denying admission to students on grounds of disability. Students having mild and moderate level of disability of seeing, hearing, loco motor and mental retardation can be given admission without any hesitation.

- That in case an NGO working in the area of disability approaches the Head Master or Head Mistresses for admission of any student with disability, the same shall be granted with the assurance of support to be provided to the disabled students and the concerned schools by the recommending NGOs.
- Offering increment to those in-service teachers who successfully complete a diploma Or a degree in the area of disability education.
- Granting study leave on priority to such in-service teacher.
- Ensuring barrier-free entrance to school buildings, classrooms laboratories, sports arena, toilets and other facilities in the school for children with disabilities. For providing barrier-free features in the school premises, respondent might approach Govt. of India, Ministry of Human Resource Development.
- Engaging one special teacher in cases where eight children with disabilities are admitted to a school. Such school shall also create a resource centre equipped with appropriate teaching learning devices for students with disabilities.

In distance education courses, where there is no restriction as to the number of seats, advertisement should mention that persons with disabilities can also apply

*In the director, Institute of open and distance education, Barkatullah University*[19] case, the respondent which was an open and distance education institute had published admission notice for several courses but no reservation for persons with disabilities was made in accordance with section 39 of the act.

The respondent submitted that in the institute of open and distance education are conducted through correspondence for which there is no restriction of number of seats. Therefore they welcome all the persons with disabilities for admission if they possessed minimum education qualifications.

In view of the material available on record and taking in the account the fact that respondent was providing seats to disabled candidates, the court decided to dispose off the matter with the advice that it should be mentioned in the future admission notice that persons with disabilities are eligible to all courses. Such information will create awareness amongst the disabled persons and their organizations about learning opportunities through Distance and Open Universities.

Sections 30 and 31 outline the special measures to create the concept of appropriate educational environment guaranteed in Section 26.

Section 30[20] mandates the preparation of a comprehensive education scheme which shall make provision for:

a) transport facilities to the children with disabilities or in the alternative financial incentives to parents or guardians to enable their children with disabilities to attend schools;

b) the removal of architectural barriers from schools, colleges or other institutions imparting vocational and professional training;

c) the supply of books, uniforms and other materials to children with disabilities attending school;

d) the grant of scholarship to students with disabilities;

e) suitable modification in the examination system to for the benefit of blind students and students with low vision;

f) restructuring of curriculum for the benefit of children with disabilities; and

g) restructuring the curriculum for the benefit of students with hearing impairment to facilitate them to take only one language as part of their curriculum.

Alternative question with equal weightage be provided in place of the question based on diagrams and figures to persons with visual disabilities

*In Ashwani Agarwal v. Secretary, Department of Education*[21] This case highlights the various difficulties faced by the blind students with regard to attempting questions based on diagrams and figures, issued relating to scribes for writing answers scripts etc. Although the complain was withdrawn because the relief sought was already given by the respondent, the brief facts of the case are mentioned below to highlight the difficulties faced by the blind students in these matters.

The Complainant affirms that the blind students are studying mathematics up to Class X with their sited counterparts. While appearing their Class X examination they face certain limitation in the paper of mathematics which allows them to attempt only 60 percent of the paper as rest 40 percent is based on visual in nature.

Complainant sought relief from the Chief Commissioner for Persons with Disabilities in advising the Ministry of Human Resource Development to issue instructions to various examination boards and agencies conducting class X and class XII examination with the CCPD

asked the Ministry to direct them to issue instructions to the paper setters to offer alternative questions in lieu of questions with diagrams and figures. The alternative questions should be of equal value to the question containing diagrams and figures.

All questions based on figures or diagrams in the paper be provided with an alternative question of equal marks from the syllabus which blind students can attempt. This will allow them to attain marks which they failed otherwise, as the questions were exclusively visual based.

The complainant alleges that the blind students be provided with extra time @ 20 minutes per hour i.e. he/she should be provided with 60 minutes of extra time to attend a three hour paper in order to provide equal opportunity.

For persons with visual disabilities, graphs should be supplemented by descriptive explanation, font size should not be less then 20, extra time should be given

*In Mohammed Asif Iqbal v. Indian Institute of Management, Calcutta and Ors*[22] Complainant who was a visually disabled candidate and a graduate in Commerce could not do well in not on data interpretation portions.

During the personal hearing, it was unanimously agreed that the guidelines/ instructions on the following lines should be framed and issued by Ministry of HRD.

a. Wherever possible, the visual graphs should be supplemented by descriptive explanation of the graphs for visually impaired candidates;

b. The font size of the question paper should not be less than 20 for the benefit of low vision candidates. They should also be allowed to use optical/ electronic low vision aids such as magnifying glass;

c. Since one of the important factors to do the question paper is stated to bo the speed for which adequate practice is necessary, persons with blindness should be allowed to use the services of a scribe of their choice who should meet the conditions that may be prescribed by the examining authorities. If the scribe is provided by the examining authorities, it should be ensured that the scribe is adequately qualified to understand the questions and to explain them to the candidate. Scribe should be allowed, to such other candidates also who cannot write themselves due to disability;

d. Extra time of 20 minutes per hour of examination currently being allowed by IIMs to visually impaired candidates who use the services of scribe, should be allowed by all the examining agencies such as IITs/ Universities/NITs etc. who conduct such entrance tests for management courses.

e. The application form should have a column for the applicant to indicate whether he/she will use the services of own scribe or would require the examining authority to arrange for it. The qualifications/eligibility conditions of the scribe should also be clearly indicated.

f. The application form should have a provision asking low vision persons to indicate the requirement of question paper in large print. The advertisement for examination as well as to provide this facility to other disabilities also in appropriate cases the application form should also clearly mention that the low vision persons would be allowed the use of magnifying glass put.

g. All the IIMs and other management institutes/Universities should ensure that their placement cells counsel/guide the candidates with disabilities for choosing the streams/area of specialization keeping in view their employability after completion of the course. While doing so, the jobs identified for different disabilities should also be kept in view.

## Amanuensis

### Cases

Right of person with Cerebral Palsy to extra time in exam

*In Dhawal s. Chotai vs. Union of India and Others*[23] This petition was filed by a person who suffered from a disorder of movement and posture which is known as "Cerebral Palsy". In view of this difficulty, it affects the normal functioning of bones, muscles and joints and also the communication skills, the Petitioner had completed his education up to graduation in commerce. Having passed the examination for foundation course for the Chartered Accounts Examination. The petitioner wanted to appear for the Intermediate Examination known as "Professional Education-II".

While giving the examinations on earlier occasions, he had requested the authorities to give him extra time and when he wrote his B. Com. examination, the University of Mumbai had granted him three extra hours. He made a similar representation to Respondent No. 2 Institution, and the Respondent No. 2 has granted him relaxation only for half an hour. Petitioner prayed that the Respondents be directed to permit the Petitioner to write the papers for three extra hours.

The court observed that in the facts of the present case, the Petitioner had undoubtedly established that on earlier occasions he did require three hours, the Petitioner would like to write the papers himself. This was because particularly the subject like Accounts would be better written if he wrote himself.

The court agreed with the contention of the petitioner and directed respondent No. 2 to permit the Petitioner to write his examination and the future examinations for the Chartered Accountants Course for three hours any time a written examination is held these three hours would be subsequent to the scheduled time in continuity on the same day. The Institute where the examination was being held would provide all co-operations to the Petitioner in continuing with the examination for these three extra hours.

### Denial of reservation of admission to paramedical courses to persons with visual impairment or hearing impairment is illegal

*In Anju Talukdar & Anr. V. State of Assam & Ors*[24] The petitioner through public interest litigation prayed to issue direction to quash the notice and suitably modify and republish the educational advertisement in so far as the same restricts the reservation for disabled candidates only to persons with loco motor disability of lower limbs having between 50% to 70% disability. This advertisement was published for the admission in paramedical courses. The respondent inter alia argued that it issued such advertisement on the basis of the guidelines issued by the Medical Council of India (MCI) which found only this category of disability to be fit for such courses.

The court after going through the submissions made by the Medical Council of India, provisions of the disability Act and various Judgment of the Supreme Court and High Court observed that it is not very clear whether there is anything in law which exclude either a person with visual impairment or hearing impairment from seeking admission to a medical course not against any reservation but purely on merit. In the absence of such restriction the learned judges said that they have no option but to reach conclusion that denying the benefit to the above mentioned two categories of disabilities is illegal. Apart from that when the language of section 39 of the Act is clear and categorical that the benefit of reservation should extend to all categories of persons with disabilities, denying the benefit appears to be wholly illegal in the absence of any legally tenable justification. Prescription of 50% to 70% disability which in turn is confined by the impugned advertisement to be disability of lower limbs is also plainly contrary to the language of the enactment. The court held that the impugned notification in so far as restricted the benefit of reservation to the loco motor disability the lower limbs is wholly unsustainable. The court directed the respondent to consider the cases of candidates falling under any one of the seven categories of disabilities recognised under the Act for admission to various courses covered under the impugned notification against the 3% of the total no. of seats sought to be filled up.

**Admission cannot been denied on the ground that the candidate failed to produce the certificate to show that he can teach students.**

*In Surinder Kumar v. Punjabi University*[25] case, an eligible blind candidate prayed for the writ of mandamus directing the respondent to admit him to B.Ed course against one of the reserved seats earmarked for physically disabled persons. The ground taken by the respondent for denying admission was that the petitioner could not produce the certificate from the chief medical officer to show that he could teach students as being one of the conditions laid down in the prospectus.

The court directed the respondent University to see that petitioner is admitted in one of the aforesaid two colleges and if the classes have already started special classes be held for the petitioner. The court held that the petitioner is seeking admission to the B.Ed course and is not seeking any appointment from the Principals of the Colleges who, as per eligibility of the petitioner are legally bound to provide him seat for the B.Ed course. By no stretch of imagination the Principle of the Colleges are competent to refuse admission to him once he has been declared successful in the combined entrance test held by the university.

If with medical aids particularly by provision of glasses or contact lenses the vision can be corrected to the standard prescribed, there is no reason why the candidate with the vision so corrected should be denied admission to the course.

*In Umesh Kumar v. State of Haryana and Others*[26] case, the petitioner took admission to the 1st year Bachelor of Engineering Mechanical course. A candidate seeking admission to the course was required to get himself medically examined and admitted to the course in case he was found to be medically fit. The petitioner was referred for medical examination. The Ophthalmologists examined the petitioner with and without classes and found him unfit for the course. In light of their findings the chief medical officer issued a certificate stating therein that on the basis of number of glasses in both eyes the petitioner was unfit for the course. On the basis of this report, the principal of the college cancelled the provisional admission of the petitioner.

The court examined the brochure of IIT and other colleges where standard of vision prescribed is 6/9 both eyes or 6/6 in better eye in the case of defective vision corrected with glasses.

### The Court Observed as Under

> "We live in the scientifically advanced age. If with medical aids particularly by provision of glasses or contact lenses the vision can be corrected to the standard prescribed, there is no reason why the candidate with the vision so corrected should be denied to the Engineering course. No reason has been assigned by the respondent as to why a candidate with power glasses above to 2.5 power be denied admission to Engineering course when such power glasses correct the defective reason up to the require standard."

The court held that the provision to this effect in the brochure which has impugned herein to Arbitrary, Unconstitutional and Unsustainable and quashed the provision and allow the petition.

### When there is reservation for a particular category, they constitute a class in itself; their inter merit cannot be ignored on the basis of the degree of disability.

*In Vimesh Jain v. Union of India and othrs*[27] The petitioner's case was that the action of respondent in making admission to MBBS course only on the basis of degree of disability is arbitrary and violation of article 14 of the constitution of India.

The court referred no. of cases including the case of Pardeep Jain v. Union of India (1984) 3 SCC 654 (AIR 1984 SC 1420) in which the court held:

> "the effort must therefore, always be to select the best and most meritorious students for admission to technical institutions and medical colleges by providing equal opportunity to all citizens in the country. It was further held by their Lordships that the primary consideration in selection of candidates for admission to the medical college must therefore be merit. The object of any rules which may be made for regulating admissions to the medical colleges must be to secure the best and most meritorious students".

The court allowed the petition and held that no distinction can be made on the basis of degree of disability. However the court disinclined to disturb the admission of other candidate and directed the respondent to create additional seat to accommodate the petitioner.

## CCPD

A pool of scribes in different discipline languages should be created so that the persons with disabilities do not suffer on account of the lack of knowledge or competence of scribe.

*In Renu Gupta v. University Grants Commission*[28] The Complainant, a visually impaired person appeared in NET examination held by UGC. She alleged that the exam coordinator provided a scribe who was not competent to read and write. She prayed to ensure provision of a competent scribe to visually impaired candidates in future.

The Respondent submitted that the visually impaired candidates were given extra time. The scribe provided was chosen from discipline other than that of the candidate. The scribe provided to the candidate was graduate in English.

The complainant in her rejoinder submitted that the scribe was slow and therefore could not complete the paper. Study of English as one of the subject in graduation is not an appropriate criterion for appointment of a person as writer. The exam coordinator should check the efficiency of a person before appointing him/her as scribe. She suggested that a junior student of the same discipline who is in practice of writing examination should be appointed as scribe because he/she would be familiar with the terms used in that discipline. The complainant also submitted that she been a commerce student it was not possible for her to teach all the symbols etc to the scribe in the examination hall during the extra time provided to her.

The court held that in the light of the facts and circumstances of the case and considering that a larger issue of providing appropriate and competent scribes to the blind/disabled persons is involved, it is necessary that a pool of scribes in different disciplines, languages be created so that the blind/disabled persons needing the help of scribes do not suffer on account of the lack of knowledge or competence of the scribe. Alternatively, the examinees should be allowed to bring their own scribes of their choice.

*In a recent case namely Ms Pallavi Kadam v. Dy, Director National Association for the Blind, Mumbai*[29]. CCPD issued a letter to respondent IBPS in which it found unreasonable the condition prescribed for the scribe by the respondent that the scribe should have lesser marks than the candidate and not more than 60% marks in his/her academic stream. The CCPD observed in this connection that this condition will put the disable candidate to serious disadvantage. Instead of such unreasonable condition proper invigilation should be ensured so that candidates using scribe do not indulge in copying.

**All the conditions relating to the qualification of the scribe etc should be indicated in the advertisement.**

*In Dharmender Parshad v. Delhi Subordinate Services Selection board*[30] The Complainant submitted that respondent held written examination for the post of DASS Grade 11. Visually disabled persons were also allowed to appear in this examination. They were not given any prior notice about the requirements of their scribes and when they turned up there with their scribes they were asked for a certificate from a Gazetted Officer declaring qualification of their scribe. Thus, many of them could not take the examination.

The court observed that the complainant was at no stage, advised by the respondent regarding qualification of the scribe, the requirement of production of certificate of educational qualifications, attestation by Gazetted Officer, etc. The respondent themselves had stated that there are no instructions regarding provision of scribe for blind candidates. Therefore, it was reasonable for the Complainant and other similarly placed candidates that they were informed by the respondent about various requirements in respect of their scribes well before the date of examination, instructions to Centre Superintendents can at best serve the Respondent's own purpose and not that of the candidates. There was, therefore, no doubt that it was the responsibility of the respondent examining body to inform the candidates regarding various requirements of examination. In the instant case, the Complainant was deprived of the opportunity to take examination and possible selection against the reserved posts for no faults of his. Because there was no complaint from any other centre or candidate does not justify deprivation of the right of the complaint to take examination.

Particularly in view of the fact that the result of the examination had been declared and respondent had already recommended three visually impaired persons, the court did not consider it expedient at that stage to direct the respondent to conduct fresh examination. The commission found that in the advertisement there was a short fall of one post to be reserved for persons with disabilities according to the roster. However the commission directed the respondent to conduct a separate examination for persons with disabilities against the vacancies which should have been reserved and backlog vacancies if any after consulting the concerned departments within four months from the receipt of this Judgment. The respondent was directed not to declare the complainant ineligible on the ground of his being over-aged for the first examination that might be conducted.

For future examinations the respondent was directed inter alia that all the conditions relating to the qualification of the scribe etc. be indicated in the advertisement itself and verification of the certificates, etc. it necessary should be done before the date of examination.

**Right of Persons with disabilities whose arms are affected or whose disability is such that they could not or have difficulty in writing to the services of scribe.**

*In Sunita Dogra v. Secretary, Department of Personnel and Training.*[31] The complainant who had bilateral congenital hyperplasia in both her upper limbs with 90% disability, filed a complaint submitting that she requested the respondent UPSC for services of scribe to write Civil Services Examination. However the respondent informed her that as per the existing rules all candidates other than those who were blind were to write the papers in their own hands. During personal hearing the complainant clarified that she could try but her speed but her speed was not enough to complete the paper with the prescribed time limit. She also had problem in continuously sitting for long duration in one posture. She could bring her own scribe.

The representative of Respondent No. 2 stated that an Expert Committee, of which Director, National Institute of Orthopaedically Handicapped and other experts from the disability sector were members, had recommended that Orthopaedically handicapped persons do not need the services of scribe as they will be appointed in the posts that require them to read and write. In the advertisement for Civil Services Examination, the Commission had indicated reading and writing as the physical requirement for the services identified for both arms affected persons. As there is no provision to allow use of scribe and extra time to Orthopaedically handicapped candidates in the rules framed by DoPT, UPSC cannot allow on its own.

The court observed:

> "That Since the services have been identified for both arms affected persons without specifying the extent of impairment, such persons who cannot write or whose speed of writing is inadequate, cannot be denied the help of a scribe to write the examination and extra time, if they request for it. The Complainant also cannot be denied the benefit of a scribe due to impairment, which is a justified request, on the ground that many other similarly placed candidates have not been allowed the services of a scribe",

The court advised the respondent to allow the complainant to use the services of the scribe and extra time as available to visually impaired persons.

The court advised the department of personnel and training to amend the relevant rules before the next advertisement and make provision to allow scribe to persons with locomotor disability, whose arms are affected and could not write by themselves or had in adequate speed and provide them the extra time also.

### A person is eligible to appear in MBBS exam even in those cases where he/she loose sight.

*In Anka Toppo* v. AIIMS[32] The aggrieved complainant on being denied the right to take the examinations for MBBS final year on losing sight by the All India Institute of Medical Sciences (AIIMS), approached the NHRC. The Respondent was of the opinion that 'in view of the severe visual loss suffered by the complainant it would not be possible for him to work in the medical profession.' After great persuasion by the NHRC and on exposing the Respondent to numerous examples of blind people successfully pursuing medical profession, the Respondent finally agreed to take steps to examine the petitioner for the MBBS course by offering a modified methodology of examination. In the light of the experience of this case the NHRC at its sitting on 28 May 2001 expressed the view that the Medical Council of India should perform a similar exercise so that the same facility and system is available in other medical institutions of the country as well.

## Reservation of Seats in Educational Institutions

This section has been the subject of litigation in the courts as well as in the commission. Some of the important cases are discussed below:

#### Cases

*In Vikas Gupta v. Indian Institute of Management and Ors*[33] The complainant sought relief to direct the respondent to provide three percent reservation in admission for M.B.A. Course as per section 39 of the act.

Complainant submitted that he was an Orthopaedically Handicapped person, who appeared in the Common Admission Test conducted by IIM. Following his success in the entrance test, he was called for Group Discussion/Interview, but could not secure a place in final merit list. The Complainant further submitted that after making representation before IIM,

Ahmedabad and Bangalore he was communicated that IIMs provide reservation only to SC/ST candidates and not to disabled candidates.

In conciliation meeting, respondents put forward various arguments in support of their stand such as:

1. Confusion prevailing to the interpretation of section 39 of the act
2. Ignorance of the provisions of reservation for persons with disabilities
3. Admission process being in advanced stage, it will be difficult to provide reservation in the current sessions. How ever they agreed to provide it from the next academic session.

Complainant expressed his dissatisfaction to the proposal offered by the Respondents to provide reservation up to three percent to candidates with disability from next academic session. Complainant maintained that he would loose out on precious year, which would have an adverse effect on his career. He also maintained that there is no ambiguity regarding provision of three percent reservation. Therefore depriving him of statutory benefit in the present academic session will tantamount to violation of his right.

The court held that since there is no ambiguity on the applicability of the provision of section 39 of the act therefore denying reservation to persons with disabilities is a clear violation of the rights of persons with disabilities. The commission suggested a number of options to respondents.

In the second conciliation meeting the respondents expressed their preference for considering the case of Complainant and other similarly situated disabled candidates for admission in the present academic session. Respondents agreed to treat Complainant and other similarly situated at par with other reserved category candidates seeking admission in the present session. Respondents also unanimously agreed to provide three percent reservation in all the courses offered by them to candidates with disabilities w.e.f. the next academic session. Respondents expressed that due to very elaborate requirement for the preparation of entrance exam, it will not be practically possible for them to conduct a special entrance test within the short period of time. They further added that advance preparation of about one year is required for conducting written test, group discussion and interviews. Respondents clarified that they will be able to consider only such candidates with disabilities who have pointed out their disability in application form and those who have represented their case before an appropriate authority for getting the benefit of reservation under Persons with Disabilities Act.

The Complainant expressed his satisfaction to the proposal offered by the Respondents. Therefore the case was settled amicably on terms and conditions proposed by court, and accepted by all the Respondents and Complainant.

**Since the teaching post in the University has been identified as suitable for Blinds /Low vision persons, they can not been denied admission to the course on the ground that special facilities for imparting education and training are not available.**

*In Sanjay Kumar Shah v. Mahatma Gandhi Kashi Vidyapeeth*[34] The complainant submitted that he was doing MA History (First year), he wanted to take admission in B.Ed course but the respondent denied him the opportunity by not providing him the application form stating that the blind/low vision persons will not be admitted. However as per the information bulletin of the said course, three percent reservation had been provided for persons with disabilities.

The respondent university was informed by the court that the government of India has identified the teaching posts in the universities as suitable for blinds/low vision persons. Therefore denial of admission to blind or low vision person is in violation of the act. Hence the complainant be allowed provisionally to appear in the Entrance Test.

In subsequent communication, Respondent submitted that in B.Ed, special education for visually handicapped special facilities for imparting education and training along with evaluation for visually handicapped are not available in the Department of Education of the University. The complainant further stated that in the information brochure the university provided that the three percent of the total seats are reserved for physically challenged persons provided that the disabilities of such persons will not interfere/restrain in the process of imparting education and training. In case of complainant it was apparent that visual impairment is directly going to interfere in the teaching, training, learning of the subject. However all other categories of physically challenged persons whose disabilities are not likely to interfere in the process of teaching, training and learning are permitted to appear in the Entrance Examination. The respondent however informed that in view of the advice of the Court the complainant is being provisionally permitted to appear in the entrance examination subject to the final settlement of his admission by this court and the respondent.

Since the issue involves wider implication of the rights of the complainant and similarly placed other blind/low vision persons, it was observed by the court that requirement of provision of additional facilities etc. cannot be the ground for not allowing them admission. The Expert Committee constituted by Ministry of Social Justice and Empowerment while identifying the jobs of TGT, PGT, Lecturer must have considered the training part for the post. Further, Section 30 (f) and (g) of the Persons with Disabilities Act also require that suitable modifications in the examination system and restructuring of curriculum for the benefit of children with disabilities should be made. Therefore, they cannot be denied admission and quality training due to delay in provisional necessary arrangements by some institutions. Many Institutions/ Universities are already imparting B.Ed, education to blind persons and a large number of them are already employed as teachers in schools/ colleges.

The Respondent University was advised to consider the Complainant and similarly placed blind candidates, if any, for admission to B.Ed, course subject to their merit in the entrance examination against three percent seats to be reserved under Section 39 of the Act and intimate the number of persons with disabilities and the blind/ low vision persons admitted to the course within 15 days from the close of admissions. The National Council for Teacher Education (NCTE) and UGC were also advised to issue necessary guidelines/instructions to all Universities and Institutions conducting B.Ed, courses to ensure that 3 percent seats are reserved for persons with disabilities including the blind/ low vision persons. The provision of necessary aids and appliances, modification in curriculum, etc should also be made so that the blind/low vision students do not suffer any disadvantage. Since the Respondent University is under Government of U.P, Secretary Higher Education, Government of U.P. was also requested to issue necessary instructions to all the notations in the State of U.P. to ensure that blind students are not denied admission to B.Ed, course and they are provided appropriate training.

## Conclusions

From the analyses of above, following principles can be deduced:

1. Right to all forms of education without discrimination
2. Inclusive education and lifelong learning
3. Reasonable accommodation of the individual's requirements
4. To learning life and social development skills to facilitate their full and equal participation in education and as members of the community.
5. Facilitating the learning of Braille, alternative script, augmentative and alternative modes, means and formats of communication and orientation and mobility skills, sign language and the promotion of the linguistic identity of the deaf community.
6. Employ teachers, including teachers with disabilities, who are qualified in sign language and/or Braille, and to train professionals and staff who work at all levels of education.
7. Free and compulsory education up to the 18 years of age.
8. Provision for making study material available in the form in which it is accessible to the different categories of persons with disabilities such as braille, audio books, e-text, large print, for persons having different kinds of visual disabilities, instructions in sign language for persons with hearing disabilities etc.
9. Accessible physical environment of the premises of educational institutions.

10. Transport facilities
11. Provision for scribe for the students with visual and other disabilities who have the difficulty in writing.
12. Provision for financial assistance
13. Adaptation in the curriculum and examination pattern.
14. Reservation of seats in educational institutions

6. With regard to the judgments of courts it has been found that although theses judgments have advanced the disability rights jurisprudence it has not gone to that extent as is the ease With Other developed legal systems of the world. There are a number of factors responsible for this.

Firstly, the provisions of the PWD act, 1995 dealing with education are not drafted in brought terms as is the ease with the above mentioned developed systems of the world. The Indian act has not been amended since 1995 when it was passed.

The UK, USA and other countries have amended their disability legislation and incorporated the fairly advanced principles of disability rights jurisprudence. For example the Equality Act, 2010 (UK) makes very elaborates provisions regarding the education of persons with disabilities. This act prohibits direct discrimination e.g. denied admission on the ground of disability, indirect discrimination e.g. providing application form in the format which is not accessible to same categories of disability, disability based discrimination e.g. putting restrictions on some categories of disability to go out during break, harassment.

Individuals disability act, 1990 (USA) provides for the special education services in cases where disability results in the students needing additional or different services to participate in school. Rehabilitation act, 1973 (USA) and Americans with Disabilities Act, 1990 also makes provisions regarding the education of persons with disabilities.

The striking feature of the above mentioned UK and US disability legislations is that they provide for the individualised treatment i.e. accommodation to be made considering the peculiar circumstance of the student with disability. As mentioned in chapter 1 of this text that these legislations define disability in broader terms as compare to Indian law. As a result a large number of students are benefited by these legislations.

India is in the process of amending the PWD act so as to harmonise it with the convention on the rights of persons with disabilities 2006 the committee appointed by the government of India for this purpose has submitted the draft of a new comprehensive legislation. This draft deals with the education of persons with disabilities extensively incorporating the provisions of the convention.

Another noteworthy development is that the courts in India have started taking note of the disability convention and have started to read the provisions of the convention in the fundamental right of the constitution. This trend will go a long way in furthering the disability rights jurisprudence in India.

## Endnotes

1. The State shall, within the limits of its economic capacity and development, make effective provision for securing the right to work, to education and to public assistance in cases of unemployment, old age, sickness and disablement, and in other cases of undeserved want.
2. Ibid. Art, 21 A: The State shall provide free and compulsory education to all children of the age of six to fourteen years in such manner as the State may, by law, determine.
3. Ibid. Art, 45: The State shall endeavour to provide early childhood care and education for all children until they complete the age of six years.
4. Ibid. Art, 51 A It shall be the duty of every citizen of India who is a parent or guardian to provide opportunities for education to his child or, as the case may be, ward between the age of six and fourteen years.
5. Quoted from National Human Rights Commission Disability Manual 2005 PP. 87-88
6. Quoted from National Human Rights Commission Disability Manual 2005 PP 85
7. Convention on the Rights of Persons with Disabilities, 2006 Art 24 2 see also Convention on the Rights of Child, 1989 Art 28 and 29 See also ibid. Art 23
8. Persons with Disability (equal opportunities Protection of Rights and Full Participation) Act, 1995 Section 26

9. National Policy for Persons with Disability, 2006
10. Ibid. section 30 (a) and (b)
11. Convention on the Rights of the Persons with Disabilities 2006 Art 24 2 (c), (d) and (e)
12. Persons with Disabilities (Equal Opportunities Protection of Rights Full Participation Act, 1995 Section 31
13. Convention on the Rights of the Persons with Disabilities 2006 Art 24 3
14. Persons with Disabilities (Equal Opportunities Protection of Rights Full Participation Act, 1995 Section 39
15. Case NO. 10315560 Dated 15.09.2010
16. Case No. 12/1034/10-11 Dated: 22nd Nov. 2010
17. 2001 CCDJ 202 Case No. 372 2000 - Decided on 24.04.2001

    See also (2002) CCDJ 492 in which respondent was directed to include separate column for physically challenged in Scholarship Form.
18. 2000 CCDJ 205 Case no. 664 of 2000 - Decided on 02.05.2001
19. 2001 CCDJ 242 Case no. 668 of 2001 - Decided on 16.05.2001
20. Ibid. Section 30
21. 2001 CCDJ 244 Case no. 667 of 2001 - Decided on 20.09.2001
22. (2004) CCDJ 347 Case no. 2559 of 2003 - Decided on 15.10.2004
23. AIR 2003 Bom 316
24. AIR 2009 GAUHATI 54
25. (2005) 1 PDD (CC) 72
26. (2005) 1 PDD (CC) 79
27. (2005) 1 PDD (CC) 79
28. 2003 I CCDJ CCDJ 7 Case no. 2312 of 2002 - Decided on 31.03. 2003

    See also (2000) CCDJ 44, Respondent was directed to tender written apology to Complainant and provide assistance of scribe as well as extra time to blind or low vision candidates (2001) CCDJ 184, Respondent was directed to refund the amount charged towards arrangement of amanuensis
29. Case No-49/104/IM2011
30. 2003CCDJ10 Case no. 26660f 2002- Decided on 19.05.2003
31. (2006)CCDJ Case no.3221 of 2006-Decided on 08.05.2006
32. No. 1754/30/2000-2001available at nhrc.nie.in/disparchive.asp

33. 2001 CCDJ 225 Case no. 518 of 2000 - Decided on 13.02.2001

34. (2005) CCDJ 13 Case no. 2887 of 2004- Decided on 14.01.2005

35. Rights of Persons with Disability bill. 2011, Section 35 Right to Education

    (I) All persons with disabilities have a right to education to enable the full development of their human potential, sense of dignity and self-worth; to develop their personality, talent and creativity, mental and physical abilities to their fullest potential; and to enable their effective participation in an inclusive society.

    (2) No person with disabilities shall be excluded from the education system on the basis of disability, and the appropriate government shall ensure that all persons with disabilities, especially girls and women with disabilities, have access to education, without discrimination on an equal basis with others, at all levels.

36. ibid. Sec.49 Right to Higher Education

    (1) No person with disability particularly women with disabilities shall be denied admission in a higher education institution on the grounds of his or her disability provided that, if a person with disability is unable to seek admission to a higher education institution at or before the age prescribed for such admission then he or she shall be given admission in such institution if he or she fulfils all other eligibility conditions.

    (2) All appropriate governments and educational authorities may if they deem fit to promote equality of opportunity relax according to the prescribed procedure and minimum qualification criteria required to be obtained by persons with disabilities who seek admission to higher educational institution.

37. Ibid. Sec 44 No Detention

    No child, who is admitted in a school, shall be held back in a class or expelled from school prior to the completion of secondary education.

38. Ibid. Sec 38 Right to Free Childhood Care and Preschool Education Every child below the age of six

39. Ibid. Sec.40 Reasonable Accommodation in Education.

    (1) The appropriate government and establishment shall ensure that reasonable accommodation of the individual requirements is provided at all levels of education system, taking into consideration both age and gender requirement needs;

    (2) The appropriate government and establishment shall ensure the persons with disabilities receive individualised support, within the education system to facilitate their effective education provided in environments that maximise academic and social development, consistent with the goal of full inclusion.

(3) In order to ensure appropriate quality education for persons with disabilities, the appropriate government and establishments shall take measures, including

(a) Facilitating the learning of Braille, alternative script, augmentative and alternative modes means and formats of communication and orientation and mobility skills, facilitating peer support and mentoring.

(b) Facilitating the learning of sign language and promotion of linguistic identity of the deaf community.

(c) Employing teachers including teachers with disabilities who are qualified in sign language and/or Braille, and to train professionals and staff who work at all levels of education.

# 4

# Disability Rights and Employment in India

Equality is the cornerstone of the human rights doctrine and is crucial to the right to work. On the one hand, discrimination on grounds of caste, race, religion, sex, place of birth or status etc. has been prohibited, and on the other, affirmative action and special measures in favour of vulnerable groups have been guaranteed. Right or work or employment is crucial for the enjoyment of various human rights. This right is equally important for persons with disabilities as without participating in economic activities and adequate means of livelihood they cannot enjoy equal and dignified status in the society.

## Constitution of India

The strategy to ensure equality adopted by the Constitution and supported by legislation is twofold. Article 16[1] deals with the right to equality of opportunity and non-discrimination in relation to work. Article 16(1)[2] guarantees equality of opportunity to all citizens in the area of public employment, and Article 16(2)[3] prohibits discrimination on grounds of race, caste, religion, sex, place of birth or status. Article 16(4)[4] empowers the State to make special provisions for the reservation in appointments to public offices in favour of any backward class of citizens which, in the opinion of the State, is not adequately represented in the services under the State.

The apex court in Indira Sawhhney v. Union of *India*[5] declared that reservation in favour of persons with disabilities is covered under Article 16(1), and said, Clause (1) of article 16 guarantees equality of opportunity for all citizens in matters of employment or appointment to any office under the State. The very concept of equality implies recourse to valid classification for preferences in favour of the disadvantaged classes of citizens to improve their conditions so as to enable them to raise themselves to positions of equality with the more fortunate classes of citizens. Extending this line of thinking to the context of persons with disability, the Court held that, to enable all to compete with each other on equal plane, it is necessary to take positive measures to equip the disadvantaged and the handicapped to bring them to the level of the fortunate advantaged. Articles 14 and Article 16(1) no doubt would by themselves permit such positive measures in favour of the disadvantaged to make real the equality guaranteed by them. With reference to the scope of Articles 16(1) and 16(2), the Courts have laid down the following principles which are now well-settled:

a) Equality of opportunity means that a citizen has an equal chance with others in matters relating to employment under the State.

b) Equality of opportunity in matters of employment means equality as between members of the same class of employees and not equality between members of separate, independent classes.

c) Clause (1) (of Article 16) is much wider in scope than Clause (2) and the grounds of discrimination mentioned in Clause (2) are not exhaustive. Discrimination alleged on grounds other than those stated in Article 16 (2) have to be weighed and judged in the light of the general principle laid down in Article 16 (1).

d) Every eligible candidate has a right to be considered. No person has a right to a post.

The right to equality in the area of work as embodied in Article 16 is however limited to public employment and does not extend to the private sector of the economy. The right to work is included in Article 41 of Part-IV of the Constitution of India, which obliges the State to ensure the right to work, subject to its economic capacity and development. Article 21 of the Constitution guarantees the right to life and liberty. The Courts have consistently maintained that the right to life does not mean mere animal existence.

The principles of Non-discrimination and Reasonable Accommodation are applicable to the right of employment of persons with disabilities. On the one hand they should have the right to participate in the economic activity including right to seek employment of their choice in government as well as private sector on an equal basis with others, at the same time the workplace environment should accommodate the special needs of the person with disability in question. These accommodations may include inter alia design of the physical environment of the workplace, provision for assistive devices, relaxed working hours, protection in case of acquiring disability during employment etc.

## Issues Relevant to the Employment of Persons with Disabilities

There are number of issues with regard to the employment of persons with disabilities which needs to be addressed. Without addressing these issues they will not be able to enjoy this right on an equal basis with others.

Firstly, there should be no discrimination against the persons with disabilities (whether the disability is acquired before on after employment) with regard to the opportunities of employment. They should be in a position to choose employment of their choice.

International Disability Convention recognises the right to work, on an equal basis with others; this includes the right to the opportunity to gain a living by work freely chosen or accepted in a labour market and work environment that is open, inclusive and accessible to persons with disabilities the convention also safeguards this right for those who acquire a disability during the course of employment. It recognises the above mentioned right in every matter such as conditions of recruitment, hiring and employment, continuance of employment, career advancement and safe and healthy working conditions to just and favourable conditions of work, including equal opportunities and equal remuneration for work of equal value, safe and healthy working conditions, including protection from harassment, and the redress of grievances etc.

The PWD Act[7] guarantees alternative employment and protection of wages in case of acquiring disability. The section also provides that persons with disabilities cannot be discriminated on the ground of disability in promotion.

Secondly, the issue of Reasonable Accommodation is crucial to the enjoyment of this right. The working environment needs to be adapted to suit the needs of various types of employees with disabilities. e.g. the architectural design of the premises of employment should be such that persons with locomotor, visual and other disabilities can negotiate with the environment with least difficulty. The international disability convention provides that reasonable accommodation should be provided to persons with disabilities in the workplace.

Thirdly, the necessary assistive aids should be provided so that they can perform the task independently. e.g. persons with visual disability should be provided with screen reading software. The PWD Act[9] provides that Governments shall make schemes to provide aids and appliances to persons with disabilities.

Fourthly, the employers should be provided incentives to encourage the employment of persons with disabilities. It becomes necessary because of the stigma attached to persons with disabilities that they cannot participate in the economic activity and thus are subject of charity.

The PWD Act[10] provides for the incentives to the employer in order to encourage the employment of persons with disabilities in public and private sector.

Fifthly, in appropriate cases, posts should be identified for various types of disabilities in which they can perform with their physical limitation and a percentage of these posts should be earmarked exclusively for them.

The convention extensively deals with this issue which provides that persons with disabilities should be enabled to have effective access to general technical and vocational guidance programmes, placement services and vocational and continuing training and employment opportunities and career advancement in the labour market, as well as assistance in finding, obtaining, maintaining and returning to employment should be promoted. They should also be employed in the public sector.

The Governments (both central and state at their respective levels) must identify posts in their establishments which can be reserved for employment of persons with disability and the list of the identified posts must be reviewed and updated at least once in three years[11].

The Governments must reserve, in every Government establishment, three percent vacancies on identified posts[12] 1% each for the following three classes respectively - (1) persons with blindness or low vision; (2) persons with hearing impairment; and (3) persons with locomotor disability or cerebral palsy.

The Act, although enumerates mental illness and mental retardation as types of disabilities, this section 33 deals with the reservation of seats for persons with disabilities does not make any provision for persons with mental disability. NHRC is aware of this fact. Annual report 2000-2001[13] makes mention of this fact. According to this report, "Over a long period of time, a major effort has been made in training to enhance the employment capabilities of persons with mental retardation. Further, the National Institute of Mental Handicap has undertaken a number of projects by which jobs have been identified in the public services, which could suitably be performed by persons with mental retardation. However, reservation in jobs has not been extended to persons with mental retardation. This is a major negation of policies, which are designed to be disability inclusive".

In the following pages judgments, orders etc. of the courts CCPD and NHRC will be analysed on above mentioned issues and other issues relating to the employment of persons with disabilities and brief account of the legal provisions dealing with employment will also be given in appropriate places.

## Employment of Persons with Disabilities the Indian Position

Employment rights of persons with disabilities are mainly covered under chapter VI of the 1995 Act containing Sections 32 to 41 (except Section 39) and pertain to various aspects through which the employment rights of disabled persons in the

Government sector are to be facilitated. In addition, the right against discrimination in Government employment is covered in Section 47 under Chapter VIII titled "Non-discrimination". Disabled persons' employment in the private sector has also been provided for in Section 41[14] of the Act while self-employment opportunities for disabled persons have been bolstered through certain affirmative action in Section 43[15] Among other related provisions, for instance, under research and manpower development, a part of Section 48[16] deals with Government promotion and sponsorship of research on job identification and on-site modifications in offices and factories, and under social security.

The National Policy for Persons with Disabilities 2006 deals with various issues of employment of persons with disabilities set out in the act.

## Identification of Posts

#### Cases Reservation of post for disabled persons is not dependent on identification of posts

*In Government of India & Anr v. Ravi Prakash Gupta &Anr*[17] The Respondent no. 1, a visually disabled person cleared the Civil Services Examination in the year 2006. He was at serial number 5 of the merit list prepared for visually disabled candidates, who has been declared successful in the examination. Although there were more than 5 vacancies available in the visually disabled category, only one post was offer under the said category and he was therefore not given appointment.

The basic contention of the respondent no. 1 before the Central Administrative Tribunal (CAT) and Delhi High Court was that since the disabilities Act came in to force in 1996 providing a statutory mandate for reservation of three percent of the posts available for persons with different kinds of disabilities enumerated in section 33 of the Act, such reservation ought to have been in force with effect from the date on which the Act came into force. If the vacancies were to be considered from the year 1996, than instead of one vacancy been declared for the year in question, there should have been at least seven vacancies from the reserved categories of disabilities which were interchangeable having regard to the number of appointments made with regard to the disabled categories reserved under section 33 of the Act since the Act came into force, there were at least seven posts which could be filled up in the year 2006. However in that year only one post from this category has been filled. Being at serial number five of the list of successful candidate amongst the disabled candidates, there were sufficient number of vacancies in which he could have been appointed and that the authorities has acted contrary to the provisions of the above Act upon the faulty reasoning that the vacancies in the reserved posts could not be declared without first identifying the same for the purposes of the Act.

The Tribunal negated his contention. Being aggrieved by the decision of the tribunal, he moved the High Court which upon accepting his case set aside the order of the Central Administrative Tribunal. The Court upon observing that a clear vacancy was available to which he could be accommodated on the basis of his position in the merit list and issued a mandamus to offer him and appointment to one of the reserved posts by issuing and appropriate appointment letter within six weeks from the date of the order. The Government of India challenged the order of the High Court in the Supreme Court.

The Supreme Court held that the submission made on behalf of the Union of India regarding the implementation of the provisions of section 33 of the Act, only after identification of posts suitable for such appointment, under section 32 thereof runs counter to legislative intent with which the Act was enacted. To accept such a submission would amount to accepting a situation where the provisions of section 33 of the aforesaid Act, could be kept deferred indefinitely by bureaucratic inaction. In view of the above observation the court saw no reason to interfere with the Judgement of the High Court impugned in the present SLP (Special Leave Petition) and dismissed the petition with cost. The petitioners were given eight weeks time to give effect to directions of the High Court. Petitioner suffering from 'MYOPIA' to the extent of 40% sat for CSE 2000 and cleared till interview but was not appointed and no reason provided therein, He sat again and cleared CSE 2001 as a General Candidate. His request for being treated as visually handicapped in 2000, 2001 exams was turned down on the ground that no posts were identified. Held, Petitioner cannot be denied appointment in the category of 'A' Services based on the rank obtained in CSE 2001.

*In Ravi Kumar Arora Vs. Union of India and Another*[19] The petitioner qualified in the written examination for the Central Civil Services (Mains) Examination, 2000 conducted by respondent No. 2 UPSC and went through the interview, but was not successful. At the time of the interview, the petitioner also underwent a medical examination but was never informed that he suffered from any physical handicap of low vision. The petitioner was however successful in the next year, was declared as a successful/qualified candidate with a rank of 325 having obtained 1184 marks and on 28.05.2002 received intimation for joining the foundation course. The specific service/ post was however, not allotted to the petitioner, which was to be subsequently done on the basis of his rank in the merit list, eligibility, preference for service given by the petitioner. In order to improve his ranking the petitioner appeared in the Preliminary examination for the year 2002 and qualified it.

The petitioner had to undergo a second medical examination and was informed that he was disqualified on account of substandard vision. He immediately represented against the same and thereafter requested that in view of the stand of the respondents, he should be treated as a disabled person and be accordingly be appointed against the suitable vacancy/post which was required to be identified under the provisions of the Act.

Since the petitioner had cleared the Preliminary Examination and was entitled to appear for the Mains Examination, he requested respondent No. 2 UPSC in writing that he may be treated as a disabled person with visual handicapped and be permitted to write the Mains Examination as such.

The request of the petitioner for being accommodated in the handicapped category was however rejected. The result of this was that he was neither being treated under the handicapped category as disable candidate nor as a general candidate.

Faced with the aforesaid position, the petitioner filed the present writ petition claiming a dual relief to write the examination in the category of partially blind/low vision and in the alternative for quashing the declaring the petitioner as unfit for selection on the ground of low vision. The petitioner was permitted in terms of the interim orders to appear in the Examination to be held for the said year as a visually challenged person but could not qualify the Mains Examination and, thus, the petitioner claimed the right to be appointed to the post meant for disabled persons for the year 2001.

After going through the facts on record and relevant provisions of the act, notification etc. the learned judge held that the petitioner is entitled to be appointed to a post in the category 'A' Services as per his merit and seniority based on the rank obtained by him for the Examination of 2001 and he be so appointed to the Indian Postal Services or an equivalent Service. He is also liable to be treated as having joined in service along with his batch-mates for purposes of determination of his seniority, monetary emoluments and promotions. However, in so far the back wages and other monetary benefits for the past are concerned since the petitioner has been working in a Group 'B' post, the petitioner will be entitled to all these monetary benefits for the past also less the amount received by the petitioner in the course of his employment.

The candidate who satisfying the conditions specified in the advertisement, his/her application cannot been rejected on the ground of his/her disability

*In Amita v. Union of India*[18] Pursuant to an advertisement by the banking services recruitment board (BSRB) for the post of Probationary officer, the petitioner who was a visually handicapped lady, applied for the said post. She possessed the requisite qualification for the post. While filling up the said application the petitioner mentioned his disability so that the board could make adequate arrangement of scribe to write in the exam. Her application was returned stating that the bank did not recruit blind candidate for the post of probationary officers.

The petitioner approached the Supreme Court under article 32 of the constitution of India praying for the direction to the respondent to hold the entrance examination for her benefit under the advertisement.

The petitioner also prayed for declaring that the denial of opportunity to contest under general category to the visually disabled person to the post of probationary officer is violative of fundamental rights enshrined under Art. 14, 16, 19 and 21 of the constitution.

The petitioner also prayed for the issuance of the writ of mandamus or an appropriate order or direction calling upon the respondent to show the steps taken by them under section 32, 33, 38, 42 and 47 of the act which mandate inter alia for identification reservation, protection in case of disablement during employment etc.

The court held that the order pass by the board rejecting the application of the petitioner on the aforesaid ground cannot be sustained. The requirement asked for by the board for writing the examination for appointment for the post of probationary officer in the bank were there that a candidate should not be less than twenty one years and not above thirty years and must possess a graduation degree. The petitioner satisfied these conditions. The petitioner applied for the post as a general candidate. Court did not find any reason why such opportunity should be refused by the board. She applied for the same post in some other bank who did not reject her application in spite of her mentioning of her disability. Thus there was a discrimination by the respondent between the petitioner and the persons who are substantially similarly circumstance. Hence she was discriminated against others who qualified for the same entrance examination. Moreover as stated by the petitioner one visually impaired person was already functioning as probationary officer. Therefore the rejection of the application by the respondent besides the ground already stated is not on reasonable ground and is arbitrary and violative of article 14 and 16 of the constitution of India.

Next, the court proceeded to consider whether the petitioner would be entitled for appointment in the post, if successful in the written examination in view of the nature of the job to be performed as probationary officer. The court noted the technological development such as access technology which enables the blind persons to use computer as an effective tool for reading hard copy printed text to create and edit document browses the web and send mail etc independently. The court also noted the fact that of various visually disabled persons are working in managerial positions. Quite a good number of posts can be identified were they can work effectively. The court expressed his pain and distressed about the fact that the list of identified post for persons with disabilities identified by the government has not been revised keeping in view the technological and other development which took place since then. The court directed the government to submit the revised list before it. Later, the government submitted its report before the court in which it was stated that the post of probationary officer is also included in the post identified as suitable for the blind. Later this report was notified.

The court order that to protect the interest of the petitioner the time spend during these proceeding should be excluded while calculating the upper age limit prescribe for appointment on any post to which the petitioner might be found eligible.

### Cases Related to Reservation of Seats

*In Sambhavana v. Delhi University*[19] The Petition was filed in public interest seeking directions against the University of Delhi and colleges affiliated with it to put in place a hundred-point roster for recruitment of persons with disability and to determine the number of vacancies available for such persons. The High Court stayed all further recruitment in colleges that had not provided for reservation for persons with disabilities and in the Respondent University till they filled-up the backlog in the three percent quota for persons with disabilities since 1994.

*In Akhila Karnataka Andha Shikshakarungala Kshemabhibriddhi Sangha v. Election Authority*[20] The Petitioner Association challenged the Government Circular calling applications for 4767 posts of primary teachers in Kannada that barred visually impaired persons from applying to the said posts on the grounds that the exclusion was completely arbitrary and unreasonable. It was submitted by the Petitioners that the Central Government had identified posts of primary teachers as suitable for blind persons and further that in all other States in the country, blind persons were being recruited as primary school teachers, particularly in Tamil Nadu where two percent of teaching posts were reserved for the blind. The High Court found the

Government Circular untenable, held that visually disabled persons were entitled to take part in the recruitment process and directed the Government to withdraw the same as they ran contrary to the provisions of the Persons with Disabilities Act.

Three percent to be computed not out of total vacancies in identified posts but of the total strength of the establishment

*In National Federation of the Blind v. Union of India*[21] The Petitioner approached the Court alleging that several advertisements that had been issued from 1996 to 2006 for government posts did not contain any provision for reservation for the blind and persons with low vision. Furthermore blind persons had been excluded from applying and being considered for appointment against the posts sought to be filled-up by these advertisements. It was further contended by the Petitioners that neither Department of Personnel and Training and Public Grievances nor Ministry of Social Justice and Empowerment nor Office of the Chief Commissioner for Persons with Disabilities was monitoring the implementation of the scheme of reservation for persons with disabilities provided under the Persons with Disabilities Act.

After having noted that the State Government had utterly failed in implementing the provisions of section 33 of the Act, the Court rejected the view of the government that 3% was to be interpreted as three percent of the vacancies in the identified posts and held that three percent was to be computed of the total posts in the establishment.

The Court directed the Respondents to constitute a Committee to compute the backlog of posts and undertake a special recruitment drive to fill up posts identified. They were further directed to modify their rules in order to interpret three percent in the manner interpreted by the Court. The Court also stayed all recruitment in departments/public sector undertakings till such time as reservation for disabled persons was provided for.

Instead of calculating posts on the basis of one advertisement only, the total number of the posts in the degree and PG colleges in the state should be calculated

*In Km. Archana Pandey VS. Respondent State of UP and Ors*[22] The petitioner who had an excellent academic record applied for the appointment as lecturer in music (Vocal) against an advertisement issued by the UP Higher Education Service Commission. It was alleged by her that though she was eligible and was fully entitled to be called for interview the Commission arbitrarily and mechanically did not call her for interview. By and interim order the petitioner was directed to be interviewed provisionally. The interview took place and it was alleged by the petitioner that she did excellently but she had not been selected.

The Commission alleged that five posts of lecturers in music in general category were advertised. The commission stated that there cannot be any reservation for handicapped category because the reservation permits only one percent quota. Since there was only five posts in general category hence there could not be any reservation. The petitioner was considered as a general candidate but she did not have the requisite merit hence could not be selected.

The court rejected this argument of respondent and held that if this stand is accepted then only if 100 posts are advertised, a handicapped person will get a chance to be selected. It will totally frustrate the intention of parliament. The court opined that the total number of lecturers in music in all the degree and PG colleges in the state have to be calculated and only thereafter the one percent quota for blind candidate have to be considered. The court allow the petition and directed the respondent to considered the petitioner application in the light of the above observation and give her the benefit of reservation under the PWD act.

## Right of the Persons with Visual Impairment to Write Civil Services Exams Either in Braille or with the Help of a Scribe

*In National Federation of Blind Vs. Union Public Service Commission and Ors*[23] *A* representative body of visually handicapped persons in India - filed the petition under Article 32 of the Constitution of India seeking a writ in the nature of mandamus directing the Union of India and the Union Public Service Commission to permit the blind candidates to compete for the Indian Administrative Service and the Allied Services and further to provide them the facility of writing the civil services examination either in Braille-script or with the help of a Scribe.

The court directed the respondent to provide such facility. The court said;

"So far as the claim of visually handicapped for writing the civil services examinations, in Braille-script or with the help of Scribe, is concerned, we are of the view that their demand is legally justified"[24].

The court observed that If some of the posts in the Indian Administrative Service and other Allied Services, as identified by the committee, can be filled from amongst the visually handicapped persons then there should be no reason why they should not be permitted to sit and write the civil services examination.

### Right of Low Vision Candidate to Get Question Paper in Bold Print

*In Parminder Pal Singh Vs. Union of India and Anr*[25] Petitioner was a visually handicapped person with some degree of sight or vision. He could, with the aid of lenses, etc., read bold print. He and some other persons who had some degree of sight or vision, were deprived from appearing in exams held by the respondent for the posts reserved for the visually disabled candidates as the respondent had decided to withdraw question papers printed in bold print. As a result, these candidates were compelled to take the paper in braille

The court agreed with the contention of the petitioner and held that he and others like him should be provided with the question papers in bold print. Merely because the respondents suspect that certain persons obtain dubious and false, certificates of being visually handicapped and may take advantage by taking the examination if the question paper is in bold print, is not sufficient reason, to deprive those visually handicapped persons not knowing Braille from taking the examination and, thus, depriving them of an opportunity to compete in an examination, where reservation has been made for them. It is for the respondents to devise ways and means to obviate or eliminate malpractices or to have further safeguards in that regard. Even at a post qualifying stage, if there are any doubts about certain candidates being visually handicapped or not, who have been successful on the basis of false medical certificates, the same can be eliminated as a result of a subsequent medical examination.

The court directed the respondents to reconsider their decision and examine the feasibility of holding a separate examination in respect of these vacancies, for those who fall within these categories of visually handicapped persons but do not possess the knowledge of Braille, by providing them an opportunity of taking the examination with the question paper in bold print, the holding of such an examination would also provide an opportunity to all those visually handicapped person who might not have applied in response to the advertisement in question since it required taking up the examination in Braille only.

#### Right of Person with Colour Blindness to Appointment to the Posts where the Perfect Vision is Not an Essential Requirement

*In Nand Kumar Narayanrao Ghodmare v. State of Maharashtra and Others*[26] The appellant, a colour blind person was selected by the Public Service Commission but appointment could not be made, the appellant filed an affidavit detailing that as per the information he had secured, there were 35 posts in the Department and only five posts required perfect vision without colour blindness.

The court held that government should consider the case of appellant to be appointed to any of the post of Agriculture officer of class II service other them the five posts mentioned by him in his affidavit within two month of the receipt of this order.

### In case of a teaching post of permanent nature, the reduction in the number of students opting for the course cannot be taken as ground for not filling post.

*In Smt. Shruti Kalrav. University of Delhi and ORS*[27] the petitioner who was a visually challenged person and who had excellent academic and practical record, applied for the post of lecturer instrumental music against the advertisement of the University which *inter alia,* provided for reservation for blind persons by stipulating three percent reservation for blind and orthopaedically handicapped candidates. She got the interview call and was interviewed by selection committee but was not selected. The respondent college filled only one post out of two posts advertised. She felt that an injustice was done to her as she not only deserved to get the said post on merit even without reservation and in any case she was bound to get the post in view of the circular of the university providing reservation. Later the second post of lecturer (Instrumental Music) which was not filled up earlier was advertised. Not to lose opportunity, petitioner applied again and was interviewed. She was placed second in the merit list. In the counter affidavit filed by the respondents it was emphasized that the petitioner only had the right to be considered for the post and was duly consider along with other candidates and selection committee did not find her suitable for the post. On a later date the affidavit was filed by the principle of the college stating that the work load in the college with respect to the subject music (Instrument Music) in the last three years has reduced and therefore only one teacher in the concerned subject was required to take classes of that subject.

The petitioner contended that not too many students seek admission for specialised subject like instrumental music and situation had not changed since filing of the present petition. In any case, appointment against the permanent post cannot be affected by the fluctuation in no. of students.

The court observed that the advertisement mentioned three percent reservation for blind and orthopaedically handicapped candidates, the consideration of the petitioner's candidature should have been keeping in view the aforesaid reservation. It should not have been an empty formality. Considering the case of the petitioner "along with other candidates", as if petitioner also belongs to "general category" itself vitiates the selection process.

The court further observed that going by the academic record and other achievements of the petitioner it is not digestible as to how she was not found suitable. No doubt it is the function of the selection committee to see the suitability of the candidate and the court cannot assume this role and substitute itself as selection committee however it is within the jurisdiction of the court to examine as to whether there is a proper consideration of the candidate by the committee. In this case the selection committee treated her like any other general candidate and that kind of consideration is not valid. The selection committee did not adhere to reservation rules. The committee even did not bother about the reservation of the university which mentioned about reservation but specifically mandated that one person should be appointed by each institution during the academic year in question. The respondent therefore did not act fairly.

Same applied to the selection procedure. Both these selection were accordingly quashed and set aside. In so far as the filling of the second post is concerned, the court observed that no doubt it is the prerogative of the employer to fill or not to fill post, the reason given for not filling the post is at all not convincing. The reduction of number of students cannot be pleaded so long as the discipline is taught in the college. Work load should not be considered on the basis of the number of students rather it should be on the basis of classes to be taught. The court questioned as to how one teacher could teach all the subject of BA (Hons.) degree course in Instrument Music of all the three years students.

The court issued the following directions:

1. To consider and decide whether the respondent college is to fill up second post of lecturer in Instrumental Music.
2. If the respondent authorities decide to fill second post, then to consider appointing the petitioner to the post of lecturer in Instrumental Music by filling the second post as well keeping in view the mandate of the Disability Act and the Resolution of the university. If this was done then Respondent No. 5 who was already teaching for the last five years can continue in her post. This should be done within a period of two months from the order.
3. In case the aforesaid is not feasible then the selection of the Respondent Nos. 5 and 6 stands quashed. The

respondent authorities are directed to fill up the post keeping in view the reservation policy contained in that Circular and Disability Act and this exercise is to be done within a period of four months from the order.

**A person after acquiring degree which is necessary for holding the post of PET cannot at a later stage be told that he is not otherwise suitable for the post.**

*In Krishna Kumar V. Secretary Govt of NCT of Delhi and others*[28] The petitioner who was a physically handicapped person applied for the post of physical education teacher against the advertisement by Delhi Subordinate services selection board (DSSB). He emerged successful and was issued appointment letter and join the service. After sometimes the Deputy Director of Education "Admin Branch" Government of NCT of Delhi "Respondent no. 3" terminated his services on the ground inter alia that he was disable to the extent of 65%, which rendered him incapacitated to impart training to the students.

On the issue of whether he was incapacitated to impart training because of his disability the court observed that it is not disputed that the petitioner suffers from the disability covered by the act and he has submitted the medical certificate issued by a duly constituted medical board. Furthermore, in the event if the physically handicapped person are totally debarred from becoming PET, such a restriction ought to have been placed if they would not have been admitted to the said courses of studies at all. A person after acquiring degree, which is necessary for holding the job of the post of PET, cannot at a later stage be told that he was not otherwise suitable. It is for the institution to see as to whether the disability of the persons concerned will be such so as to disable him from performing his duties for which he have been taking training . Once they have passed the examination, it must be held that they are physically fit to perform their duties.

The court held that the termination of the services of the petitioner is clearly unjust, illegal and arbitrary. The petitioner was duly selected and joined the service. The termination order was issued when the petitioner had rendered services for more than four years. The termination of the service of the handicapped person like petitioner after such a long period of service amounts to adding insult to the injury. In the view of above discussion the court set aside the order of termination of the petitioner and directed the respondents to reinstate him with all consequential benefits. The respondent can give him light duties having regard to disabilities.

### A candidate who is otherwise high up in the merit list and should be appointed as a general category candidate.

*In all India Confederation of the Blind Vs. Govt, of NCT of Delhi and Ors*[29] In this case, the court held that the respondents could not adjust a candidate who is otherwise high up in the merit list and would be to appointment in the general category against the three percent reservation earmarked for PWDs under the act.

The direction was issued to the respondents to ensure that while preparing the select list, such person calming the benefit of the three percent reservation who even otherwise are entitled to be appointed of the basis of their own merit should be treated as general category candidate and should not be adjusted in the three percent quota which should be left for other persons eligible to claim under it.

### Mother of a Mentally Retarded Child Should not be Transferred

*In Rosily v. Registration Inspector General*[30] The Petitioner, a mother of a child diagnosed as 90% mentally retarded, was working with the District Registration Office in Ernakulam. She was transferred to the office in Kottayam and requested to be posted back in Ernakulam as her child was undergoing treatment and rehabilitation at a centre in Ernakulam. The Petitioner relied on a Government Order, which included parents of mentally retarded children in the preferential category for posting in places of their choice.

The Court held that this was one of the few cases where the request ought to have been accepted without delay and directed the Respondent to take a decision in light of the Court's observations within three weeks of the order.

## Person Denied Post Because of a Medical Condition Challenges Action of Respondent Petition Allowed Employer Directed to Offer Petitioner Employment

*In Ranjit Kumar Rajak v. State Bank of India*[2] The Petitioner had applied for and was selected for the post of Probationary Officer with Respondent. Subsequently, he was called for a medical examination and was informed that he was not eligible for the post of Probationary Officer in the bank due to a renal transplant he had undergone in 2004. He approached the Court against the said action of the bank and relied on medical reports to confirm his fitness and good health to work in the said post and contended that it was clear that denial of employment was on account of his medical history of renal transplant although his present medical profile did not interfere with his job responsibilities. He challenged the action of the respondent in refusing employment as irrational and discriminatory.

The Bank submitted inter alia that the Petitioner would require continuous mediation and periodical check-up throughout his life, the cost of which would have to be borne by the bank. An officer of the bank may be posted anywhere in India including rural branches and that the Petitioner, if appointed would request for posting at places where medical and check-up facilities were available and that such a request cannot be acceded to as a probationary officer was required to work anywhere in India including at rural branches.

The Court, after a detailed consideration of the provisions of the UN Convention on the Rights of Persons with Disabilities that India had ratified and the meaning of the term Reasonable Accommodation therein, concluded that in the absence of a Municipal law on the matter, the Convention can be read into Article 21 as it did not in any way conflict with the Municipal law. It found that in the absence of a statutory definition of reasonable accommodation, the reasonable accommodation as set out in the protocol in the first instance could be considered. But however that it would have to have a nexus with the financial burden on the institution and/or undertaking which will have to bear the burden and further the extent to which reasonable accommodation can be provided for. The Court held that it would, therefore no longer be open to the State merely on account of past or present medical problems if otherwise, a person is fit to work and can be reasonably accommodated without undue hardship, to deprive a person otherwise qualified and successful, the right to employment.

Reliance was placed on an order of the High Court in the case of a person with HIV who was denied employment on account of his condition, where the Court concluded that in every such case, the test of medical fitness prior to employment or even during employment has necessarily to be correlated with the person's ability to perform the normal job requirements and any risk of health hazard he may pose to others at the work place.

The Court concluded that there is no material to show that the burden cast on the Respondent for the medical expenses which were likely to be about Rs. 13,000 per month would result in an undue hardship to the respondents. Hence the petition was allowed and it was directed that the petitioner be offered employment within sixty days.

**Vacancy reserved for persons with disabilities can lapse only if there have been an effective recruitment and inter change has been attempted.**

*In Shri Ram Bahadur Rai v. Employee Provident Fund Organisation*[33] The complainant submitted that he was appointed as Chair Trainer in the respondent organisation. After thirteen years of working he was promoted to the post of peon. Thereafter he was not given the benefit of promotion from peon to Daftry though he was eligible for the same.

The respondent submitted inter alia that his case for promotion was considered under the reservation for persons with disabilities. When he became eligible for promotion three years were over and as per the instruction of the government of India under the rotation of vacancy and due to non-availability of persons with disability during those three years the post reserved might be treated as lapsed and the complainant is not eligible for promotion under the reservation policy of the disabilities Act.

During hearing, the respondent submitted that the post of Daftry is not identified for persons with low vision therefore the complainant was not considered eligible for promotion. Going through the roster submitted by the respondent the court found that the reservation roster for persons with disabilities was not updated and maintained properly. The court found that the persons appointed against reservation for persons with disabilities who were holding the post of Daftry might have been promoted or retired since a long time his past when they were appointed to that post. Therefore the post of Daftry might be vacant to which the complainant could be promoted.

The court also found that the submission of the respondent that the post of Daftry is not identified for persons with low vision is incorrect. Therefore he should not have been denied promotion on that ground. The court rejected the submission of the respondent with regard to the reservation of post after three years. The court observed in this connection that a vacancy reserved for persons with disabilities can lapse only if there have been an effective recruitment and inter change has been attempted. Unless there were eligible persons with disabilities to be considered against the reservation vacancy, reservation of a vacancy would of no consequence.

In view of the above the court observed that the complainant was very much eligible for promotion to the post of Daftry in the year 1997 (almost thirteen[th] years before) and also the post is identified for persons with low vision. It seems inadvertently, there has been violation of the Persons with Disabilities Act, 1995 by not providing the complainant, the benefit or reservation in promoting to the post of Daftry. Also, the Complainant belongs to SC category and he should have been considered for promotion to the post of Daftry either against the post reserved for SC or for Persons with Disabilities. There has been ignorance on the part of EPFO and this cannot be considered an excuse for not providing him the benefit under the Persons with Disabilities Act.

As the complainant would be retiring very soon the respondent was directed to promote him to the post of Daftry from the date when his promotion was due and the consequential benefits be given to him as per rules. All the dues on account of notional promotion should be settled on or before the date of retirement. The action taken report might be submitted to this court within forty five days.

**Right of person with hearing impairment to be provided with the necessary arrangements such as sign language interpreter, overhead projection and be allowed to speak in the language in which he/she is comfortable.**

*In Chandra Kishore Joshi v. Secretary, Union Public Service Commission and ors*[4], the respondent Union Public Service Commission issued and employment notice for recruitment of extra Assistant Director Directorate of Coordination (Police wireless) in Ministry of Home Affairs in the category of physically handicapped (hearing impaired)

Complainant alleged that during the interview, members of interview board neither provided questions in writing nor an interpreter and therefore he could not understand questions properly. The court observed that since the interview did not materialise as the interviewee could not comprehend the speech of interviewers hence the interview conducted could be termed as null and void. Therefore the commission might conduct a fresh interview, in which complainant should be provided with the necessary arrangement for example sigh language, overhead projection to show written version or oral version. Since the complainant had the ability to speak in Hindi therefore he should be allowed to give answer in Hindi or mixture of Hindi and English orally.

The respondent no. 2 confirmed that the post was kept unfilled since they had already forwarded the requisition for filling the vacant post. Therefore the complainant should avail of the opportunity or appearing in the interview once again.

The Respondent no. 1 assured of all support during the interview. The complainant accepted the proposal put forth by the respondent therefore the case was settled accordingly.

The reservation is to be worked out against the vacancies that were filled since 1996 and not only on the basis of one advertisement

*In Jawaharlal Nehru port trust*[31] case, the respondent submitted that the number of sanctioned posts were only eight out of which to were meant for promotion. Therefore three percent of eight post is only 0.25 and thus reservation cannot be provided.

On considering the reply, the court informed the respondent inter alia that reservation for persons with disabilities under Section 33 of the Act, which is mandatory, is to be worked out against the vacancies that were filled since 1996 when the Persons with Disabilities act came into effect. The reservation should be distributed, as far as possible, amongst all the identified jobs. It was thus clarified that quota for persons with disabilities is not based on mathematical computation of three percent of the vacancies, but to be calculated on the basis of point earmarked in the rosters.

Upon considering the facts and circumstances, the case was disposed of with the following directions inter alia:

- To issue corrigendum for reserving a vacancy of Accounts Officer for persons with disabilities and submit copy of the corrigendum within 30 days of the receipt of this Order;
- To submit action plan to clear backlog reservation;
- To maintain separate vacancy based 100 point reservation rosters in each group for persons with disabilities and to submit photocopies of first and last page of each of the rosters to this Court within 60 days of the issue of this Order.

Since the selection of candidates with disabilities is made by UPSC based on the requisitions placed by the CCAs, there should not be any scope for mismatch between the categories of disabilities and the vertical category of the recommended candidates

*In Sumit Kaur v. Department of Personnel and Training*[36] The complainant submitted that she was declared successful in Civil Service (Main) Examination. She appeared in the interview and was also medically examined. She was declared successful in the interview and was informed on enquiry on telephone by the DOPT that she had been selected for the post of Section Officer Grade 'B' in Armed forces Head Quarters. After waiting for almost one week, she was informed that her case was still under consideration before the competent authority. After another ten days, she was informed on telephone that no service would be allocated to her. She was also informed that her selection was in disabled category and vacancies reserved category had exhausted as her rank was lowest amongst general category candidates.

She argued before the court inter alia that she was ignored as a person with disability because she was a general category candidate which is in utter violation of fundamental rights guaranteed under article 14 and 16 of the constitution of India. She was declared successful based on her marks of general standard and had not availed any concession/relaxation on the basis of disability; therefore she is entitled to get the service even in general category.

Although the case was closed on the request of the complainant as she had taken the matter before the CAT Principal Bench, New Delhi, however the court made the following observation:

This Court is of the view that since the selection of candidates with disabilities is made by UPSC based on the requisitions placed by the CCAs, there should not be any scope for mismatch between the categories of disabilities and the vertical category of the recommended candidates. Further, denial of reservation to persons with disabilities in a large number of services on the ground that these are yet to be identified is also not justified particularly when the CCAs of other services have been doing it since 2001 when Ministry of Social Justice and Empowerment issued the list of identified jobs vide Notification No. 16-25/99-N.I.-I dated 31.05.2001. Therefore, the Complainant and other similarly placed persons with disabilities can be considered against the backlog vacancies since 2001, if not 1996, the year the Act came into effect or the vacancies caused due to dropouts.

**If a blind person can be appointed to the post, there is no justification to deny appointment to a person with hearing impairment on the ground that she had myopia and had undergone LASIK surgery.**

*In Ms. Jasreen Singh v. Bharat Petroleum Corporation Ltd. Mumbai*[37] The complainant who had 100% hearing disability was selected for the post of Management Trainee "HR" in the respondent organisation but was rejected as she was found to have myopia above (-) 4.00D. After LASIK Surgery, her vision is 6/6. It may be mentioned here that the said post has been identified as suitable for persons with hearing impairments as well as for persons with visual impairment.

The respondent submitted inter-alia that they are guided by the norms and standards prescribed by Oil industries safety directorate (OISD) for medical fitness.

Also Clause 51(7) (d)(1) of OISD states as under, "the total amount of myopia (including the cylinder) shall not exceed (-) 4.00 D,. The total amount of hypermetropia (including the cylinder) shall not exceed (+) 4.00 D, in each eye". During medical examination, it was found that her Myopia exceeded the permissible limit. She was provisionally selected against the post reserved for hearing disabled but as per OISD norms clause 5.0 (9) stated above, she otherwise did not satisfy other physical standards as prescribed with regard to myopia. The respondent further stated that although the post is also identified for the visually handicapped category, selecting the complainant against this would tantamount to treating her as visually handicapped. Respondent stated that they referred the matter for medical opinion by furnishing the criteria of blindness/low vision as per the disabilities Act to the ophthalmologist who opined that she did not satisfy the criteria. Under these circumstances the respondent sought the commission's advice.

After hearing both the parties and perusing various advertisement produced by the parties, the court observed that in respondent organisation, a far more stringent standard for vision is being applied to the post of Management Trainee (HR) than the post of flying Pilots in Indian Air Force and to various posts in Indian oil corporation. Therefore it may not be justified to apply the stringent medical standards as are being followed by a Police Force like ITBP especially in case of a post identified as suitable for persons with disabilities. If LASIK surgery for correction of vision can be permitted for pilots, the same should not be denied to the complainant. Further in the oil industry itself if the Indian oil corporation (IOC) which is also governed by the guidelines of the OISD can allow corrected myopia upto 6.00, there appears no reason why the complainant with a better vision (6/6) after LASIK surgery, should not be considered medically fit in respondent organisation.

With regard to the relaxation in the standard of vision in case of the complainant who has been selected for a post i.e. identified for persons with hearing impairment as well as for visual impairment, the court observed that the purpose of identifying the post is to ensure that a person with his/her disability should be able to perform the duties attached to the post. The court further observed that if person with blindness can perform the function of the post there is no justification to deny appointment to the complainant against a reserved vacancy for persons with hearing impairment on the ground that she had myopia and had undergone LASIK surgery. If the medical standard are not relaxed, than the persons with disabilities would never be able to enter any government/public service even if they acquire necessary qualification against all odds and the handicapping environment and the purpose of the act will be defeated.

In view of the above observations the court directed the respondent to issue offer of appointment to the complainant within 30 days and submit an action taken report to this court.

The court also advised OISD to suitably modify/update their guidelines in this matter.

The post of Probationary Officer as well as the clerical posts in the bank are identified for persons with disabilities including those with blindness and low vision, therefore it would not be justified to denied appointment of one- eyed persons to those posts.

*In Shri Ashwini Kumar Gupta, Ms. Shweta Kaur Chhatwal v. State Bank of India, Mumbai, State Bank of India, Lucknow, State Bank of India, New Delhi, and Ministry of Finance, New and others*[32] The complainant qualified the written exam and interview for the post of Probationary Officer in the respondent organisation against the vacancy earmarked for persons with locomotor disability. Subsequently respondent cancel his appointment on the ground that he was visually impaired which he did not disclosed. The submission of the complainant was that his right eye was non-functional but he is neither a persons with blindness nor low vision as per the disability Act. The appointment of Complainant no. 2 was also cancelled by the respondent on the similar ground. The respondent submitted that as per policy guidelines about medical fitness in force in the bank, one-eye persons are not eligible for recruitment in the bank The issue relating to the change of policy in this matter had been taken up with the Ministry of Finance and the Indian Bank Association on receipt of the advised the cases of both the complainants would be re-examined.

During the course of hearing, respondents were informed that the post of Probationary Officer as well as the clerical posts in the banks is identified for persons with disabilities including those with blindness and low vision. Therefore it would not be justified to deny appointment of one- eyed persons to those posts. After a number of hearings, the respondent informed the court that the policy in this respect has been formulated and approved by the Executive Committee of Central Board.

Subsequently the respondent informed the court that complainant no. 1 had been advised to complete the pre appointment formalities. Complainant no. 2 also informed the court that she had got appointment in the respondent organisation.

**There is no bar to appoint a person with disability with muscular dystrophy to the identified posts.**

*In Ms. Meenakshi Singh v. IDBI Bank Ltd*[33] The complainant a persons with 70% locomotor disability filed a complaint alleging that she was selected as Assistant Manager - Centralised Operation under PH category on the basis of Personal Technical Interview. Subsequently, respondent sent her for pre employment health check up and later on she was sent for MRI and Blood Test, she was declared medically unfit for the job of Assistant Manager because of Multiple Sclerosis, though in her disability certificate submitted with application form, it was clearly mentioned that she was having Multiple Sclerosis. During hearing the respondent stated inter alia that the job of the post in question needs frequent movement to visit various places, collection of cash, maintaining the database and clearing of the cheques within a time bound period. After hearing and going through the written submissions of the parties and perusing the relevant guidelines, the court observed that the managerial jobs involving financial responsibilities of the banks have been identified. Nothing has been produced to effect that the person with disability due to muscular dystrophy (to which the complainant was suffering) cannot be appointed to an identified post. Para 23 of DOP&T O.M. No. 36035/3/2004-Estt (Res) dated 29.12.2005 provides inter alia that in case of medical examination of a person with disability for appointment to a post identified as suitable to be held by persons with particular kind of disability, the concerned medical officer or board shall be informed beforehand that the post is identified and suitable to be held by person with disability of the relevant category and the candidate shall then be examined medically keeping this fact in view.

In the light of the above the court saw no justification to deny appointment to the said post to the complainant on the ground of her disability. The respondent bank was therefore advised to appoint her to the post of Assistant Manager- Centralised Operation, if she is otherwise fit.

**The employer should specifically mention the provision of reservation for persons with disabilities in advertisement, If there is any short fall, the vacancies should be kept for persons with disabilities.**

*In the Chief Commissioner, Disabilities v. Medical Superintendent-cum-joint Director Health Services General Hospital Chandigarh 2000*[40] The respondent published a notice in the employment news for certain post in which no provision for reservation for persons with disabilities was provided.

The court sought clarification on two points namely

1. Date of year on which reservation to persons with disability in Group C and D came into effect in the state.
2. Whether the five ward servant/Nursing orderly mentioned in the reply was appointed against reserved quota for the disabled it yes. Mark the copy of the Employment notice in response to which the recruitment of 5 disabled candidates was made.

In view of the material on record, the court was of the view that the respondent was not exempted from filling up the vacancies advertised. It further observed that between year 1996 and 2000 a total of 63 vacancies were advertised. Out of them, at least. 2 vacancies should have been earmarked but only one vacancy was allotted to person with disability. The respondent was accordingly directed to keep one vacancy out of the total vacancies advertised.

*In Employees Provident fund Organisation* Suo motu - Notice taken of the advertisement issued by the Respondent for the post of Supervisor (Computer) - No reservation as per *Section 33* provided - Respondent's took the defence that the notification issued by the Department of Personal Training does not identify the said post suitable for reservation for the disabled - In the facts of the case the post of Supervisor (Computer) was held to be comparable to that of Computer Operation Officer and E-Commerce Professional which have already been identified for reservation - Held, the relevant notification was issued pursuant to an expert committee report which has held that any reference to a particular post identified as suitable for reservation will also include any nomenclature used for a comparable post with identical functions - Further, detailed guidelines issued for compliance with the provisions of the Act and Respondent directed to maintain 100 point roster to provide reservation.

## The List of Identified Jobs Should be Updated and Revised Periodically

*In General Secretary, National Federation of the Blind v. Secretary to the Government of Maharashtra*[34] the respondent submitted that as per the list of identified jobs, the post of Stenographer is not identified as suitable for persons with disabilities. On the basis of record the commission found that the list was out dated and was not revised as mandated by the act.

In the light of the above, the Respondent was advised to either adopt the list of identified jobs published by the Ministry of Social Justice and Empowerment, Government of India based on the recommendations of the Expert Committee or carry out a comprehensive review of the jobs and notify/issue the list within six months. While notifying the list, it should be kept in mind that the jobs that have been identified by the Government of India are not excluded unless there are valid reasons for their exclusion.

As regards the consideration of Complainant No. 2 and other similarly placed persons for the post of stenographer, the Respondent should advise Maharashtra Public Service Commission to consider them for the posts of stenographer if they are otherwise eligible. Respondent should submit an interim report on the action being taken in the matter. A copy of this Order was sent to Commissioner for Persons with Disabilities, Government of Maharashtra who is directed to coordinate and monitor the progress of identification and in issuing the list of posts for persons with disabilities so that the interests of persons with disabilities are not adversely affected. The Commissioner will keep this Court informed of the progress on monthly basis.

**The nomenclature used for respective jobs shall also mean and include any nomenclature used for the comparable post with identical functions of the identified posts.**

*In R.B. Singh v. Ordnance Factory Board*[35] The complainant who was working as supervisor in the respondent factory filed a complaint alleging that he had requested the respondent for his promotion as Chargerman II (Non-technical & store) but his request was not consider as somebody else from general category was promoted to the post. The respondent submitted that the post in question was identified for certain categories of disabilities and the respondent was not considered for promotion in terms of the criteria adopted in this matter. During the hearing of the case, the respondent informed that the work situation varies from factory to factory in the ordnance department. The organisation would not put to risk a person with disability by making him work in a post that was not identified for him.

The court argues with approval the following para one B of the report of expert committee recommendation which reads: "The nomenclature used for respective jobs in these recommendations shall also mean and include any nomenclature used for the comparable post with identical functions of the identified posts".

Further, para 5 of the said notification says that the list of jobs identified by the committee is no means exhaustive and

Ministries/Departments etc. may have to further supplement that. The identified jobs cannot be pruned unless the concern department/organisation has been exempted by the competent authority specified in the notification itself.

The court referred its earlier decision namely case no. 2480 of 2002 and held that the complainant is entitled to be considered for promotion to the post against the reserved vacancy by the DPC that takes place immediately after he became eligible for the post as per the relevant recruitment rules and if found fit should be considered for promotion from retrospective date with the admissible benefits under government of India. The respondent was directed to submit a report to this court within three months from the date of receipt of this communication.

**The reservation is applicable even if the organisation does not receive any grant from the consolidated fund of India or is a small organisation.**

*In The National Centre for Radio Astrophysics*[36] The submission of the respondent inter alia was that NCRA is a Research Centre of the Tata Institute of Fundamental Research and conducting Doctoral and Post-Graduate Research in Astronomy and Astrophysics. Most of the engineers, technicians and other staff members are expected to maintain the systems for ensuring 24 hrs. observation and as such, it would not be desirable to employ the disabled in such un-conducive terrains. Earlier, the register indicating the reservations were maintained by TIFR, Mumbai. It was also submitted by the Respondent that on advice of this Court, they has started maintaining the separate 100 point reservation rosters meant for persons with disabilities and identified certain posts and would be able to employ them as and when reservation point reaches as per norms. In view of the facts stated above and positive action taken by the Respondent, the court closed the case with the direction that while advertising the vacancies in future, certain details should be indicated to ensure the safeguards available to persons with disabilities under the act and various orders of the government.

*In Navodaya Vidyalaya Samiti*[5] case, the employment advertisement issued by the respondent did not provide for reservation for persons with disabilities in accordance with the

Act. The submission made by the respondent showed that it did not specify the number of vacancy reserved for persons with disabilities. Further, from the details of group C and D posts, it was noticed that recruitment exercise for the advertised posts had been completed but no person with disability was appointed. During personal hearing, the respondent was informed by the court inter alia that the Act came into force w.e.f. 1996. Therefore recruitment/ promotions are applicable on or after 01.01.1996 which needs to be indicated in the 100 point rosters and backlog worked out from that date. As per the instructions of DoPT, separate 100 point reservation rosters are to be maintained for the post/ group, i.e., Group 'A', 'B', 'C and 'D' to calculate the reservation for persons with disabilities for implementing Section 33 of the Act. In the said, rosters points no. 1 and 67 are to be reserved for them. The first cycle of the roster is to be closed after point no. 100 has been reached. Further, in Group 'C and 'D' posts, the reservation is to be calculated against the entire sanctioned posts, i.e., identified as well as unidentified, and both in direct recruitment as well as in promotion. However, in Group 'A' and 'B' posts, the sanctioned strength in respect of only identified posts was to be taken into account. The notification of the Ministry of Social Justice and Empowerment containing the list of identified jobs for persons with disabilities. In Group 'C and 'D' posts, reservation for persons with disabilities is applicable in promotion also. Further, reservation for persons with disabilities is horizontal and therefore, if a vacancy is reserved for SCs/ STs/ OBCs, the same can also be reserved for persons with disabilities, if the said vacancy falls against the reserved points in both the rosters.

While advertising the vacancies for persons with disabilities, the following must invariably be indicated:

(i) Sub-categories of disabilities - whether the post is reserved for blind or low vision;

Hearing impaired; locomotor disabled; or cerebral palsy;

(ii) Eligibility of persons having 40 percent or more disability;

(iii) Number of vacancies reserved for persons with disabilities in each category; and

(iv) Relaxation of age, application fee and eligibility criteria, if any.

*In central WAKF council*[46] case, the submission of the respondent was that the council is a statutory autonomous body established by the government of India under the provision of the Wakf act, 1995 for the purpose of advising it on matters pertaining to working of a Wakf Boards and proper administration of the Wakfs in the country. No grant is received by the council from the consolidated fund of India. Respondent also submitted that the council, in its educational schemes has special consideration for the physically challenged persons in the form of Scholarship and Ad-hoc grant on priority basis, only the remaining seats are distributed among the other categories. Respondent further submitted that the notification of the Ministry of Social Justice and Empowerment and other rules/laws concerning reservation for persons with disabilities referred to in the notice are not intimated to the Council and hence they remained completely unaware about the provisions, otherwise they would have certainly acted on it much earlier. Nonetheless, no physically challenged candidate ever applied for any post. The Respondent is a small organization having a sanctioned strength of thirty two staff only. In many cases, there is only one post for a particular job. In some cases, there is one post to look after more than one job. With regard to the currently advertised posts, the Respondent stated that the Asstt. Programmer has to be responsible not only for operating the data bank and maintenance of computers and creation of LAN etc., but also for organizing training programmes for the staff of the Council as well as for the staff of the State Wakf Boards. Similarly, the Library, Documentation and Reference Assistant will be in-charge of the Reference Library being created by the Council and would be responsible for procurement of Books, Journals of Court Judgments and other documents, which are frequently required by the Council in its day to day functioning. He will also be responsible for the documentation of the valuable record, which has been piling up in the Council. He has also to assist the Council members, consisting of eminent Jurists, Members of Parliament, Retired Judges of Supreme Court and High Courts etc., as Reference Assistant in their day to day work. The person has to be physically fit to cope with the job requirements. Therefore, reservation in case of these two posts will defeat the purpose for which these posts have been created. The respondent was informed about the provisions of the act and related orders etc issued by the Ministry of Social Justice and Empowerment. The respondent was also informed that provisions of the act applied to all establishments under the government whether or not they received grant from the consolidated fund of India. Upon considering the facts of the case and the undertaking given by the Respondent to reserve two vacant posts of Accounts Clerk for persons with disabilities and to also reserve vacancies in Group A and B posts in future, the case is disposed of with the following directions inter alia:

- to advertise the vacancies proposed to be reserved for persons with disabilities within three months from the date of receipt of this Order;
- to submit names, addresses and categories of disability of persons appointed against vacancies reserved for persons with disabilities within 15 days of their joining;

**The Reservation is also Applicable in Apprenticeship Training**

*In The Director, Instruments Research and Development Establishment,* The court took a Suo moto notice of an advertisement published by the respondent for three years apprenticeship training under apprenticeship act 1961 in various trades. In the said advertisement reservation for persons with disabilities was not made in accordance with the act. The respondent submitted that the advertisement was issued for intake candidates for trade apprenticeship for one year and not for giving employment. The court observed that the provision of the act relating to reservation is applicable in this kind of situation also. The court observed:

> "During the apprenticeship, training is imparted to the apprentices which prepares them for employment. They are also paid stipend. Therefore, in our view, reservation under Section 39 of the Act should be provided to persons with disabilities to ensure equal opportunities to them".

As the proposed apprentice training had been closed, this case was closed. However, for future it was advised by the court that reservation for persons with disabilities should be provided under section 39 of the act.

Candidate from disability category, unless recruited against reserved vacancies should not be considered as having been recruited under the reserved category

*In Registrar, Dr. Babasaheb Ambedkar University*[48] In this case, the respondent published and advertisement for the post of Assistant Professor and Lecturers. In said advertisement no provision for reservation was made for persons with disabilities.

The respondent submitted that in the process of recruitment of teaching and non-teaching posts and admission of students they strictly followed the rules and regulations and reservation policy of the state. This being a comparatively new university the total number of the sanctioned post is reasonably small. The court relied on the Supreme Court Judgement in R. K. Sabarwal versus State of Punjab 1997 which inter alia held that the appointment of candidate which are made on merit and not due to reservation are not to be counted towards reservation so far as the direct recruitment is concerned. They are to be treated as general category appointment. In the present case, the persons with disabilities who were appointed by the university are not appointed against the reserved post hence will not be treated as appointment against the reservation made for persons with disabilities.

The court also issued guidelines regarding the maintenance of rosters.

Cancellation of the appointment of one eyed person against a post that has been found suitable even for blind/low vision person results in injustice

*In Sonika v. LIC Housing Finance Limited*[19] The complainant applied for the post of Junior Executive Assistant in the respondent organisation. On having declared qualified in the written test, computer skill test and interview, she was given an appointment letter by respondent along with medical report form. She alleged that after being medically examined by the Doctor, she was declared medically fit with nil vision in left eye due to accident in childhood, the respondent cancelled her appointment stating that she is medically unfit on the basis of medical report. Respondent submitted that the petition is not sustainable under the Persons with Disabilities Act, as the definition of disability provided in Section 2 does not cover one eyed persons. Complainant herself claimed that as per the uniform definition of blindness, she is not a disabled person. The expression "Low Vision" may include a person who had lost one eye-Accordingly the averments of the Complainant will be applicable only if the post is reserved for blind or low vision person. On the contrary, the post for which the Complainant has applied is a regular post in the general category. Further the appointment of complainant was subject to being found medically fit. The Regional Manager cancelled the appointment of the complainant observing that she had not been found medically fit.

**Post Offered to the Complainant Required**

- Moving out in the field for various jobs.
- Ability to work on computers for long hours dealing with sensitive and intricate data, various statements of accounts and connected matters.
- Appearing for a test on Computer once in a while.

The complainant submitted that she has disability of one eye but this does not constitute any disability for the job for which she is selected; she further stated that as per instructions of Government of India, loss of one eye is not considered as disqualification on medical grounds. Complainant claimed that since the respondent has disqualified her on account of lost vision in one eye, her petition very much comes under the purview of act. Moreover she has been declared fit by the doctor in the medical examination.

The court referred the reports of various committees an agreed with the respondent that the one eyed person with thirty percent visual impairment is not covered under the definition of persons with disabilities as defined in section 2 (t) of the act. However it cannot be overlooked that cancellation of the appointment in respect of the complainant on the ground that she is one eyed person against a post that have been found suitable for even blind/low vision person has resulted injustice. It cannot be denied that she suffered from disability. She certainly is not entitled to the benefit/concessions available to persons with disabilities but cannot be denied appointment against open vacancies. If it is done, it will result in double jeopardy. In view of the above facts, the court advised the respondent to appoint the complainant to the post within thirty days from the receipt of the Judgement and order.

**The amount of compensation for extra cost in respect of transportation should be commensurate with the level of employee the extra expenditure in respect of additional cost of accessories of the personal vehicle, fuel, maintenance cost.**

*In Laxmikant Vijayvargiya v. Bharat Heavy Electrical Limited and ors*[37] The complainant, a person with locomotor disability of more than 50% submitted that his entire left leg is affected with polio which made him to use a crutch to walk. The respondent company is paying transport allowance to its employees who are blind or orthopaedically disabled of lower extremities @ five percent of basic pay subject to a maximum of Rs. 100 per month over and above the transport subsidy/ subsidized transport/conveyance reimbursement facilities. The complainant justified his claim for additional transport allowance on the ground that he, as a person with disability has to pay more for the car with additional features. The cost of scooters specially designed for persons with disabilities is also more. Further, the maintenance and operating cost of special vehicles is more as these were less fuel efficient. The township where the company had allotted him accommodation is spread over a large area and therefore could not be said to be a campus. The distance between his residence and place of work is more than two Km. The court upheld the contention of the complainant and made following observation that there is no dispute that the eligible blind and employees with locomotor disability need to be compensated for the extra cost they have to incur for transportation whether the journey is performed to commute between residence and place of work or for any other official work except when the official vehicle is provided. The amount of compensation for extra cost should also be commensurate with the level of the employee, the pay and the amount of transport allowance/conveyance expenditure to other employees. Govt. of India and PSEs following CDA pattern have found the compensation amount to be double the normal rate as reasonable. The amount of Rs.100/- being given by Bharat Heavy Electrical Limited (BHEL) to its employees with disabilities irrespective of their level in the hierarchy in the organisation and the amount of normal conveyance expenditure they are entitled to cannot be reasonable for an eligible employee with disability who is entitled to reimbursement of conveyance the expenditure an between Rs.2,200/- and Rs.2,290/-. A reasonable amount can be double conveyance expenditure or an amount that takes care of the extra expenditure employee with disability is forced to incur on travel to office and back or for any official work, as compared to non-disabled employees. The extra expenditure could be account of additional cost of accessories of the personal vehicle, fuel, maintenance of the vehicle, etc. The court advised the respondent to insure that the complainant was compensated for the extra expenditure he has to incur on account of the accessories in the car, extra fuel and maintenance which could be up to double the normal rate of transport allowance subject to his fulfilling the required conditions.

### Right of Persons with Disabilities to be Posted Near their Native Places

*In Ved Prakash v. Kendriya Vidyalaya Sangathan*[38] The complainant submitted that his daughter, a person with 70% locomotor disability who was posted as PGT "Commerce" at the respondent Kendriya Vidyalaya. be posted near her native place.

After going through the records and submission made by the respondent, the court observed that from the said note that while deciding about the choices for posting no consideration appears to have been given to the needs of persons with disabilities an policy of Department of Personnel and Training, Govt, of India that persons with disabilities should be posted near their native places within the region and requests from them for transfer to or near their native places should also be given preference. It is also observed that the policy decision has not been published /notified for information of the Complainant. This policy is being followed by all the government organisations including Public Sector Undertakings, Autonomous Bodies, etc. It may also not be practical for a person with disability who requires the assistance of other person for day-to-day needs, to accept a contractual job for a limited period far away from their native place. Appointment against the reserved vacancies in accordance with Section 33 of the Act is the right of persons with disabilities and the HR policies that inhibit persons with disabilities from joining the post can be treated as infringement of their rights, It is therefore, necessary that such policies need to be modified to enable and facilitate persons with disabilities to actually avail their rights and entitlements under the Act. The Respondent was directed to change the policy to enable and facilitate persons with disabilities to opt for their state of domicile in consonance with the instructions of Department of Personnel and Training and consider them for posting to their home town accordingly.

The court further directed the respondent that those persons with disabilities, who were appointed but could not opt for posting in their state of domicile due to policy of KVS, be allowed to give fresh option for posting. Based on their options, the Respondent should consider them against the available vacancies and transfer them accordingly and submit a report to this Court.

### Right of the Parents of Child Suffering from Autism Not to be Transferred

*In Dheeraj Kumar v. Director, Intelligence Bureau*[52] The complainant submitted that his daughter was suffering from Autism and was undergoing treatment at AIIMS. He had been asked to go on transfer to Chandigarh, though he had requested the Special Director/S, LB. that due to treatment of his daughter for Autism at AIIMS, he should not be transferred. The Complainant emphasized that shifting his daughter from Delhi at this stage when her bone age was 2 years more than her age i.e. eight years, is not safe. It took five years for the special educator to establish rapport with the child. The effort made so far might go waste, if she was shifted and put under a new structured setting and environment. The protection and the facilities that were likely to have positive effect on the life of the child should not be denied to her and the family. Shifting such a child could also shatter the family. The Complainant also added that it was not possible for him to specify the period during which his daughter may require to be in Delhi for appropriate treatment/therapy.

In the light of the facts and circumstances of the case, the Respondent was advised by the court to cancel the transfer of the Complainant and allow him to stay in Delhi until his daughter required the treatment/rehabilitation services by specialist. The Respondent might however, shift him from one office to another within Delhi for security reasons, if necessary.

## Non-Discrimination in Case of Acquiring Disability

Section 47 of the act of the PWD act guarantees certain rights to though people who acquire disability in the course of employment. This section provides that no such people cannot be remove from service or reduced in rank in the event of acquiring disability. If such person is not suitable to the post which he was holding before acquiring disability, he may be shifted to some other post with the same pay scale and service benefits. If it is not possible to adjust him against any post, he may be kept on a supernumerary post until a suitable post is available or he is retired whichever is earlier. This section also provides that the promotion cannot be denied to such person on the ground of disability only. However in appropriate cases the government can exempt any establishment from the provisions of this section.

## Cases

Section 47 expression "person with disability" is distinct from the expression "employee who acquired disability during his service" -Act of management in discontinuing driver from service subsequent to a 12% disability incurred during service held to be in violation of section 47

*In Municipal Corporation of Greater Mumbai v. Srirang Anandrao Jadhav*[39] The Respondent, a driver with the BEST, was rendered disabled while performing his duties on account of stone throwing during the arrest of a political leader. He was subsequently deemed unfit for his duties and shifted to an alternate post. However he was later told not to report for work although no order of termination was served upon him. The Respondent moved the Labour Court which held that the termination was in violation of section 47 of the Persons with Disabilities Act and directed his reinstatement. The order was challenged by the Petitioner in the Industrial Court by way of a Revision Application but the same was dismissed.

It was urged by the Petitioner that the Respondent's disability had been certified as only 12% and hence that he was not a person with a disability under the Act and therefore not entitled to the benefit of section 47, which in any event they contended was not pleaded before the Labour Court. Furthermore, the workman had since then reached the age of superannuation. It was also pleaded that the workman had been offered an alternate post for re-employment as and when a vacancy arose in the future which he initially accepted but later declined. The Respondent on the other hand contended that it was pertinent to note that the expression, "person with disability" in section 2(t) had not been used by Parliament in section 47 of the Act and that therefore there was a clear distinction between a person with disability and an employee who acquires disability and hence that the Respondent could not have been removed from service.

Upon a detailed examination of the background to the legislation, the provisions of the law and precedent, the Court concluded that the Respondents entitled to the protection available under section 47 of the act.

**Even if the person suffers injury outside the course of employment, he/she is entitled to the protection available under section 47 of the Act.**

*In Belliyappa Gowda v. Karnataka state Road Transport Corporation, Bangalore & Anr*[40] The petitioner joined service as a conductor in the respondent corporation, during the course of his employment, he met with an accident and sustained injuries by way of fracture to knew join and right thigh and he was hospitalised and underwent an operation. On account of injuries sustained by him, he became disabled and was not in a position to perform his duties as a conductor. Later he submitted representation along with the medical certificates which was sympathetically considered by the authorities and he was allotted alternative and sedentary jobs were he was not required frequent movements. The medical certificate stated that he suffered 40% of permanent physical disability. According to the petitioner, he was also due for promotion as a traffic controller which was not consider by the authorities, as a result, he continue to work as a stand duty conductor. Subsequently the petitioner was issued with a memo stating that he was required to work as a line duty conductor, for which he submitted representation stating that having regard to the injuries sustained by him and also due to the permanent disablement, he was enable to perform the duties of a line duty conductor. As such he sought to work as a stand duty conductor. Later, he filed a writ petition before the High Court praying for the issuance of the writ of mandamus directing the respondents to allot him duties of working at controller points and other duties like issuing passes etc. The said petition was dispose off. The court formed the opinion that the regulation of the respondent provides for providing alternative jobs befitting physical condition for an employee in capacitated during the discharge of his duties and directed the authorities to consider the case of the petitioner for allotment of alternative jobs. Later he filed contempt proceedings stated that the authorities have not consider his case as per the direction of the court. Later he was directed by the authorities to appear before a medical board and on the basis of the report of the medical board, he was compulsorily retired.

On the basis of the above facts and circumstances, the court observed that in the instant case, the petitioner had sustained injury outside the course of employment, might be in some quarrel and that a complaint also came to be lodged in this regard. The petitioner suffered disabilities during the year 1992 much before the act came into force and his case was not considered by the authorities. The corporation having considered the representation of the petitioner has accommodated alternative jobs without reducing any rank at the first instance. Later, by whimsical decision taken subsequently he was once again asked to discharge the duty as line duty conductor without considering his request to continue in the suitable alternative post, during the year 1999 he was compulsorily retired. At that time the Act, was very much in force. It was for the respondent's authorities to Act, properly having understood the provisions of the Act.

The court declared regulation of the respondent which provided to accommodate for alternative job for such person who suffer disability during the course of employment alone as ultra vires to the disability Act. The respondent was directed to reinstate the petitioner with 50% back wages with continuity of service to the alternative suitable post and also to consider is entitlement for promotional opportunity within four weeks from the date of the receipt of a copy of this order.

**The protection of section 47 of the act, is available even in those cases where the person has got the invalidity pension on account of his/her disability.**

*In Kunal Singh V. Union of India and ors*[41] The appellant was recruited as a Constable in the Special Service Bureau (for short 'the SSB'). When he was on duty, he suffered an injury in his left leg. The medical aid given to him did not help. Ultimately, his left leg was amputated on account of gangrene which had developed from the injury. He was invalidated from service by the respondents.

In the Supreme Court the appellant raised a specific ground based on section 47 of the act.

According to the petitioner, his disability falls under section 2 (i) (v) namely locomotor disability. The court observe that it is clear from the facts that the appellant suffered from the disability covered by section 2 (i) (v) read with section 2 (c) of the act and he acquired it during his service.

The court further observed that the act is an special legislation hence rule 38 of the Central Civil Services "Pension" Rules cannot override Section 47 of the Act which provided safe guards in case of disablement. The court allowed the appeal. The learned judge made the following observations:

Merely because under Rule 38 of CCS (Pension) Rules, 1972, the appellant got invalidity pension is no ground to deny the protection, mandatory made available to the appellant under Section 47 of the Act. Once it is held that the appellant has acquired disability during his service and is found not suitable for the post he was holding, he could be shifted to some other post with same pay scale and service benefits; if it was not possible to adjust him against any post, he could be kept on a supernumerary post until a suitable post was available or he attains the age of superannuation, whichever is earlier. It appears that no such efforts were made by the respondents. They have proceeded to hold that he was permanently incapacitated to continue in service without considering the effect of other provision of Section 47 of the Act.

*In Jaikumar Jagannath Kulkarni v. State of Maharashtra & orsr*[42] In this case, the petitioner was appointed as compounder. After working for almost 16 years. He was declared as permanently incapacitated by the medical board for rendering services.

On the basis of this report, the respondent no. 2 retired him compulsorily on the ground that he was medically unfit to perform duties as compounder. The petitioner contended inter alia that under the provisions of the disabilities Act 1995 his services ought not to have been discontinued. Instead he ought to be shifted to some other post and with same pay scale and service benefits and if suitable post was not available, he should be have been accommodated supernumerary post. After hearing both the parties and looking in to the facts and circumstances, the court observed that the petitioner was a disabled person under the Act. He is therefore entitled to the protection of section 47 of the Act. Apparently, the termination order issued by the respondent is reach of the mandate of section 47 of the Act therefore said termination order is liable to be quashed and set aside. The certificate issued by the civil surgeon showed that the petitioner is capable of doing light work. Therefore the respondent will have to adjust him by giving him same light work if it is available. If no such light work is available, he is entitled to be kept on a supernumerary post until suitable post is available or he attains superannuation whichever is earlier.

*In Maharashtra Road Transport Corporation & Anr. V. Deepak Shrikrishna Pandit*[43] In this case, the respondent was serving with the petitioner as a driver. He was beaten by a Motor cycle rider due to which he suffered severe injuries and therefore was found unfit to serve as a driver. For few months the petitioner allowed the respondent to work as a traffic controller. After some times the petitioner asked the respondent to resume duties as driver. The respondent filed complaint before the industrial court which by and interim order permitted the respondent to work as traffic controller. The respondent was declared medically unfit for the post of driver therefore the petitioner terminated his services later, the petitioner offered him the post of Peon as alternate employment. Thereafter the industrial court passed the impugned order directing the petitioner to protect the wages last drawn by the respondent even if he was appointed as a peon.

After hearing both the parties and analysing various judgments, the court observed that the petitioner had no option but to accommodate the respondent on the post carrying equal pay and if not so accommodated go on paying him the salary of the post Of driver on which he was working before he acquired disability even if it might cause loss to the petitioner corporation.

With regard to the offering of the post of peon to the respondent by the petitioner, court observed that the respondent should have accepted the appointment to the said post of under protest since the respondent was not qualified to be appointed as traffic controller. In that case, the respondent would have been entitled to difference of wages in view of the provisions of section 47 of the Act. Since he did not accept the offer, the petitioner cannot be burden with the liability to pay entire wages for the period for which the respondent was out of employment. The petitioner would be liable to pay only difference of pay of peon and pay of the post of driver.

*In Delhi Transport Corporation v. Harpal Singh, Ex. Security Guard*[44] The respondent no. 1 was appointed as a security guard on 12 November 1982. In June 1991 he met with an accident while in service and suffered disability. He was retired from service on 29 January 1994. The labour court by its order reinstating him noticed the provision of section 47 an referred to and applied a judgement of the Delhi High Court. The petitioner contended that since the Act came into force on the 7th February 1996 and the respondent was retired prematurely on 26th February 1994, the said Act could not have any retrospective effect so as to come to the aid of the respondent. The court rejected the contention of the petitioner and dismissed the petition. The court observed:

It is not in dispute that while the respondent No. l/workman was relieved from service on 22nd February, 1994, the espousal pertaining to his termination by way of the present reference was made after the day when the Act came into force on 7th February, 1996. The Act being a social welfare measure and enacted with a view to benefit disabled persons, the plea of the DTC which is an authority of the State, to the effect that the Act cannot be made retrospective, cannot be countenanced. Any statutory enactment incorporating a welfare measure particularly for the weaker sections of society has to be given foil effect. In any case since the reference was made after the Act came into force, the benefit of the Act is available to the respondent No. 1 and giving the benefit under the Act to the respondent No. 1 cannot in any event be termed as retrospective operation of the Act.

**A Person can not be Given Lower Post After Acquiring Disability as Per the Section 47 of the Act.**

*In Rupender Singh vs. State of Haryana and Ors*[45] The petitioner had joined as driver with the Haryana Roadways. When he was on duty while driving the Bus, an accident occurred with another Bus. The petitioner sustained injuries. He was medically examined by the Medical Board and declared 'unfit for driving duty. Consequently respondent no. 3 passed the order of retirement from the post of driver and gave him alternative job of helper-tyreman in the lower pay scale. The petitioner argued that in face of Section 47 of the Disability Act, 1995, the petitioner cannot be retired from the post of driver by giving him a lower post of helper-tyreman. If he is to be posted to another post then his pay scale can not be reduced nor can any promotion be denied to him.

The court observed: When the facts of the present case are examined in the light of the observation made by the Supreme Court in the case of Kunal Singh v. Union of India, and the provisions of Section 47, it becomes evident that order ... cannot be sustained in the eyes of law and has to be held as violative of Section 47 of the Disability Act, 1995. The prohibition against retirement of an employee who acquired disability while in harness has been completely ignored by respondent No. 3 while passing the impugned order .... Firstly, the petitioner cannot be retired, and secondly efforts ought to have been made to adjust him on a post carrying equal pay scale and thirdly if no post is available, an employee like the petitioner has to be permitted to work on a supernumerary post.

*In O.P. Sharma v. Delhi Transport Corporation and othrs*[1] The petitioner joined the services of DTC as a Conductor. At the time of joining he was physically disabled on account of deformity in his left leg. While in service, the petitioner suffered a paralytic attack, which led to severe impairment of movement of his leg. He was ill for about five months. The medical board found him to be unfit for the post. The petitioner sought for assigning of other duties and he was assigned the duty of Ticket Tally Clerk (TTC). He even applied to the post of Assistant cashier. The petitioner had been even prior to his medical examination, performing the duties of the TTC. He was posted to some other place and since joining that place he was obstructed in the discharge of his duties. The petitioner made allegations against the second respondents that he did not permit smooth discharge of the function by the petitioner and that eventually in an arbitrary manner issued the impugned order. He also stated that his disability did not come in the way of his continuing in the DTC.

The petitioner submitted that the respondents had nowhere disputed that for a period of four year from the date of impugned order the petitioner was working as a Ticket Tally Clerk (TTC). No attempt was made to offer alternative employment in view of the section 47 of the PWD act and various judgment of the Supreme Court and High Courts. The petitioner was a graduate and was even at the stage of recruitment, appointed as a disabled person.

The petitioner further urged that relief and complete consequential benefit should not be withheld in these proceeding merely because the act came in to force after the disability was incurred by the petitioner.

After analysing various judgments the court observed that It would appear that where by an enactment, beneficial measures are introduced, a litigant is entitled to avail of its benefits, certainly in pending proceedings. In the present case, the DTC, an instrumentality of the State, and admittedly bound by Article 14, is under an obligation to behave in a non-discriminatory and non-arbitrary manner. During the pendancy of litigation, the Act was brought into force; it gave statutory shape to the principle of non-discrimination at the workplace. Hence, its application cannot be construed as retrospective application of a later law.

The petitioner admittedly worked for about four years after incurring his disability. There is no reason why DTC could not have continued the arrangement, and given him assignments which does not require him to move around. Its insensitivity, led to the premature retirement of the petitioner, who was 39 years at that stage. The Act requires assignment of other duties, if the disabled employee cannot perform the duties assigned earlier. That obligation was admittedly not followed. The DTC stated that another, alternative employment was offered; the post of peon was offered to the petitioner, who agreed to it, but requiring that the DTC ought to protect his pay. Even this was not acceptable to the respondent. The facts show that even aside from the obligations under the Act, the DTC did not attempt to ensure alternative employment, or take into account the intervening four years employment of the petitioner in the capacity of TTC. It acted upon an old medical report, which stated that the petitioner could not work as conductor.

In the light of the facts of the case and the position of law discussed in various judgments. The learned judged was of the view that the DTC denied alternative employment for arbitrary reasons. Equally it terminated the services of the petitioner in a high handed manner.

The impugned order was accordingly quashed. The DTC was directed to reinstate the petitioner and assigned him suitable duties in accordance with Section 47 of the act. The petitioner is entitled to continuity of service for all purposes, including grant of annual increment, consideration for promotion etc. the petitioner is also entitle to back wages.

**It is the duty of the employer to inform the person who has become disabled during employment about the benefit contained in section 47 of the Act especially if the person is and uneducated class IV employee.**

*In Bhagwan Dass & Anr. V. Punjab State Electricity Board*[46] The appellant was working as assistant lineman with the respondent. While in service he became totally blind. After the disabilities Act, came into force, the government of Punjab, department of Personnel and Administrative Reforms, issued a letter directing all the heads of departments to comply with section 47 of the Act. The respondent also adopted the government letter under its circular. The respondents stated that the appellant remained absent from duty without any sanctioned leave from January 18, 1994 to March 21, 1997. He was directed by the Executive Engineer to resume duties. He however failed to report for duty therefore a charge - sheet was issued initiating disciplinary proceedings against him for gross miss conduct under the regulation of the respondent. Respondent stated that the appellant by his letter sought to explain his absence from duty and requested the respondent board to retired him from service. He further requested that his wife be appointed in his place. The letter clearly stated the fact that he requested his retirement because he was unable to perform his duty due to the loss of vision. Some internal correspondences took place between the officers of the respondent board over the question as to how to deal with the issue. Later on, the charge sheet issued against the appellant was withdrawn and he was asked to submit leave application for the period of absence.

The appellant than filed an affidavit before the concern officer in which he pleaded that he had no knowledge about the rules of the respondent electricity board and represented for retirement unknowingly. He further stated that when he came to know about these rules, he again represented that he might not be retired and might be retained in service as per the instructions of the department. The respondent did not respond to his affidavit and he was retired by making payment of his terminal dues.

The Supreme Court observed that from the material it is clear that notwithstanding the clear and definite legislative mandate, some officer of the respondent board took the view that it was not right to continue disabled person in the service And they accordingly took the view that the appellant had himself asked for retirement and therefore he was not entitled to the protection of the disabilities Act.

The letter, on the basis of which the officer of the respondent board took this stand, was written when a charge sheet was issued to him and in the letter he was trying to explain his absence to duty. The court observed that it was impossible to read that letter as a voluntary offer for retirement. Appellant was a class IV employee. He was not aware of any legal protection available to him and apparently believed that the blindness would cause him to lose his job, the source of livelihood of his family. The enormous mental pressure under which he would have been at that time is not difficult to imagine. In those circumstances it was the duty of the superior officers to explain to him the correct legal position and to tell him about his legal rights.

In light of the above discussion the court held that the action of the respondent board in terminating the service of the disabled employee is illegal. In view of the provisions of section 47 of the disability Act, the appellant must be deemed to be in service and he will be entitled to all service benefits including annual increment and promotion etc. The amount of terminal benefits paid to him should be adjusted against the amount of his salary if any balance remains that should be adjusted in easy monthly instalment from his future salary.

### Alternative Employment to be Provided Even where Disability is Less than 40%

*In Dilbag Singh v. DTC*[47] The Petitioner, a bus driver with DTC was surrounded by a mob that pelted stones on the bus and set the bus on fire. The Petitioner was hit by lathis and suffered injuries on his head. By an order, the Petitioner was given premature retirement on medical grounds. The Petitioner approached the High Court for quashing of the same. The petition was disposed of with liberty to approach the office of the Commissioner of Disabilities. The Commissioner rejected the Petitioner's complaint on the ground that the Petitioner's disability is less than 40 per cent, and hence that section 47 of the Act has no application. The order of the Commissioner was challenged before the High Court. The High Court in construing the scope of section 47 of the Persons with Disabilities Act, held that the provision does not use the term 'person with disability' but use the words 'an employee who acquires disability'. The term 'disability' has a wider definition than the term 'person with disability'. Hence the fact that the disability is less than 40 per cent. Is of no relevance for the purpose of section 47. The order of the Chief Commissioner was quashed and the Petitioner was ordered to be reinstated to a suitable post of equivalent rank with arrears and continuity of salary and increments.

The promotion can be denied if disability affects the discharge of functions or performance in a higher post or if disability would pose a threat to the safety of the co-employees, members of the public or the employee himself, or to the assets and equipments of the employer

*In Union of India Vs. Devender Kumar Pant*[48] The Respondent was selected for the higher post of Chief Research Assistant in the Research Designs and Standards Organization (RDSO), Ministry of Railways and by an order, he was promoted to the said post with the condition that his promotion will be effective from the date of submission of fitness certificate in B-l medical category.

The medical classifications for various categories of non-gazetted staff of RDSO, revised with a view to rationalize the medical standards, were notified by the RDSO, Ministry of Railways. According to these guidelines, the main distinction between B-l and B-2 medical categories was that colour perception was a requirement prescribed for B-l category but not for B-2 category. The promotion order required the respondent to submit B-l Medical Category 'fit' certificate, the respondent filed objections contending that in the existing RDSO environment, the nature of work prescribed for the posts of JRA, SRA and CRA is the same, and as he has already cleared for B2 medical category, it is not necessary for him to secure fitness in the higher medical category of Bl. By several replies the Directorate informed him that the different medical categories are prescribed in pursuance of rationalisation of medical standards, taking into account the requirements of the job, as also the safety and welfare of the public, fellow workers and the concerned employee himself. He was therefore once again called upon to present himself before the authorized Medical Officer for medical test and certification. The question that arose for consideration before the supreme court was that whether refusal by the appellant to give effect to the promotion of respondent unless he obtains fit certificate in B-l medical category, violates section 47(2) of the Act. The court held that if the disability will affect the discharge of functions or performance in a higher post or if the disability will pose a threat to the safety of the co-employees, members of the public or the employee himself, or to the assets and equipments of the employer And promotion is denied on these grounds, then it is not denial of promotion merely on the ground of disability, but is denial of promotion by reason of the disability plus something more, that is adverse effect of the disability upon the employee's performance of the higher duties or functions attached to the promotional post. It is significant that section 47(2) does not provide that even if the disability comes in the way of performance of higher duties and functions associated with the promotional post, promotion shall not be denied. Section 47(2) bars promotion being denied to a person on the ground of disability, only if the disability does not affect his capacity to discharge the higher functions of a promotional post. This would mean that a person who is otherwise eligible for promotion shall not be denied promotion ***merely or only*** on the ground that he suffers from a disability. Thus Section 47(2) bars disability per *se* being made a disqualification for promotion.

The promotion should not be withdrawn without deciding upon the representation of a person with disability for retention at the place where he was posted before promotion

*In P. Rathinavelu v. Steel Authority of India Limited*[49] case, the complainant, a person with 55% locomotor disability, working as a Executive Assistant Gr. Ill with the respondent filed a complaint submitting that on promotion to the post of Junior Executive (Finance/Marketing). He was transferred to another place. He requested the respondent for retention at the same place where he was working before promotion. The court advised the respondent to reconsider the transfer of the complainant and intimate the decision to the court. The respondent informed to the court that the two senior employees promoted along with the complainant were retained because of the experience in the relevant areas of their working, as the complainant did not joined at the place where he was transferred, another employee was promoted who had joined that office. The Respondent further submitted that the complainant, being one of the senior employees was provided with an opportunity for movement to the executive cadre by promoting him against the limited vacancies that were available only in the marketing. The court observed that from the facts of the case submitted by the Respondent, *it is* revealed that the Respondent withdrew the promotion of the Complainant without deciding upon his representation for retention at Salem (the place where he was posted before promotion). There does not appear to be any sound reason for not retaining him at Salem as two more persons were retained who were promoted with the complainant. The Respondent, knowingly or unknowingly, did not give due consideration to disability of the Complainant vis-a-vis others. Seniority was given overriding priority, which is not in line with the spirit of the act and DoPT's OM No.AB-14017/41/90-Estt.(RR) dated 10.05.1990, as per which persons with disabilities appointed under the Govt. should preferably be posted in their native places. In the facts and circumstances of the case, the Respondent was advised to promote the Complainant from the date when two persons were promoted and retained at Salem from the same panel and retain him at Salem and submit an action taken report within one month from the date of receipt of this Order.

Were the DPC has the knowledge that the person with disability is not doing the work that his counterparts were doing and the employers themselves deployed him on particular kinds of jobs without his asking for it, it can not grade him below average and declare him unfit for promotion

*In Nandkumar J. Dalvi v. Employees State Insurance Corporation*[50] The complainant who became visually impaired after rendering 14 years of service with the Respondent, submitted that he was denied promotion to the post of

Superintendent on the ground of his visual impairment. The respondent submitted that the promotional cadre post is only an alternative functional designation for Insurance Inspectors who are statutory authorities under Section 45(1) of the ESI Act, 1948. The post of Insurance Inspectors, Managers Gr. II and Superintendents are interchangeable. The Local Office Manager is also a statutory functionary as could be seen from the definition under Regulation 2(9) of the ESI (General) Regulations, 1950. The court informed the Respondent that the job of Inspector/Local Office Manager/Superintendent in ESI Corporation involved indoor and outdoor work that was comparable to the jobs of the identified posts and that as per Section 47 of the Act, promotion should not be denied to a person merely on the ground of his disability. After going through the representations make by both the parties, the court make following observations:

> "Upon considering facts and circumstances of this case, this Court has observed that the DPC had the ACRs of the Complainant on his performance of the job he was assigned. It also had the knowledge that he was not doing the work that his counterparts were doing. It needs to be noted that the Respondent themselves deployed the Complainant on particular kinds of jobs without his asking for it. He apparently performed the task assigned to him satisfactorily as nothing adverse was communicated to him nor the reporting/reviewing officers graded him 'below average'. Therefore, with the inputs available in his ACRs, it was clearly his disability because of which the DPC decided to grade him 'below average' and declared him unfit for promotion. Such a decision would amount to discrimination on account of disability, as it was the Respondent who decided to assign him a particular work. Further, as submitted by the Respondent, the post of Insurance Inspector, Manager Grade-II and Superintendent are interchangeable. Therefore, it should not be impossible for the Respondent to post him in the office as Superintendent not involving the job of an Insurance Inspector".

In view of the above facts, The Court directed the Employees State Insurance Corporation to consider the complainant for promotion to the post of Superintendent and promote him to that post, if otherwise found fit, from the date when the post of Superintendent was added to the regulations as an interchangeable post to Insurance Inspector within 3 months from the date of receipt of this Order. It should also be ensured that the Complainant is not declared unfit on the ground that he did not perform the duties of the post, which was not assigned to him.

## Conclusion

From the above, discussion following points can be deduced:

1. Right to work on an equal basis with others
2. Prohibition of discrimination on the basis of disability with regard to all matters concerning all forms of employment, including conditions of recruitment, hiring and employment, continuance of employment, career advancement and safe and healthy working conditions.
3. To enable persons with disabilities to have effective access to general technical and vocational guidance programmes.
4. Right to exercise the labour and trade union rights on an equal basis with others.
5. Right to self-employment, entrepreneurship, the development of cooperatives and starting one's own business.
6. Employment in the private sector through appropriate policies and measures, which may include affirmative action programmes, incentives and other measures.
7. Right to reasonable accommodation is provided to persons with disabilities in the workplace.
8. Right against slavery or in servitude, and are protected, on an equal basis with others, from forced or compulsory labour
9. Identification and reservation of posts suitable to the different kinds of disabilities.

10. Provision for accessible/ assistive devises suitable for different kind of disabilities so that they can perform their task effectively.

11. Accessible environment in the work place

Indian disability law deals with a limited number of issues with regard to the employment of persons with disabilities, these issues are mainly related to reservation of posts in public employment, protection of employment if a person becomes disabled during the course of employment to private employers for the purpose of encouraging employment of persons with disabilities in private sector.

As compare to the provisions of the advanced legal systems of the world such as UK and USA and the provision of disability convention, these provision does not covered a number of issues which are necessary to promote and protect the employment interests of persons with disabilities, for example there is no "Non -discrimination-clause in Indian law to expressly prohibit discrimination on the ground of disability Similarly the concept of "Reasonable Accommodation" is not fully incorporated in Indian law.

As mentioned in previous paras, UK and US disability laws are a very broad in scope. Some of the important points are mentioned below in this connection.

UK and US law prohibit discrimination on the ground of disability. These legislation also provide that the employer can not asked about the disability of a person while employing him/her and all the medical information is confidential. Only those questions can be asked which are related to the nature of employment in question.

The provisions relating to the reasonable accommodation are very broad in these legislations. They are on similar lines as contained in the disability convention. Title one of Americans with disabilities Act, 1990 (ADA) prohibits private employers, state and local governments, and employment agencies and labour unions from discriminating against qualified individuals with disabilities in job application procedure, hiring, firing, advancement, compensation, job training and other terms, conditions and privileges of employment. A qualified employee or applicant with a disability is an individual who, with or without reasonable accommodation, can perform the essential functions of the job in question. Thus it is not limited to government and public sector employment only but also includes in id ambit the private employers with fifteen or more employees. The definition of disability is also very wide in ADA. According to this act, and individual with a disability is a person who:

- Has a physical or mental impairment that substantially limits one or more major life activities;
- Has a record of such in impairment; or
- Is regarded as having such and impairment

Similarly the Equality Act, 2010 (UK) is wider in scope as compare to its predecessor i.e. Disability Discrimination Act, 1995.

- The different tests used to justify discrimination are replaced by a single "Objective Justification" tests which means that the employer must show that its conduct was a proportionate means of achieving a legitimate aim.
- Direct discrimination or harassment based on "Perceived" disability is made unlawful for e.g. the employer may be liable even if the effect of impairment on normal day to day activity or not substantial.
- Direct discrimination or harassment based on association (e.g. where a friend of a disabled person is harassed) is made unlawful.

It is submitted here that apart from looking into the draft Rights of Persons with disabilities bill 2011, the government should look into the provision of these legislation also.

Section 62 provides for the grievance redressed mechanism in every establishment. The positive trend in Indian judiciary to read the convention into the fundament rights enshrined in the constitution of India combined with the proposed new disability law will certainly help in advancing the disability rights jurisprudence in India.

## Endnotes

1. Constitution of India, Art 16, Equality of opportunity in matters of public employment
2. Ibid. Article 16 (1) There shall be quality of opportunity for all citizens in matters relating to employment or appointment to any office under the state.
3. Ibid. Art 16 (2) No citizen shall, on grounds only of religion, race, caste, sex, descent, place of birth, residence or any of them, be ineligible for, or discriminated against in respect of, any employment or office under the state.
4. Ibid. Article 16 (4) Nothing in this article shall prevent the State from making any provision for the reservation of appointments or posts in favour of any backward class of citizens which, in the opinion of the State, is not adequately represented in the services under the State.
5. 1992 Supp (3) SCC
6. Convention on the Rights of Persons with Disabilities, 2006 Art 27 1

   See also International covenant on Economic, Social and Cultural Rights, 1966 Arts 6 and 7
7. Persons with Disabilities (Equal Opportunities Protection of Rights and Full Participation Act) 1995 Section 47
8. Ibid. Art 27 1 (i)
9. Persons with Disabilities (Equal Opportunities Protection of Rights and Full Participation Act,) 1995 section 42
10. Ibid. section 41
11. Persons with Disabilities (Equal Opportunities Protection of Rights and Full Participation Act) 1995 section 32.
12. Ibid. section 33.
13. NHRC annual report 2000-2001
14. Persons with Disabilities (Equal Opportunities, Protection of Rights and Full Participation), Act. 1993. Sec 41. The appropriate Governments and the local authorities shall, within the limits of their economic capacity and development, provide incentives to employers both in public and private sectors to ensure that at least five per cent, of their work force is composed of persons with disabilities.
15. Ibid. Sec 43 The appropriate Governments and local authorities shall by notification frame schemes m favour of persons with disabilities, for the preferential allotment of land at concession] rates for-
    (a) House
    (b) Setting up business;
    (c) Setting up of special recreation centers;
    (d) Establishment of special schools;
    (e) Establishment of research centers;
    (f) Establishment of factories by entrepreneurs with disabilities

16. "Ibid. Sec 48 The appropriate Governments and local authorities shall promote and sponsor research inter alia,, in the following areas-
    (a) Prevention of disability;
    (b) Rehabilitation including community based rehabilitation;
    (c) Development of assistive devices including their psychosocial aspects;
    (d) Job identification;
    (e) On site modifications in offices and factories.
17. 2011 AIR SCW 416
18. Manu/SC/0481/2005, 2005 (4) ESC497, [2005 (4) JCR 240 (SC), JT 2005 (7) SC 288, (2005) IIIL LJ 749SC, (2005) 13 SCC721, 2005 (3) SLJ410 (SC) See also Bedanga Talukdar v. Saifudaullah Khan and Ors. SC Civil Appeal nos. 8383-8344 of 2011 Decided on 28/09/2011 in which it was held that there can not be any relaxation in terms and conditions such as protection of disability certificate alongwith application, contained in the advertisement of competitive exams unless power of relaxation is duly reserved in relevant rules or in such advertisement.
19. WPno.16258 of 2006 (Del HC)
20. WP No. 16396 of 2006(kant HC) See Also Manoj Kumar V The University of Hyderabad
21. 156 (2009) DLT 446 (Del HC)
22. Manu/UP/0666/2004,2004(4)AWC3264, 2004( 102)FLR821] See also Smt. Anu Bath v. State of Uttar Pradesh and Ors. Allahabad High Court Special Appeal
24. (1993) 2 SCC 411
25. (2205)1 PDD(CC)284
26. (1995) 6 SCC 720
27. 90 (2001) DLT 262
28. Manu/DE/8974/2007, 2008(101)DRJ733
29. Manu/DE/1052/2005, 123(2005)DLT244, 2005(84)DRJ44, [2005(107)FLR811], (2006) IILLJ43Del
30. WP 30387 of 2007 (Ker HC)
31. (2006) CCDJ 374 Case no. 3157 of 2006 - Decided on 24.07.2006 See also (2000) CCDJ 59 (2004) CCDJ 377 (2006) CCDJ 337 (2006) CCDJ 340 (2006) CCDJ 343 (2006) CCDJ 372 (2005) CCDJ 137
32. CCPD Case No. 25/1012.08-09 Case no. 28/1012/08-09 dated 27.10.2010
33. CCPD Case no. 39/1013-09-10 dated 25th June 2010
34. (2004) CCDJ 377 Case no. 1475 of 2001 - Decided on 09.02.2004
35. (2205) CCJD case no.3116 of 2005-decided on 0812.2005
36. (2005) CCDJ 111 Case no. 3100 of 2005 - Decided on 29.12.2005
37. (2006)CCDJ 499 Case no. MP/A/CCD/2005-decided on 26.06.2006
38. (2006) CCDJ 420 Case no. 3056 of 2005 - Decided on 23.05.2006
39. 2011 IICLR 601 (BOM HC)
40. 2008(i)AIR Kar R 77
41. (2003) 4 SSC 524

42. 2007(5) ABR(NOC) 705 (BOM)(DB)
43. 2010 (6) ABR (NOC) 576(BOM)
44. 105(2003) DLT 113
45. Manu/PH/0197/2006, [2006(110)FLR758], (2007) ILLJ61P&H, (2006)143PLR469

    See also Delhi Transport Corporation v. Sh. Manmohan Delhi High Court WP (C) NO 7696/2010 and CM 19998/2010 Decided on 07.03/2011 in which after becoming disabled
46. 2008 AIR SCW534
47. 2005 (84) DRJ 208: 123 (2005) DLT 318: (2006) I LLJ 480 (Del HC)
48. Manu/SC/l 167/2009, AIR2010SC1253, JT2009 (9) SC552, (2009) IVLLJ310SC, (2009) 8 MLJ134 (SC), 2009(9) SCALE504, 2010 (1) SLJ91 (SC)
49. (2006) CCDJ 487 Case no.3106 of 2003-decided on 08/02.2206
50. (2006)CCDJ case no.2930 of 2004–decided on 11.10.2006.
51. Ibid Sec 57 Reservations
    a. Persons with blindness;
    b. Persons with hearing impairment and speech impairment;
    c. Persons with locomotor disability and leprosy cured;
    d. Persons with cerebral palsy and muscular dystrophy;
    e. Persons with autism, intellectual disability and mental illness;
    f. Persons with multiple disabilities, deaf-blindness and multiple sclerosis.
    g. Persons with Low vision and persons who are hard of hearing

       Provided that posts identified under Section 32 of the Persons with Disabilities (Equal Opportunities Protection of Right to and Full Participation) Act of 1995 (Act No 1 of 1996) shall operate ^g guidelines for implementing this reservation. 6

    (2) The percentage stated can be renewed and the classification altered upon review once every 3 years.

    (3) If sufficient number of qualified persons with disabilities are not available in a particular year then the reservation may be carried forward to the subsequent year, and if in the subsequent recruitment year also a suitable person with disability is not available, then the post may be first filled by interchange among the categories, and if the vacancy is still not filled then the establishment shall identify train and then induct persons with disabilities on the post. In no case shall a post to which a person with disability is entitled to be appointed be allowed to lapse.

    (4) The entitlement outlined in sub section (2) and the process in sub section (3) shall also extend to schemes guaranteeing employment, or the creation of posts for employment, by way of any legislation notification or rule formulated by the appropriate government, including but not limited to the Mahatma Gandhi National Rural Employment Guarantee Act, 2005.

# 5

# Disability Law and Accessibility in India

## Introduction

Accessibility is a good example of the principle of reasonable accommodation. It is crucial for them to live independently and with dignity. Accessibility in the context of persons with disabilities means that the design of physical environment such as buildings, roads, buses, railway stations, rail compartments, airports aircraft etc. should be made in a manner that persons with various types of disabilities can negotiate them independently and without much difficulty. For example, there should be the facility of ramps and lifts so that people with locomotor disability can go to any part of the building.

Accessibility is not limited to the physical environment only. It also includes within its preview the accessibility of Information and Communication. For example, educational institutions should make study material available in Braille, 'urge print, audio books, e-text so that the pupil with visual disability can read the material. These institutions should provide the facility of sign language interpreter so that pupil with hearing disability is able to follow the instructions in the class.

In recent years, new dimensions have been added to the concept of accessibility. Now, accessibility also means that the websites should follow certain standards so as to make them accessible to various types of disabilities such as blind people who use screen-reader software. Similarly, for persons with visual disabilities, images need to be described in text. For persons with hearing disability, audio needs to be interpreted in sign language various electronic consumer items which have digital panels should also provide tactile buttons so that people with visual disability can operate them independently.

## Constitution of India

The Constitution of India[1] in Article 15(2) says,

No citizen shall, on grounds only of religion, race, caste, sex, place of birth or any of them, be subject to any disability, liability, restriction or condition with regard to-access to shops, public restaurants, hotels and places of public entertainment; or the use of wells, tanks, bathing Ghats, roads and places of public resort maintained wholly or partly out of State funds or dedicated to the use of the general public.

Articles 15(3) and 15(4) of the Constitution[2] establish a very positive role for the State. They encourage introduction of special measures in favour of women, children, Scheduled castes and Scheduled tribes, and other members of socially and educationally backward classes.

For persons with disabilities, accessible environment is necessary so they can enjoy various human rights on an equal basis with others. These rights include, education, employment, participation in social, political and cultural life, rights relating to sports and other recreational activities.

The UNCRPD[3] deals with the various types of accessibility. It provides that to enable persons with disabilities to live independently and participate fully in all aspects of life, States shall take appropriate measures to ensure access, on an equal basis with others, to the physical environment, to transportation, to information and communications, including information and communications technologies and systems, and to other facilities and services open or provided to the public, both in urban and in rural areas.

In India, access without discrimination to public facilities, roads, places of culture and entertainment for persons with disabilities came into focus only with the enactment of Persons with Disabilities Act, 1995, which lays down duties of various Government authorities. It is submitted that the Indian law, apart from keeping in view the UNCRPD should also take into consideration the laws of various countries which are broader and scope.

Section 44-46 of the act deal with various aspects of accessibility. These Sections are actually build upon Articles 15 and 16 of the Constitution as the element of non-discrimination to achieve equality of opportunity and access to public places, including transport systems is guaranteed in very clear terms for persons with disabilities. These provisions mainly deal with the accessibility of physical environment only the other aspects of accessibility such as reformation and communication etc are not covered by these sections another limitation of these provisions is tea) like the Directive Principles of State Policy enshrined in the constitution of India, the enforcement of these provisions is subject to Economic Capacity and Development. No Time-frame is prescribed for there implementation.

Section 44[4] mandates the establishments in the transport sector to take special measures to-

(a) adapt rail compartments, buses, vessels and akcraits in such a way as to permit easy access to orthopaedically disabled people;

(b) Adapt toilets in rail compartments, vessels, aircrafts and waiting rooms in such a way as to permit the wheel chair users to use then conveniently.

Section 45 provides -

1) installation of auditory signals at red lights in the public roads for the benefit of persons with visual disability ;
2) causing curb cuts and slopes to be made in pavements for the easy access of wheel chairs users;
3) engraving on the surface of the zebra crossing for the blind or for persons with low vision
4) engraving on the edges of railway platforms for the blind or for persons with low vision
5) devising appropriate symbols of disability; and
6) Warning signals at appropriate places.
7) Section 46[5] mandates to provide for-

(a) ramps in public buildings;

(b) adaptation of toilets for wheel chair users;

(c) Braille symbols and auditory signals in elevators or lifts;

(d) ramps in hospitals,, primary health centers and other medical care and rehabilitation institutions.

The National policy for Persons with Disabilities[6] also deals with the issue of accessibility on similar line.

NHRC in its 2000-2001[7] report recognises the significance of this right the report states:

> "(ix) Access is not only a problem for persons with locomotor disability. There was need to launch a scheme to provide support services such as escort and interpretation to persons with sensory disability".

Further the 2003-2004[8] annual report states:

> "2.11 Accessibility is has been the overriding concern in the disability rights debate throughout the world. If access is guaranteed, persons with disabilities can use, interact and participate in social institutions and environments to the same extent as others. The capacity of people with disability to fully participate in all aspects of community life is not so much hampered by the impairments as due to inflexible systems, processes and structures. A study commissioned by the office of the UN High Commissioner for Human Rights notes that "all points of access to the structures, of everyday life - the world of education, of work, of family or of social interaction - are set largely by reference to the dominant norm of the able bodied." Therefore, discrimination occurs when the difference of disability is discounted while regulating the terms of access and participation".

### Cases

### Access to Religious Places

*In B. Meenakshi v. State of Tamil Nadu*[9] The petitioner sought to highlight the inaccessibility of the temples in Tamil Nadu.

Pursuant to the filing of the Petition, the Hindu Religious and Charitable Endowment Department of the Respondent issued a circular to all executive offices of temples under its centre[1] to make temples accessible and to submit periodical reports to the department of the progress made. The High Court directed that the said circular be widely publicized and that the department ensure due compliance of the orders.

The orthopaedically handicapped person with locomotor disability should be provided concession by the airlines at par with blind traveller, the facility of ambulifting should also be provided to them

*In Javed Abidi v. Union of India and Ors*[10] In this case the petitioner enter and prayed for the following relief

(a) Direct the Indian Airlines to immediately provide for aisle chairs in every aircraft,

(b) Direct the Indian Airlines to provide ambulift on aII the airports of the country,

(c) Direct the Indian Airlines to provide 50% concession to all the disabled persons as defined in Section 2 (i) of the Act because to provide this concession only to visually impaired persons is discriminatory and directly violative of the fundamental rights of the other disabled, as guaranteed under Article 14 of the Constitution of India.

The petitioner argued inter alia that like blind persons,, The orthopaedically disabled persons with locomotor disability require the relief of concession for their travel by air more as it becomes an impossible task for them to travel from one corner to die other corner of the county by train and there is no justification for the Airlines net to grant such concession to such people when the concession is made available to the blind people.

The court observed that the objective of the act is to create earner free environment for persons with disability *and to* make special provision for their integrator into the social main stream.

When we consider the different types of disabilities mentioned is Section 2 (a) of the act and examines the same in relation to the difficulties one faces (b) train to far-off places, Those who are suffering from locomotor disability would stand by a separate class itself because of their immobility and the restriction of the limbs.

The court issued direction to the Indian airlines to grant them the same concession which the airlines giving to those suffering from blindness. But the court clarified that each and every person suffering from such disabilities would not be entitled to concession. Who have locomotor disability to the extent the 80% and above entitle to such concession.

## Accessibility in Election

*In Disabled Rights Group vs. Chief Election Commissioner*[11] the petitioner approached the Chief Justice of India after several failed attempts of securing accessibility for disabled voters from the Chief Election Commissioner. A letter outlining government's action, along with a copy of the Government Order, was sent only days before polling was scheduled to begin. On notifying the letter of the petition as a Public Interest Litigation. The Court directed the Chief Secretaries of respective States to ensure that wooden ramps were made available for elections in April 2004, as far as possible. However, as regards foe elections to be held in May 2004, wooden ramps should be provided at polling stations - at least in the cities and urban areas - to enable disabled persons to reach the polling stations and cast their votes.

In the commuter system of the city, some important point such as inter -platform transfer facility for the wheel chair user, spacious compartments inside the boggy, height of the coaches for easy access etc should be kept in mind

*In P. Sudhakara Reddy v. Railway Board and ors*[12] The complainant submitted that the memorandum of understanding between Government of Andhra Pradesh and Railway Board for Multimodal Suburban Transportation Systems (MSCTS) had been signed. The MOU was also to provide a few buses plying on fixed routes with accessible parking lots, bus terminal to take care of the entire mobility chain. As per his survey, Railway stations in Hyderabad and the rail coaches were inaccessible to persons with disabilities particularly to wheel chair users. The complainant requested the court to seek commitment from me concerned authorities for taking specific measures to make MSCTS fully accessible for persons with disabilities as mandated by the act.

Respondent no. 1 submitted inter alia that lay out of CNLR type coach had been developed by RDSO to provide for disable friendly coaches. Since Ministry of Social Justice and Empowerment during a review meeting desired that the facilities for visually impaired and hearing impaired should also be provided, the complainant no. 1 approaching the Ministry for providing finance for the design and manufacturing of a few proto-type CNLR coaches,

This Court, after hearing the parties, proposed that since the new commuter system like MSCT was being developed, some important points such as inter-platform transfer facility for the wheel chair users, spacious compartments inside the boggy, height of the coaches for easy access for persons on wheel chairs should be kept in mind. Efforts should also be made to make rail and road modes of transport complementary to each other,

Respondent no. 1 submitted the action taken report as per this, the regular production of SLR type coaches specially adapted to permit barrier free use by disabled passengers had been started.

The court pointed out that it had been taking up the issue with Railways and the response of the railways had been positive. Due to this the Ministry of Railway and government of Andhra Pradesh would ensure the provision and adequate accessible features in the MSCTS Hyderabad.

The court advised the Government of Andhra Pradesh to plan for appropriate accessible connectivity of MSCTS by accessible road transport i.e. buses for developing disabled friendly buses. The court advised the Commissioner for Persons with Disabilities, Gent, of Andhra Pradesh to monitor the issue of accessible MSCTS in Hyderabad and introduction of barrier free buses in Andhra Pradesh and submit a report to this Court from time to time.

## Accessibility in Public Transport for Disabled Commuters

*In Dinesk Gupta vs. Ministry of Transport & Ors*[13] This complaint was from person with physical disability who was using tricycle for short distances. However, he faced great difficulties in using buses in Delhi when he had to travel from He approached the CCD in early 2001. Requesting that the DTC buses should be converted like the ones used by *Akshya Pratisthan,* an NGO in Delhi.

The CCD held several hearings with all the respondents, as result of which the technical group under the Ministry of Social Justice & Empowerment with TATA and Askok Leyland were constituted to research and develop comprehensive design for buses design of buses for persons with disabilities. The Project Director, Science & Technology Mission Mode submitted the report of the Committee stating that 2-3 options for barrier free accessible buses are under development. An order of six buses was placed with TATA Motors, which should have been on the road by December 2004 DTC and Government of NCT assured the CCD that by 2010 all the buses plying in Delhi would be converted to low floor, high capacity buses, including the existing ones.

The persons with disabilities should not be transferred to the place where there is no facility for wheel chair users, architectural harriers should be removed from the premises to make the building accessible for the different categories of disability.

*In Saira Parveen and Anr. V. head Master, Jawahar Lal Pratmicvidalaya.*[14] The complainant No. 1 submitted that her husband (Complainant NO. 2) who was working as Assisted Teacher with the respondent suffering from 80 percent of disability. He was using wheel chair. Her husband was providing with facilities including easy accessibility by the former Headmaster at the premises occupied by the department. He had been regularly attending his duty at the allotted premises before the Authorities decided to stop all the facilities and directed him to perform the duty at the new premises. The new place of work had no facilities for the wheel chair users. Due to the adamant attitude of the Authorities, her husband was passing through serious mental agony and prayed that his rights be protected.

In view of the material available on the record and the fact that the authorities had restored the facilities provided to the husband of the complainant, the petition was dismissed with the advice to respondent to continue existing arrangements and the architectural barriers, it any should be remove from the school premises to make the building accessible for all categories of physically handicapped persons.

In order to ensure that persons with disabilities benefit equally from the scientific and technical advancement, the Persons with Disabilities Act in Section 48 encourages appropriate Governments and local authorities to promote and sponsor research in the following areas inter alia:

- development of assistive devices including their psycho-sock, aspects; job identification; and
- on-site modifications in offices and factories.

The NHRC is alive to the fact that telecommunications, broadcasting and other systems of information are out of the reach of a vast majority of persons with disabilities due to their cost and standards of design and delivery. Hence, in January 2003 it recommended that Government of India and State Governments should elaborate and adopt a National/State policy on accessible infrastructure for persons with disabilities in order to ensure barrier free access to built environment, transport system, telecommunications and information technology development in the field of disability.

## Conclusions

From the other analysis following points emerge:

1. Right to persons with disabilities to live independently and participate fully in all aspects of life.
2. Right of persons with disabilities to access Buildings, roads, transportation and other indoor and outdoor facilities, including schools housing, medical facilities and workplaces.
3. Right to accessible Information, communications and other services, including electronic services and emergency services.

4. To develop, and monitor the implementation of minimum standards and guidelines for the accessibility of facilities and services open or provided to the public.
5. Right to forms of live assistance and intermediaries, including guides, readers and professional sign language interpreters, to facilitate accessibility to buildings and other facilities open to the public
6. To promote other appropriate forms of assistance and support to persons with disabilities to ensure their access to information.
7. To promote access for persons with disabilities to new' information and communications technologies and systems, including the Internet.

As compared to the convention provisions and laws of the developed countries such as UK and US A, the Indian disability rights jurisprudence on accessibility of persons with disabilities has not developed to that extent as is the case with the above mentioned legal systems. There are several reasons for this.

Firstly, the provisions of the PWD act are into as wide as the provisions of the always of these countries. The act talks about the physical accessibility only if it does not other types of accessibility such as the accessibility of information and communication.

Secondly, there is no time frame prescribed for implementing the provisions relating to accessibility. There is a rider inbuilt in these provisions. This rider is that is that the authorities shall implement these provisions subject to their economic capacity and development.

In contrast to the Indian law, the Americans with disabilities Act (ADA) is very specific in this matter. The act requires the states and local governments to follow specific architectural standards in the new construction and alteration of their buildings. They also must relocate programs or otherwise provide access in inaccessible older buildings and communicate effectively with people who have hearing, vision or speech disabilities. When streets and roads are newly built re altered by & municipality, they must have ramps wherever there are curbs or other barriers to entry from a pedestrian walkway. Likewise, when new sidewalks or walkways are built or altered, they must contain curb ramps or slopes areas wherever they intersect with streets or roads.

However, public entities are not required to take actions that would result in undue financial and administrative burdens. They are only required to make reasonable modifications to policies, practices, and procedures where necessary to avoid discrimination, unless they can demonstrate that doing so would fundamentally alter the nature of the service, program, or activity being provided. Another limitation on the ADA Title 11 requirements is that not ever/ existing municipal building must be retrofitted in order to meet the accessibility requirements - the man requirement is that a public entity make its programs accessible, not necessary each facility or each part of a facility. For example, each rest room in a facility need not be made accessible. However, signs directing people with disabilities to the accessible tea areas and spaces in a fancily should be provided.

In addition to structural requirements, State and Iocal Government- must ensure effective communication with individuals with disability, Wherever necessary to ensure that communications with individuals with hearing., vision, and speech impairments are as effective as communications with others, the public entity must provide appropriate auxiliary aids, such as listening headsets, television captioning, large print materials, etc. However, governments are not required to take any actions that with result in a fundamental alteration or in undue financial and administrative burden.

Apart from this there are other legislation- which deal with specific issues of accessibility. They are Architectural Barrier act of 1968 (as amended in 1988), Air Carrier Access Act of 1986 Section 504 of the Rehabilitation Act of 1973.

The Disability Discrimination act, 1995 "DBA" (UK) aid recently passed equality act, 2010 (UK) which improved upon the DDA is almost on similar lines

All persons with disabilities have the right on equal basis with others to the physical environment, transportation, information and communications, including appropriate technologies and systems, and other facilities and services provided to the public, both in urban and in rural area.

## Endnotes

1. Constitution of India, Art 15 (2) No citizen shall on ground only of religion, race, cast, sex, place of birth or any of them, be subject to any disability, liability, restriction or condition with regard to;
   (a) access to shops, public restaurants, hotels and places of public entertainment or
   (b) the use of wells, tanks, battling ghats, roads and places of public maintained wholly or partly out of State funds or dedicated to the use of the general public.
2. Ibid Article 15 (3) and Article 15 (4) 15 (3) Nothing in this article shall prevent the State from making ay special provision for women and children. 15 (4) Nothing in this article or in clause (2) of Article 29 shall orevdraft the State from making any special provision for the advancement of any socially and educationally backward classes of citizens or for the Scheduled Castes and the Scheduled Tribes,
3. Convention on the Rights of Persons with disability 2006 Art 9. See also International! Covenant on Economic Social and Cultural rights Art 15 See also Convention on the Rights of Child, 1989 Art 23
4. Persons with Disabilities (Equal Opportunities Protection of Rights and Full Participation) Act, 1995, Sec 44
5. Ibid Sec45
6. Ibid sec46
7. NHRC annual report 2000-2001
8. NHRC annual report 2002-2004
9. Writ petition 7027 of 2006 (Mad HC)
10. (1999)SCC467
11. CPW No. 182/2004
12. (2004) CCDJ 334 Case no.705 of 2001-decided on 12..05.2004
13. Case No. 58/1999, CCPD, 06.06.2034
14. 2003 CCDJ 15 Case no. 1467 of 2001-decided on 6.10.13
    (1) All persons with disabilities have the right on an equal basis with others to the physical environment, transportation, information and communications, including appropriate technologies and systems, and other facilities and services open or provided to the public, both in, urban at: in rurrt wear.
    (2) All appropriate governments and establishments shall be required to ensure drat the rights of persons with disabilities. To accessibility as outlined .U sub sect on (1; of uif sec.ou ,ae iiT. pwuekd).

# 6

# Disability Law and Social Security in India

## Introduction

The primary purpose of social security measures is to give individuals and families the confidence that their standard of living and quality of life will not be eroded by social or economic eventualities and to provide medical care and income security against defined contingencies. For persons with disabilities, social security measures additionally aim to facilitate physical and vocational rehabilitation, protect against unemployment by allowances and job creation and provide benefits such as insurance, compensation, rehabilitation and maintenance of their dependants. The issue of social security becomes an important issue for persons with disabilities because disability and poverty work in cyclic pattern which means that disability leads to poverty as disabled people are deprived of participating in the economic activities due to various reasons such as lack of opportunity of education and training, social stigma attached to disability etc. The reason for including the chapter on social security in this book is that persons with disability being one of the marginalised sections of the society will not be able to reap the benefits of other rights such as education, employment etc. unless they are provided with the basic facility to lead a dignified life.

## Constitution of India and Social Security

The social security measures in India draw their strength from the Directive Principles of State Policy[1], which inter alia, enjoin the State to strive to promote the welfare of the people by securing and protecting, as effectively as it may, a just economic and social order. The Government has put in place a security net for the workers so that they are secure in times of contingencies such as retirement, resignation, retrenchment, death and disability. The security of the family members, particularly dependent children and disabled children, is also guaranteed in the event of the death of an earning member of a family.

UNCRPD[2] deals with this right. It recognises inter alia the right to an adequate standard of living for persons with disabilities and their families, including adequate food, clothing, and housing, and to the continuous improvement of living conditions, without discrimination on the basis of disability.

In India, For persons with disabilities, special security measures are outlined in Sections 66, 67 and 68 of the Persons with Disabilities Act, 1995. Section 66[3] mandates the government at all levels to undertake or cause to be undertaken rehabilitation schemes for persons with disabilities through its financial support. Further, Section 67[4] obliges the government to frame insurance schemes for the benefit of its disabled employees.

Section 68[5] obliges the government to frame a scheme for payment of unemployment allowance to persons with disabilities.

Apart from these provisions, the Act entitles persons with disabilities to poverty alleviation schemes, assistive devices, 3% housing for the poor disabled persons[6].

Another important enactment that elaborates a comprehensive social security provisions for persons with disabilities is the National Trust Act. This Act aims to:

1. Deal with problems of persons with disabilities who do not have a family support;
2. Promote measures for the care and protection of persons with disabilities in the event of death of their parent or guardian;
3. Evolve procedures for the appointment of guardians and trustees for persons with disabilities requiring such protection;

4. Extend support to registered organizations to provide need based services during the period of crisis in the family of persons with disabilities; and
5. Strengthen facilities to provide support to persons with disabilities to live within their own families.

NHRC in its annual report of 2000-2001[7] states:

> "(viii) There are no floor-level legislative guarantees regarding care and protection, which have been left totally to the discretion of the executive. The nutritional, residential, medical, developmental and educational needs of children without careers must be the joint and several responsibilities of the Central and State Governments and Local Authorities. Similar facilities could be extended to destitute persons with disabilities, aged persons with disabilities and without careers, and persons with multiple disabilities".

The National Policy for Persons with Disabilities also deals with the issue of social security of persons with disabilities.

Apart from the above, a number of public interest litigations have come up before the Supreme Court.

## Social Security for Persons with Disabilities

### Continuation of pregnancy should be permitted of the mentally challenged lady

*In Suchita Srivastava v. Chandigarh Administration*[8] The woman in question is an orphan who had been abandoned by her parents at an early age and subsequently she had been under the guardianship of the Missionaries of Charity, New Delhi. Thereafter, she had been admitted in the Government Institute for Mentally Retarded Children in Chandigarh and was later on brought to the 'Nari Niketan' a welfare institution. Later she was shifted to 'Ashreya' a newly established welfare institution.

A medical social worker and a staff nurse observed that the victim was showing signs of nausea and had complained about pain in her lower abdomen in addition to disclosing the fact that she had missed her last two menstrual periods. Acting on their own initiative they conducted a pregnancy test with a urine sample and found it to be positive. Following this development, a medical board consisting of two gynaecologists and a radiologist was constituted. The board concluded that she had been pregnant for 8-10 weeks at the time.

The Director-Principal of the GMCH thereafter constituted a three-member medical board whose task was to evaluate the mental status of the victim and they opined that the victim's condition was that of 'mild mental retardation'. Thereafter another multi-disciplinary Medical Board was constituted by the same authority. This Board was asked to submit its considered opinion as to the consequences of continuation of pregnancy and the capability of the victim to cope with the same. The board recommended the termination of the victim's pregnancy.

Since there was no clear statutory basis for proceeding with the abortion, the Chandigarh Administration moved the High Court of Punjab and Haryana seeking a judicial opinion on the said matter. In its order the High Court had taken note of the opinion given by the multi-disciplinary Medical Board. However, as a measure of abundant caution the High Court directed the authorities to constitute an Expert Body consisting of medical experts independent from the administrative control or any form of influence by the Chandigarh Administration.

Even though the Expert Body's findings were in favour of continuation of the pregnancy, the High Court decided to direct the termination of the same. On the ground that it is in the best interests of a mentally retarded woman to undergo an abortion, keeping in mind that in addition to being mentally retarded she was also an orphan who did not have any parent or guardian to look after her or her prospective child.

Aggrieved by these orders, the appellants moved the Supreme Court. The second appellant an advocate appeared in person and sought a hearing on an urgent basis because the woman in question had been pregnant for more than 19 weeks at that point of time.

The Supreme Court over rued the decision of the high court. The court placed reliance on the section 3 of the Medical Termination of Pregnancy Act, 1971 and observed that since the victim had clearly expressed her willingness to bear a child. Her reproductive choice should be respected in spite of other factors such as the lack of understanding of the sexual act as well as apprehensions about her capacity to carry the pregnancy to its full term and the assumption of maternal responsibilities thereafter.

The court observed that there is no doubt that a woman's right to make reproductive choices is also a dimension of 'personal liberty' as understood under Article 21 of the Constitution of India. It is important to recognise that reproductive choices can be exercised to procreate as well as to abstain from procreating. The crucial consideration is that a woman's right to privacy, dignity and bodily integrity should be respected Taken to their logical conclusion, reproductive rights include a woman's entitlement to carry a pregnancy to its full term, to give birth and to subsequently raise children

The court further said that It is evident that the woman in question will need care and assistance which will in turn entail some costs. However, that cannot be a ground for denying the exercise of reproductive rights.

Performing an abortion at such a late-stage could have endangered the victims' physical health and the same could have also caused further mental anguish to the victim since she had not consented to such a procedure. Proceeding with an abortion at such a late stage (19-20 weeks of gestation period) poses significant risks to the physical health of the victim.

The court noted that the findings recorded by the Expert body which had examined the victim indicate that the continuation of the pregnancy dues not pose any grave risk to the physical or mental health of the victim and that there is no indication that the prospective child is likely to suffer from a congenital disorder. However, concerns have been expressed about the victim's mental capacity to cope with the demands of carrying the pregnancy to its full term, the act of delivering a child and subsequent congenital disorder. In this regard, the court directed that the best medical facilities be made available so as to ensure proper care and supervision during the period of pregnancy as well as for postnatal care. Since there is an apprehension that the woman in question may find it difficult to cope with maternal responsibilities, the Chairperson of the National Trust for Welfare of Persons with Autism, Cerebral Palsy, Mental Retardation and Multiple Disabilities (constituted under the similarly named 1999 Act) has stated in an affidavit that the said Trust is prepared to look after the interests of the woman in question which will include assistance with childcare. In the said affidavit, it has been stated that this Trust will consult the Chandigarh Administration as well as experts from the Post Graduate Institute of Medical Education and Research (PGIMER) in order to ensure proper care and supervision. If any grievances arise with respect to the same subject-matter in the future, the respondent can seek directions from the High Court of Punjab and Haryana under its writ jurisdiction.

### Protection and Care of Mentally ill Persons to be in Accordance with the Law

*In Re Death of 25 Chained Inmates in Asylum Fire in Tamil Nadu vs Union of India*[9] The Supreme Court issued the following directions pursuant to directions suggestions of the Amicus Curiae appointed by the Court, to investigate the plight of mentally ill persons in various mental asylums, pursuant to an unfortunate event in which 25 inmates died in a fire as they were chained to their beds and could not escape:

i. District-wise survey of all registered/ unregistered bodies offering psychiatric/ mental health care. No unregistered body will function.

ii. No mentally challenged person will be chained in any part of the State,

iii. Chief Secretary or Additional Chief Secretary designated by him the State level, and Cabinet Secretary, Government of India or any Secretary designated by him at the Central level, shall be the nodal agency to coordinate all activities involved in implementation of the Mental Health Act, 1987, the Persons with Disability (Equal Opportunities, Protection of Rights and Full Participation) Act, 1995 and the National Trust for Welfare of Persons with Autism. Cerebral Palsy. Mental Retardation and Multiple Disability Act, 1999

iv. National Trust should be formed under the 1999 Act and contribution made for it.

vi. One Central Government-run mental hospital in each State and Union Territory must be established within a definite time frame.

vii. State Government & Union Territory Government set up at least one mental hospital within a definite time frame.

viii. Both Central & State Government shall undertake a comprehensive awareness campaign with a special rural focus to educate people as to provisions of law relating to mental health, rights of mentally challenged persons, the fact that chaining of mentally challenged persons is illegal and that mental patients should be sent to doctors and not religious places such as temples or dargahs.

## Procedure of Admission, Release and Treatment to be Followed for Mentally ill Inmates by State Protective Homes

*In Dr. Upendra Baxi vs. State of Uttar Pradesh & Anr*[10] Through this public interest litigation, Dr. Baxi and Mrs. Lotika Sarkar sought to enforce the human rights of the occupants of state protective homes under Article 21 of the Constitution. The Supreme Court ordered a panel of doctors to examine the inmates at the Agra home and submit a report to the Court. The report of the Psychiatric Department In-charge showed that 33 out of the 50 inmates had varying degrees of mental retardation and had not been examined at the time of admission into the Home. Despite this report, the Superintendent had released 14 of them, without determining their mental state and with no money to cover even the train fare to their hometowns.

The Court held that firstly it is necessary for the Magistrate ordering the release to ascertain whether the circumstances justify the release of the inmates of state homes. Thereafter, the Superintendent is required to make relevant entries in the inmates Register regarding the physical and mental health of the inmates at the time of release. The Court expressed regret that the Superintendent had not personally, as per rules as well as on humane grounds, enquired from the inmates released recently as to where they proposed to go, for which railway tickets ought to have been supplied. The Court also suggested that the Superintendent in this regard could make an application to the Magistrate.

The Court also recommended that psychiatric treatment be provided to the mentally ill inmates, for which a record of the time and place of treatment should be maintained. Further, it was directed that vocational training aimed at rehabilitation ought to be provided and separate accommodation should be made available to these inmates. The State Government and the Superintendent were directed to transfer the mentally ill inmates of the home to a mental health institute, after consulting a psychiatric doctor for deciding the category and determining whether the inmates were required to be in an institute. All costs, charges and expenses incurred for providing accommodation in special institutes for these inmates should be borne by the State Government.

## Proper Civic Amenities for Running State Owned Mental Hospitals

*In Rakesh Chandra Narayan vs. State of Bihar*[11] A letter addressed to the Chief Justice from two citizens of Patna in regard to the mental hospital at Kanke near Ranchi was considered as public interest litigation under Article 32 of the constitution. Taking cognizance of a letter addressed to the Chief Justice of India, the Court treated it as a PIL under Article 32 of the Constitution as it spoke of the conditions in the mental health institution in Bihar. The report submitted by the Chief Judicial Magistrate appointed by the court to visit the home in question revealed shocking and inhuman conditions in the hospital in which a large number of patient were living. The Court observed that it is the obligation of the State to provide medical attention to even' citizen and that it would be difficult for the Supreme Court to monitor the management of a hospital located far away. However, in light of the State Government's indifferent attitude and in spite of several interim Supreme Court orders and assurances held out by the State, defects have still not been remedied, though the Court's intervention has led to some improvements. A Committee of Management was appointed with a sitting High Court Judge as its Chairman, with powers to look after all aspects of the institution. Directions were given to the Committee for proper functioning, management, funds, etc. Observing that a hospital is not a place where cured people should be allowed to stay, the Court directed the Committee to take immediate steps to set up a rehabilitation centre at a convenient place around Ranchi, for those who after being cured are not in a position to return to their families or to seek useful employment on their own. Parties including the Committee were granted liberty to move the court from time to time for clarifications or more orders.

The Court also directed that various implementation reports that are furnished by the respondent States from time to time should be placed before the Court, For this purpose, the Court directed that the matter shall be deemed to be pending to monitor the progress as also to facilitate passing of further orders. The court observed:

> "29. In a welfare State and we take it that the State of Bihar considers itself to be one such, it is the obligation of the State to provide medical attention to every citizen. Running of the mental hospital, therefore, is in the discharge of the State's obligation to the citizens and the fact that lakhs of rupees have been spent from the public exchequer (perhaps without, or with inadequate, return) is not of any consequence. The State has to realise its obligation and the Government of the day has got to perform its duties by running the hospital in a perfect manner and serve the patients in an appropriate way. The reports and affidavits of the Government of Bihar and its officers (not the reports furnished to the court by the judicial officers) have not given us the satisfaction of the touch of appropriate sincerity in action".

"30. The scheme which was furnished to the court was a half-hearted one and no attempt therein was made to bring about any improvement except attending to certain obvious deficiencies and shortfalls. The hospital has been in existence from pre-independence period. There have been epoch making breakthroughs in the field of psychiatry and treatment of psychiatry patients. The approach to mental health and the techniques of psychiatry have changed. Psychologists have developed their art and tools. The method of care and attention for the mentally ill has also undergone a sea change. When we had called upon the State of Bihar to give a scheme for improving, the conditions of the hospital, this Court had not intended a scheme for removing the deficiencies in the old hospital; we had really intended to look forward to a scheme of reorientation which the scheme did not even remotely touch except to say that NIMHANS at Bangalore has been contracted".

## Choice between Payment of Additional Compensatory amount or Alternative Job

*In Anand Bihari & Ors. vs. Rajasthan State Road Transport Corporation & Anr*[12] The petitioners were employees of Rajasthan State Road Transport Corporation. During the course of employment, their eyesight became defective and they were discharged from service. The Supreme Court held that the Corporation should give each of me retired workmen their retirement benefits, and in addition offer them any available alternative job, which they are eligible to perform. It was further stated that in case no such alternative job is available, each of the workmen should be paid an additional compensatory amount along with their retirement benefits. If the alternative job becomes available at a later date, the Corporation may offer it to the workmen provided they refund the proportionate, compensatory amount

## Computation of Compensation

*In R.D. Haitangadi vs. M/s. Pest Control (India) Pvt. Ltd.*[13] the appellant met with an accident while travelling, as a result of which he suffered serious injuries resulting in 100% disability and paraplegia below the waist. A practising advocate before the accident, he was unable to resume his practice due to the disability. The Supreme Court stated that while fixing an amount of compensation payable co a victim of an accident, the damages have to be assessed separately as pecuniary damages and special damages. Pecuniary damages are those, which the victim has actually incurred and which are capable of being calculated in terms of money, whereas non-pecuniary/ damages are those, which are incapable of being assessed by arithmetical calculations.

In order to appreciate the two concepts, pecuniary damages may include expenses incurred by the claimant: (i) medical attendance; (ii) loss of earnings of profit up to the date of trial; (iii) other material loss. So far as non-pecuniary damages are concerned, they may include: (i) damages for mental and physical shock, pain suffering, already suffered or likely to be suffered in future; (ii) damages to compensate for the loss of amenities of life which may include a variety of situations, e.g. the claimant may not be able to walk, run or sit on account of injury; (iii) damages for the loss of expectation of life, i.e., on account of injury the normal life-span of the person concerned is shortened; and (iv) for inconvenience, hardship, discomfort, disappointment, frustration and mental stress.

## No Fault Compensation Principles Applied in Cases of Disability in Motor Accidents

*In K. Nandakumar vs. Thanthal Periyar Transport Corporation*[14] The appellant was injured in a motor accident and sustained permanent disability as a result. Since it was found that the appellant himself was negligent he was denied compensation by the Tribunal as well as the High Court. The Supreme Court, applying section 92-A of the Motor Vehicles Act, 1939, which lays down the principle of no-fault compensation, held that a claim for compensation under the Section is not defeated by reasons of any wrongful act, neglect or default of the person who had died or suffered permanent disablement. It was farther stated that the quantum or compensation is not to be diminished even if the person who died or suffered permanent disablement bore some responsibility for his death or disablement.

## Loss of Future Income, Prolonged Medical Treatment and Hospitalisation Should be Taken into Consideration for Condoning Delay and Awarding Additional Compensation

*In Swatantra Kumar vs. Qamar AH & Ors*[15] The claimant, a pillion-rider and the respondent suffered permanent partial disabilities as a result of a vehicular collision between them. The Tribunal awarded them compensation under the Motor

Vehicles Act, 1939, which the High Court increased. The Supreme Court increased the amount of compensation for both, after consideration of future economic loss doe to die permanent partial disability as well as for pain, shock and suffering,

**Compensation in Lieu of Future Earnings for Disability Due to Accident, is Allowable Even when there is no Formal Employment**

*In Ashwani Kumar Mishra vs. P. Muniam Babu & Ors*[16] The appellant was 23 years of age when he met with an accident, received severe injuries and became permanently disabled. Both the Tribunal and High Court granted him some compensation. Before the Supreme Court, the appellant pressed for compensation in lieu of future earnings on the basis of his monthly income. The insurance company submitted that there was no proof of his income and it was not proven that he was employed under his father for the work for which the vehicle was being utilised at the time of the accident, he was however, not disputed that at the time of the accident, the appellant was assisting his father in construction work.

The Supreme Court stated that even though the appellant was not formally employed, the amount of compensation could be fixed on the basis of "some guess work some hypothetical consideration, some amount of sympathy' linked with the disability caused". Hence the Supreme Court enhanced the amount of compensation.

**A Person who is in Regular *Army* there is *no reason why he Should* not be Treated on Duty when he was on Casual Leave**

*In Lance Dafadar Joginder Singh V. Union of India and Others*[17] The appellant was serving as Lance Dafadar in regular Army. He served for more man 17 years as a combatant soldier and had served in the operational area during the 1965 and 1971 Indo-Pak wars. When he was proceeding on casual leave from Babina, his duty station to his home in district Faridkot (Punjab), While boarding the train at Babina Railway Station he got involved in an unfortunate accident as a result of which he fell down from the train and suffered severe injuries. His right leg came under the wheels of moving fain and as such he was crushed below the knee. The leg was amputated at the military hospital. He was discharged from Army and he was being paid the pension due to him. Although the appellant was given Army pension but he was denied disability tension under the Pension Regulations. The disability pension was denied to the appellant on the ground that the injury was not attributable to military service. The appellant challenged the denial of disability pension.

The court agreed with the contention of the appellant that he being in the regular army, there is no reason why he should not be treated as on duty when he was on casual leave. No army regulation rule was brought to the notice of the court to show that he was not entitled to disability pension The court saw no justification in denying the disability pension and ordered accordingly.

**Payment *of* Disability *Pension and invalid pension to a member of* the Security Forces declared medically *unfit to serve despite long delay,* Court orders payment to be made to the *Petitioner***

*In Abdul Majid Shah* v. *Union of India*[18] This Writ Petition was filed seeking directions against the Respondents for grant of invalid pension to the petitioner. He was a Constable with the Border Security Force, suffered from schizophrenia was treated in the base hospital. Due to his mental ailment the Petitioner was produced before a medical board, which found him completely and permanently, incapacitated for further services of any kind in BSF. The Petitioner was accordingly compulsorily retired from service. The Petitioner was not granted the invalid pension as prescribed under the relevant rule nor given disability pension. The Petitioner thereafter approached the authorities through various representations for grant of invalid pension and disability pension but no heed was given to any of his representations. The Petitioner then approached the High Court after a long delay, owing to the nature of his disability. After hearing the arguments of both the sides the Court allowed the Writ Petition and directed the Respondents to grant invalid pension to the Petitioner from the day he was compulsorily retired from service.

### The Court may Award Compensation in a Writ Petition *in* Addition to any Compensation to which the Person is Entitled under any other Law Such as Workmen Compensation Act

*In J. B. Kumar vs. Secretary Labour and Anr*[19] In this case, the appellant was working as an assistant steward on monthly salary of Rs. 3108/- with the respondent no 2. He met with road accident and thereafter was absent from the duty. After waiting for one year and four months to enable the workman to recover from the accident injury, the management directed him to report on duty. The appellant workman however failed to inform the management about his state of health. The management deputed its doctor to visit the residence of the appellant. The doctor examined him and gave his opinion that the appellant would not be able to perform the duties at all even after recovery. Consequently the workman was terminated on the ground of his continued illness and medical unfitness to perform duties. The workman challenged the said order on the ground that it was in unjustified and illegal termination. The court held that from the records it is clear that the appellant is unable to discharge the duty as an assistant steward, as the job involves physical movement inside the hotel/restaurant. And amount of Rs. 70,000, which has already been received by the appellant is independent of any liability under the workman compensation act.

Considering the peculiar circumstances of the case the petitioner should be exempted from appearing in the written test and her case for regular employment should be considered even though she was appointed without following the proper procedure.

*In Anubha Bhargava vs. Union of India and Ors*[20] The petitioner was one of those 130 employees, working in different offices of the respondent Airport Authority of India, whose services were terminated, inter alia, on the ground that all these persons were appointed on ad hoc basis without any advertisement or calling candidates from Employment Exchange or following recruitment rules. The petitioner filed an application stating the peculiar facts related to her. These facts inter alia were:

The petitioner, a Convent educated commerce graduate and Computer literate is a visually challenged girl who was appointed as a Receptionist under the Physically Handicapped Category, she lost her eye sight during employment;

b) She cannot read Newspapers which carry objective questions and answers by way of puzzles and other materials;

d) She cannot/does not watch TV, where she could benefit from the programmes especially the one which enhances General Knowledge;

The court stated that the petitioner could not show that her appointment was made after the following the proper procedure. Moreover she was appointed only on ad hoc basis hence her status remained as that of an ad hoc employee. Her contention that after six months she is to be treated as a probationer and after two years as a regular employee cannot be accepted.

In view of the above facts, The court past following directives:

> Court however noted the peculiar facts concerning the petitioner as mentioned above. It also noted the fact that only two post were reserved for persons with disabilities and no post was reserved for visually disabled candidate. The respondents were not able to show that the quota meant for visually handicapped persons i.e. 1% of the posts have already been filled.
>
> 1. The petitioner is entitled to be exempted from appearing in the written test.
>
> 2. On the basis of service record, since she had served from 25.9.2002 to 30.11.2004, her case for regular employment should be considered. She should be given the job which she can conveniently handle keeping in view her aforesaid disability. Though she became totally blind when she was still in service, she continued to discharge her duties as a Receptionist to the satisfaction of her employer, therefore, it is not a case where the petitioner will not be able to perform any duties, It will be up to the respondents to take this vacancy from the general quota prescribed and adjust it against the quota reserved for physically disabled persons after undertaking the exercise as to how many posts under the said quota are still

> available. Alternatively, it will, be open for the respondents to create a supernumerary post for the petitioner immediately, to be adjusted against the disability quota. However, she will not be entitled to any salary for the interim period. The appointment would be treated as a fresh appointment without giving any benefit of the past service rendered.

**Even in those cases where a person with disability is appointed for a fixed period, his case may be considered sympathetically and he may be adjusted against the seats reserved for persons with disabilities**

*In Dilip Baruah V. State of Assam and Ors*[21] Petitioner was a disabled person suffering from 60 percent disablement of traumatic paralysis of the left hand. Respondent appointed him as Surveillance Worker in his establishment for a period of 30 days. The services of the petitioner was extended after the initial period of one month for other 15 days. Till the year 1996 the services of the petitioner was availed by the department by providing extension time and again. Thereafter he was not allowed to continue in the said capacity. After discussing the history, objectives and provisions of the PWD Act and the provisions of the constitution the court observed that the basic purpose of the act is to improve the socio-economic conditions of the persons removing any discrimination in protection of rights provisions of medical care, education, training employment and rehabilitation and for equal opportunities for adequate means of livelihood and employment.

Considering the facts and circumstances of the case vis-a-vis, the relevant provisions of law and on perusal of the material on records, the court directed the respondents to consider the case of the petitioner for appointment in reserved quota of disabled persons (loco motor disability) with the similarly situated persons taking into account his experience as other factors within a period of two months from the date of receipt of the order.

**Governments and local authorities were directed to give preferential treatment to disabled persons in allotment of land at concessional rates**

*In Prajwala v. Union of India & Ors*[22] The petitioner filed a public interest litigation alleging that Section 43 of the disabilities Act has not been fully implemented by various states. This section provides for concessional allotment of land for various purposes. The counter affidavit filed by a number of states showed that the provision has not been fully implemented.

The court directed that whenever the state governments or local authority allot land for various purposes indicated in section 43 of the Act and various items indicated in this section, preferential treatment be given to the disabled be given at concessional rate. The percentage of reservation may be left to she d'serefior of the state governments/local authorities. However, total percentages of disabled persons shall be taken into account while deciding the percentage.

**Where the disability of a person is to such an extent that he/she cannot discharge his/her duties regularly and independently, relief can be moulded in the interest of justice and compensation can be guaranteed so that the persons and his dependents can lead a life with dignity.**

*In Bihari Lai Thaw ait v. State of Chhattisgarh and othrs*[23] the petitioner was suffering from polio in both of his lower limbs. He was able tc move with the support of his hands. Under the order of the district collector, he underwent operation in a private hospital free of cost but the operation was unsuccessful and his condition worsened. The district medical board certified the extent of disability as 75%. The petitioner submitted application to the district collector for providing unemployment. The district collector promised him all assistance for his rehabilitation and passed and order for his employment as assistant teacher but his order was not implemented.

In these circumstances the petitioner approached the National Human Rights Commission with the prayer for compensation of Rs. 15 lacks, a direction for treatment of his heart ailment and management of his disability and also his employment to the job of an Assistant Teacher. The commission observed that the well intentioned action initiated by the collector did not materialize and the petitioner could not get a substantial relief. Neither his disability was cured nor he got the employment. The commission made following recommendations.

i. To grant ex-gratia monetary relief to the true of Rs. One Lac the petitioner.

ii. To offer a job to him commensurate with his academic qualification and physical ability in accordance with the provisions of the disability act of 1995

iii. To arrange for the medical treatment, management and care of the petitioner for the ailments with which he was suffering at state expense.

**These recommendations were to be Complied within Six Weeks**

The grievance of the petitioner before the court was that the recommendations of the commission have not been complied with even after more than 7 years, employment has not been provided to him. Upon considering all the facts including the medical report of the petitioner, the court observed that the petitioner was entitled for employment, as per the recommendation of the commission. However, since both the parties had agreed that no meaningful purpose will be served by providing employment to the petitioner as the disability of the petitioner is of such and extend that he cannot perform his duties regularly and independently, therefore it will be just and proper to mould the relief in the interest of the justice so that the petitioner and his dependant can lead a life with dignity.

Considering the fact that the petitioner was living with his old widow mother who is infirm sick lady, the court opined that ends of justice would be served if a monitory compensation of Rs. 3 lakhs was paid to the petitioner. Accordingly the respondent no. 1 was directed to set aside a some of Rs. 3 lakhs as a monetary compensation to the petitioner and invest the same in one of its equities or deposit for a monthly income of not less than Rs. 2500 for period of 7 years and pay to the petitioner each month fee amount of interest accruing on such deposit. The state was also directed to provide fee petitioner suitable medical treatment as per advice of the specialist free of cost.

## Conclusions

From the above discussion the following rights emerge:

1. Adequate standard of living for persons with disabilities and their families.
2. Access by persons with disabilities, in particular women and girls to social protection programmes and poverty reduction programmes.
3. Access by persons with disabilities and their families living In situations of poverty to assistance from the State wife disability related expenses, including adequate training, counselling, financial assistance and respite care.

In USA the Social Security Administration, a Federal administrative agency, provides monthly cash benefits to people who are unable to work for a year or more because of a disability. Individuals who qualify as disabled under the Social Security" Act may be entitled to either disability insurance benefits or Supplemental Security Income.

All persons with disabilities shall have a right to social security which includes but is not limited to securing adequate standard of living for persons with disabilities and their families in terms of food security, shelter, housing, social care, pension, unemployment allowance, health care, medical support, medical and life insurance;

- Any refusal of insurance on the grounds of disability is unlawful. Any rule in standard form contracts that persons with disabilities constitute higher or unacceptable risk constitutes discrimination and is invalidated; and any practice to that effect stands invalidated;
- In furtherance of right to live independently and in community the appropriate government shall *inter alia*
- frame disability pension, schemes to cover persons with disabilities requiring support in all such schemes, the person with disability shall be the recipient for award of disability pension:
- Frame rules for making provisions for transfer of tension benefits of government employees to theft children with disabilities;

- Provide for special initiatives such as enhanced disability pension for persons with multiple disabilities, persons needing high support, women and elderly persons with disabilities;
- Provide an unemployment allowance to all persons with disabilities proportionate to a uniform applied standard of qualification and skill; irrespective of the tenure of registration with the employment exchanges;
- Provide adequate care-giver allowance to all persons with disabilities meeting high support;
- Pay enhanced post retirement benefits to persons with disabilities;
- For not less than six percent reservation of and housing to persons with disabilities in all government housing schemes and/or urban or rural development programmes with priority to women and elderly persons with disabilities;
- Ensure that not less than six percent of the beneficiaries, in all poverty alleviation and various developmental schemes, shall be persons with disabilities with priority to women and elderly persons with disabilities
- Provide for not less than six percent reservation in allotment of land on concessional rate, where such land shall be used for the purpose of promoting housing, shelter, setting of occupations, businesses, enterprises, self help groups gainful occupations, recreation centers, production centers exclusively for persons with disabilities whether or not such facilities are owned and managed by persons with disabilities;
- To provide incentives to house owners by way of reduction in property for who lease out premises to persons with disability for residential and commercial purposes.

The need for social security for disabled can hardly be overemphasized. However, we need to understand that the family has been the primary producer of welfare even before the birth of a welfare state on the lines of modern welfare approach. Later community, membership institutions, markets, and finally

States provided welfare facilities. Particularly in democratic states, it has been the political necessity to produce and distribute welfare for the vulnerable groups in the society. The magnitude of the woes of the persons with disabilities is vast and its impact on the individual, family and community is severe. The most vulnerable groups among the persons with disabilities include very young children, women and the aged with disabilities. Their existence and livelihood requirements have to be taken care of by some agency in the society-that agency could be the state in the absence of benevolent markets and communities and more so when the families of the persons with disabilities cannot do so. Further it is apart of social justice that a State may assure to its subjects. In the United States the Social Security Administration, United States (SSA) considers one as disabled under Social Security Rules, if on cannot do work that he did before and SSA decides that he cannot adjust to other work because of his medical condition(s). A person's disability must also last or be expected to last for at least one year or to result in death. Social security programme rules assume that working families have access to other resources to provide support during periods of short-term disabilities, including workers' compensation, insurance, savings and investments. The Persons with Disabilities (Equal Opportunities, Protection of Rights and Full Participation) Act, 1995, inter-alia and strives to promote empowerment of persons with disabilities. The right to received support and assistance, although essential to improving the quality of life of people with disabilities.

## Data

NSSO 58th Round, undertaken in 2002, estimates that about 1.85 percent of population suffer from some kind of disability or other. However, detail data are available now for designing a comprehensive social security system for persons with disabilities. In contrast, detailed statistics on the disabled population in Europe is available on the basis of which social security is planned and implemented. Some of the fundamental rights contained in the European Convention on human Rights and its Protocols, and the Revised European Social Charter include the right to education; the right to work; the right to private and family life; the right to protection of health and social security; the right to protection against poverty and social exclusion; the right to adequate housing etc. based on these statistics the European countries are working hard to make their disabled people enjoy the fruit of the policies. Therefore, availability of detailed data on the disabled population in India is a pre-requisite for better planning and implementation of social security schemes. Data on the following aspects as regards the disabled population in the country will be useful in this regard:

- Parents with disabled children below poverty line : This is required to design some additional social assistance schemes.
- Unemployed disabled persons who can be gainfully employed: This is required to design special employment schemes and employment drives and to evolve income generation strategies for the disabled persons and ultimately make them eligible for protective type of Social Security Schemes.
- Non-employable disabled persons who always require support of the Family/Community or the State: This is required to design State assisted/funded schemes as well as to rehabilitate them in the homes for disabled persons.
- Disabled persons above 60 years of Age: This is required to help mitigate the hardships of the disabled senior citizens through Old Age Pension Schemes in the form of Social Assistance and State assisted health care.
- Disabled women : This is required to understand whether the disabled women are dependent on their parents or on their husbands and the poverty status of their family/ parents and to design schemes of Assistance or Insurance Accordingly. This will also help us to understand the requirements of the disabled women in the child bearing age and making provisions for their maternity care.
- Disabled widows: This will help planners to understand the dependency levels of the widows, if they are pensioners, their economic status etc.

- Disabled persons engaged in agriculture and informal sector: This data will enable the Government to design programmes of skill upgradation for the workers in the informal employment and self employment and create backward and forward linkages for their economic activities. It is also possible to specially brand the products produced by the disabled and grant export concessions and subsidies.
- Disabled persons retired from armed forces and capable of being re-employed: This data will enable planners to assess the assistance required for this category of people.

## Required Social Security Programmes for the Disabled Persons in India

Assistance and benefits both in the form of cash and kind will help ameliorate the condition of the disabled persons who have to bear additional economic and social cost due to their disability. Granting benefits for the persons with disabilities is a necessary condition but not a sufficient one for their empowerment and overall development. People with disabilities, like all people, require love and affection that is most often best provided by their families. Specific measures and assistance are therefore essential to help these families overcome the threat of many possible sources of deprivation and provide and caring home as a much better and more natural alternative to life in large institutions/homes for disabled for disabled. If the family itself is poor, it may not be able to extend any kind of support to the disabled members but rather treat him as an extra burden. Before designing the programmes suggested hereunder, this fundamental social understanding should not be overlooked. The cash benefits by way of assistance could be in the form of the following:

- Scholarships to the disabled children
- Old age pension to the aged and widows
- Unemployment assistance to the education disabled
- Cash subsidies for self employed
- Disablement pension

- Retirement pension The benefits in the form of kind could be in the form of:
- Concessions and support in various activities and concessions in transport
- Medical assistance
- Medical insurance where employer liability schemes are possible
- Compensation in the case of work injury resulting in disability
- Maternity care for the disabled mother
- Compulsory provision of crèches in all the work places for the children of disabled mothers
- Reservations and Concessions in services
- Special skill upgradation programmes
- Special schools and Teacher Training centers
- Tax rebates for the disabled persons as well as the parents of the disabled children

## Available Programme for the Disabled

Currently reservations in services, concessions in employment, disability pension under the Employees' provident Funds and Miscellaneous Provisions Act 1952, medical and maternity benefits under Employees' State Insurance Act 1948, benefits under the Workmen's Compensation Act 1923, special schools for the disabled children, disability specific assistance programmes are available in the country, through the coverage is not comprehensive. Ironically three major Social Security Acts listed above are the employer liability and employment related benefit schemes. They are operative only in the case of disability during the course of employment. There are no programmes for old age and survivor benefits in the case of the disabled who cannot be employed or the disabled person who are not employed even after crossing the employable age. There are no programmes for the disabled, dependent and aged widows excepting some very meagre assistance given by some State Governments such as old age pension of Rs. 75 per month. In addition we find that multiplicity of agencies and duplicity of benefits are very common to all the social security programmes available in India, and the plight of the persons with disabilities has no exception to this rule. Annexure II gives the status of pension/unemployment allowances for the persons with disabilities, State/union Territory wise-source: Chief Commissioner Disabilities.

## Programmes/Schemes Required to be Designed for the Disabled Persons

Currently available schemes or programmes do not comprehensively address the problems of the disabled persons. The major Social Security Acts available in India aim only at employment related disability. In fact a large number of the disabled persons are outside employment or in informal economic activities or simply dependent on their parents, children and/or spouses. In some of the Rural Development and other programmes there are some disabled beneficiaries. However, keeping in view the statutory provision of 3% reservation for persons with disabilities and all poverty alleviation schemes, the coverage is negligible. This provision needs to be effectively implemented. In the United States the Social Security and Supplemental Security Income disability programmes are the largest of several Federal Programmes that provide assistance to people with disabilities. While these two programmes are different in many ways. Both are administered by the Social Security Administration and only individuals who have a disability and meet medical criteria may qualify for benefits under either programme. Supplemented Security Income (SSI) is a Federal income supplement programme funded by general tax revenues (not Social Security taxes) it is designed to help aged, blind and disabled people, who have little or no income; and it provides cash to meet basic needs for food, clothing, and shelter. Based on the international best practices and the India specific requirements the urgent need is to formulate the following types of benefits and programmes:

i) Universal old age defined benefit Pension Scheme for the disabled without any means test (As Social Assistance) should be thought of based on national average wage that guarantees poverty alleviation among the persons with disabilities;

ii) Universal medical benefits (possibility of establishing opening separate out patient windows for the disabled should be seen to lessen the hardships of the disabled patients who stand in the general queues in the public hospitals), free treatment to the disabled persons by corporate hospitals could be thought of a precondition for grant of license to the corporate hospitals;

iii) Universal Unemployment Assistance to the disabled persons with means test will definitely alleviate poverty among the persons with disabilities and employable. However, a scheme of discontinuance of the benefit in the event of non-acceptance of employment may be thought of to protect them from falling into unemployment trap;

iv) Trying up with corporate hospitals to extend medical care at a confessional rate to the disabled, where the disabled have a capacity to pay, and subsidizing cost of surgical treatments in the hospitals;

v) Social assistance to the disabled children and scholarship schemes for them if they are school going. Pre-examination training to enable them to sit of competitive examinations along with other candidates;

vi) Special Employment and Skill upgradation programmes

vii) Bank credit at subsidized rate of interest for the self-employment projects taken up by the disabled persons (NHFDC activities needs to be expanded)

viii) Reservations in services ad other concessions provided needs to be effective implemented

ix) Incentives to be given to employers encouraging employment of the disabled persons in consonance the provisions in the PWD Act, 1995.

### Financing of the Schemes

The approach to financing the schemes designed for the disabled persons as also launching of new social security schemes for persons with disabilities should be broadened and the following options including the traditional budget allocations out of the Government funds need to be explored:

- Finance from the general revenues or tax financed as a major source;
- Collection of cess from the industries, employment in which leads to occupational diseases and work hazards;
- Special tax on luxury items and those items consumption of which are injurious to health
- Contribution from employed parents of the disabled to establish a separate fund for Disability welfare;
- Donations from charitable organizations;
- Donations from international donors and agencies;
- Employer share of contribution at enhanced rates for the programmes designed to address contingent poverty;

## Administrative Arrangements

The current Administrative arrangements for delivery of support and benefits to the persons with disabilities are scattered. There is neither a uniform benefit formula nor is there any single agency that administers or guides the programme. It is suggested that multiplicity of agencies or departments currently looking after disability benefits need to be integrated together to have comprehensive programme design and implementation policy under one umbrella wit a Chief Executive officer. However disability specific branches under that agency may be designed to continue the professional approach. As per the Act, one of the jobs of the office of Chief Commissioner for persons with disabilities is to monitor utilization of funds disbursed by Central Government. This needs to be ensured. A National Commission has also been set up recently to aid and advice the Government regarding disability and rehabilitation matters and to recommend action. Date may be collected through census as also NSSO surveys at regular intervals. A national Unique Identification Number on the lines of National Social Security Number may be thought of to avoid duplicity in benefit delivery. The State Governments may start, in right earnest issue of identify cards, preferably, SMART cards with assigning such numbers. All the States may appoint independent State Commissioners, who, as per the Act., may perform their quasi-judicial function in supervising and implementation of various provisions of the

Act., and redressing grievances. Administration arrangements may be made for collection and recording of contributions and donations for developing a fund for social security programmes for disabled. The current system of collection of contributions under protective Social Security schemes need not be disturbed; investment of funds and budgetary allocations made for the purpose need to be enhanced and designing effective income generating schemes may be given attention. Suitable schemes along with administrative arrangements may be made for delivery of benefits including medical benefits, old age pension and benefits in cash or kind. Conclusion The current Social Security programmes are employment related and do not appear to have any special attention to the disabled persons. To be eligible for the benefits one has to become disabled after getting into employment. This approach does not address the disability ab-intio and major problems of non-employment and poverty among the disabled persons. Disabled persons in India are the most vulnerable group. Unfortunately, disabled persons irrespective of their economic status are subjected to social exclusion in the society. Economic, psychological and social confidence building is therefore immediately necessary. Social Security programmes for the disabled, to some extent will relieve the pain of being dependent. Comprehensive administrative arrangement, polling up funds form various sources and delivering the benefit under professional supervision and control are the other immediate requirements. Lack of information and dissemination and absence of a single window approach make persons with disabilities often unaware of what benefits and schemes are available to them. Besides ensuring that available benefits reach them, more resources from local state, national and international agencies, Government and Non-Government Organisations need to be mobilized. For example, resources available under various Departments/Ministries and schemes such as Rural Development, HRD Ministry, Labour Ministry, DRDA Programmes, grant in aid schemes for special schools, pension schemes, UNDP programmes, CARART, NHFDC, and international funding organisations such as NORAD, Action Aid, SIDA, DANIDA and others need to be harnessed.

## Endnotes

1. Constitution of India part 4
2. Convention on the Rights for Persons with Disabilities Art 28, 25 and 26

   See also International covenant on Economic, Social and Cultural Rights, 1966 Art 9
3. Persons with Disabilities (Equal Opportunities Protection of Rights and Full Participation) Act, 1995, Sec 66
4. Ibid Sec 67
5. Ibid Sec 68
6. Ibid Sec 43
7. NHRC annual report 2000-2001
8. JT 2009(11) SC409
9. (2002) 3 SCC 31
10. (1983) 2 SCC 308
11. 1989 Supp (1) SCC 644
12. (1991) 1SCC 731
13. (1991)1 SCC 551
14. (1996) 2 SCC 736
15. (1998)5 SCC 308
16. (1999) 4 SCC 232
17. 1995 Supp(3) SCC 232

    See also Gurnam Singh v. Union of India and ors (2005) 1 PDD (CC) 174, Petitioner enrolled as sepoy discharged form service as he got epileptic fits, held this disability is attributable to military service hence he is entitled to disability pension.

    Bhagwant Singh S/o Nanak Singh v. Union of India, Ministry of Defence, New Delhi 2005) iPDD (CC) 182, Petitioner, a civilian clerk in Army developed diabetes Medical board declared him unfit was granted permanent disability pension - Subsequently, this pension was cancelled as the Board
18. 2008(2)JKJ 240(J&K HC)
19. Manu/DE/0268/2008
20. Manu/DE/8770/2007
21. (2005) 1PDD(CC) 197
22. AIR2009 SC2288
23. 2007 (3) AJHR (NOC)930(CHH); AIR 2007(NOC) 1201 (CHH)

# 7

# The Way Ahead in Lieu of Conclusions

Disability is part of the human condition. Almost everyone will be temporarily or permanently impaired at some point in life, and those who survive to old age will experience increasing difficulties in functioning. Disability is complex and the interventions required to overcome disability disadvantage are multiple, systemic, and will vary depending on context.

The evidence from the studies sources in this work suggests that many of the barriers people with disabilities face are avoidable and the disadvantages associated with disability can be overcome. The following nine recommendations for action are cross-cutting and guided by the more specific recommendations at the end of each chapter. Implementing the recommendations requires involving different sectors – health, education, social protection, labour, transport, and housing – and different actors – governments, civil society organizations (including disabled people's organizations), professionals, the private sector, and people with disabilities and their families. It is essential that law tailors their actions to their specific contexts. Since there is a resource constraint in our country to fight disability , some of the priority actions, particularly those requiring technical assistance and capacity-building, can be included within the framework of law and policy on disability in the new bill. The following few measures are suggested to improve the condition of disabled.

## Enable access to all mainstream policies, systems and services

People with disabilities have ordinary needs – for health and well-being, for economic and social security, to learn and develop skills, and to live in their communities. These needs can and should be met in mainstream programmes and services. Mainstreaming not only fulfils the human rights of persons with disabilities, it is also more effective. Mainstreaming is the process by which government and other stakeholders ensure that persons with disabilities participate equally with others in any activity and service intended for the general public, such as education, health, employment, and social services. Barriers to participation need to be identified and removed, possibly requiring changes to laws, policies, institutions, and environments. Mainstreaming requires a commitment at all levels, and needs to be considered across all sectors and built into new and existing legislation, standards, policies, strategies, and plans. Adopting universal design and implementing reasonable accommodations are two important strategies. Mainstreaming also requires effective planning, adequate human resources, and sufficient financial investment – accompanied by specific measures such as targeted programmes and services.

### Invest in specific programmes and services for people with disabilities

In addition to mainstream services, some people with disabilities may require access to specific measures, such as rehabilitation, support services, or training. Rehabilitation – including assistive technologies such as wheelchairs, hearing aids, and white canes – improves functioning and independence. A range of well-regulated assistance and support services in the community can meet needs for care, enabling people to live independently and to participate in the economic, social, and cultural lives of their communities. Vocational rehabilitation and training can open labour market opportunities. While there is a need for more services, there is also a need for better, more accessible, flexible, integrated, and well-coordinated multidisciplinary services, particularly at times of transition such as between child and adult services. Existing programmes and services need to be reviewed to assess their performance and make changes to improve their coverage, effectiveness, and efficiency. The changes should be based on sound evidence, appropriate in terms of culture and other local contexts, and tested locally

### Adopt a national disability strategy and plan of action

While disability should be a part of all development strategies and action plans, it is also recommended that a national disability strategy and plan of action be adopted. A national disability strategy sets out a consolidated and comprehensive long-term vision for improving the well-being of persons with disabilities and should cover both mainstream policy and programme areas and specific services for persons with disabilities. The development, implementation, and monitoring of a national strategy should bring together a broad range of stakeholders including relevant government ministries, nongovernmental organizations, professional groups, disabled people and their representative organizations, the general public, and the private sector. The strategy and action plan should be informed by a situation analysis, taking into account such factors as the prevalence of disability, needs for services, social and economic status, effectiveness and gaps in current services, and environmental and social barriers. The strategy should establish priorities and have measurable outcomes. The plan of action operationalizes the strategy in short and medium terms by laying out concrete actions and timelines for implementation, defining targets, assigning responsible agencies, and planning and allocating needed resources. Mechanisms are needed to make it clear where the responsibility lies for coordination, decision-making, regular monitoring and reporting, and control of resources.

### Involve People with Disabilities

People with disabilities often have unique insights about their disability and their situation. In formulating and implementing policies, laws, and services, people with disabilities should be consulted and actively involved. Disabled people's organizations may need capacity-building and support to empower people with disabilities and advocate for their needs. When suitably developed and funded, they can also play a role in service delivery – for example, in information provision, peer support, and independent living .At an individual level, persons with disabilities are entitled to control over their lives and therefore need to be consulted on issues that concern them directly – whether in health, education, rehabilitation, or community living.

Supported decision-making may be necessary to enable some individuals to communicate their needs and choices.

## Improve Human Resource Capacity

The attitudes and knowledge of people working in, for example, education, health care, rehabilitation, social protection, labour, law enforcement, and the media are particularly important for ensuring non-discrimination and participation. Human resource capacity can be improved through effective education, training, and recruitment. A review of the knowledge and competencies of staff in relevant areas can provide a starting point for developing appropriate measures to improve them. Relevant training on disability, which incorporates human rights principles, should be integrated into current curricula and accreditation programmes. In-service training should be provided to current practitioners providing and managing services. For example, strengthening the capacity of primary health care workers, and ensuring availability of specialist staff where required, contribute to effective and affordable health care for people with disabilities. Many countries have too few staff working in fields such as rehabilitation and special education. Developing standards in training for different types and levels of rehabilitation personnel can assist in addressing resource gaps. There are also shortages of care workers and sign language interpreters. Measures to improve staff retention may be relevant in some settings and sectors.

## Provide Adequate Funding and Improve Affordability

Existing public services for people with disabilities are often inadequately funded, affecting the availability and quality of such services. Adequate and sustainable funding of publicly provided services is needed to ensure that they reach all targeted beneficiaries and that good quality services are provided. Contracting out service provision, fostering public-private partnerships, notably with not-for profit organizations, and devolving budgets to persons with disabilities for consumer-directed care can contribute to better service provision. During the development of the national disability strategy and related action plans, the affordability and sustainability of the proposed measures should be considered and adequately funded through relevant budgets. Programme costs and outcomes should be monitored and evaluated, so that more cost-effective solutions are developed and implemented. Often people with disabilities and their families have excessive out-of-pocket expenses. To improve the affordability of goods and services for people with disabilities and to offset the extra costs associated with disability, particularly for poor and vulnerable persons with disabilities, consideration should be given to expanding health and social insurance coverage, ensuring that people with disabilities have equal access to public social services, ensuring that poor and vulnerable people with disabilities benefit from poverty-targeted safety net programmes, and introducing fee-waivers, reduced transport fares, and reduced import taxes and duties on assistive technologies.

### Increase Public Awareness and Understanding of Disability

Mutual respect and understanding contribute to an inclusive society. Therefore it is vital to improve public understanding of disability, confront negative perceptions, and represent disability fairly. For example, education authorities should ensure that schools are inclusive and have an ethos of valuing diversity. Employers should be encouraged to accept their responsibilities towards staff with disabilities. Collecting information on knowledge, beliefs and attitudes about disability can help identify gaps in public understanding that can be bridged through education and public information. Governments, voluntary organizations, and professional associations should consider running social marketing campaigns that change attitudes on stigmatized issues such as HIV, mental illness, and leprosy. Involving the media is vital to the success of these campaigns and to ensuring the dissemination of positive stories about persons with disabilities and their families.

### Improve Disability Data Collection

Methodologies for collecting data on people with disabilities need to be developed, tested cross-culturally, and applied consistently. Data need to be standardized and internationally comparable for benchmarking and monitoring progress on disability policies and for the implementation of the laws uniformly. Nationally, disability should be included in data collection. Uniform definitions of disability, based on the ICF, can allow for internationally comparable data. Understanding the numbers of people with disabilities and their circumstances can improve country efforts to remove disabling barriers and provide appropriate services for people with disabilities. As a first step, national population census data can be collected in line with recommendations from the United Nations Washington Group on Disability and the United Nations Statistical Commission. A cost-effective and efficient approach is to include disability questions – or a disability module – in existing sample surveys such as a national household survey, national health survey, general social survey, or labour force survey. Data need to be disaggregated by population features, such as age, sex, race, and socioeconomic status, to uncover patterns, trends, and information about subgroups of persons with disabilities. Dedicated disability surveys can also gain more comprehensive information on disability characteristics, such as prevalence, health conditions associated with disability, and use of and need for services including rehabilitation. Administrative data collection can be a useful source of information on users and on types, amounts, and cost of services, if standard disability identifiers are included.

## Strengthen and Support Research on Disability

Research is essential for increasing public understanding about disability issues, informing disability policy and programmes, and efficiently allocating resources. This work recommends several areas for research on disability including:

- the impact of environmental factors (policies, physical environment, attitudes) on disability and how to measure it;
- the quality of life and well-being of people with disabilities;
- barriers to mainstream and specific services, and what works in overcoming them in different contexts;
- accessibility and universal design programmes appropriate for low-income settings;
- the interactions among environmental factors, health conditions, and disability – and between disability and poverty;

- the cost of disability and the cost–effectiveness of public spending on disability programmes.

Research requires focused investments in human and technical capacity, particularly in low-income and middle-income countries. A critical mass of trained researchers on disability needs to be built. Research skills should be strengthened in a range of disciplines, including epidemiology, disability studies, health and rehabilitation, special education, economics, sociology, and public policy. International learning and research opportunities, linking universities in developing countries with those in high-income and middle-income countries, can also be useful.

# List of Cases

- Union of India v. Devender Kumar Pant
- Chameli Singh v. State of U.P
- Indra Sawheny & Ors. v. Union of India & Ors
- Shri Umesh Kumar v. The Secretary Department of Elementary Education & Literacy, Department of Ministry of Human Resource Development, New Delhi
- Shri Kishan Lai v. Kathak Kendra
- Parvathi Ramakrishnan v. The Chief Secretary, Govt, of NCT of Delhi and Ors
- Mahesh Sharma v. Commissioner Municipal Corporation of Delhi
- Ashwani Agarwal v. Secretary, Department of Education
- Mohammed Asif Iqbal v. Indian Institute of Management, Calcutta and Ors
- Dhawal s. Chotai vs. Union of India and Others
- Anju Talukdar & Anr. V. State of Assam & Ors
- Surinder Kumar v. Punjabi University
- Umesh Kumar v. State of Haryana and Others
- Vimesh Jain v. Union of India and othrs
- Pardeep Jain v. Union of India
- Renu Gupta v. University Grants Commission
- Ms Pallavi Kadam v. Dy, Director National Association for the Blind, Mumbai
- Dharmender Parshad v. Delhi Subordinate Services Selection board
- Sunita Dogra v. Secretary, Department of Personnel and Training.
- Anka Toppo v. AIIMS
- Vikas Gupta v. Indian Institute of Management and Ors
- Sanjay Kumar Shah v. Mahatma Gandhi Kashi Vidyapeeth
- Indira Sawhhney v. Union of India
- Government of India & Anr v. Ravi Prakash Gupta &Anr
- Amita v. Union of India
- Sambhavana v. Delhi University
- Akhila Karnataka Andha Shikshakarungala Kshemabhibriddhi Sangha v. Election Authority

- Ravi Kumar Arora Vs. Union of India and Another
- National Federation of the Blind v. Union of India
- Km. Archana Pandey VS. Respondent State of UP and Ors
- National Federation of Blind Vs. Union Public Service Commission and Ors
- Parminder Pal Singh Vs. Union of India and Anr
- Nand Kumar Narayanrao Ghodmare v. State of Maharashtra and Others
- Krishna Kumar V. Secretary Govt of NCT of Delhi and others
- All India Confederation of the Blind Vs. Govt, of NCT of Delhi and Ors
- Rosily v. Registration Inspector General
  Ranjit Kumar Rajak v. State Bank of India
- Shri Ram Bahadur Rai v. Employee Provident Fund Organisation
- Chandra Kishore Joshi v. Secretary, Union Public Service Commission and And ors
- Sumit Kaur v. Department of Personnel and Training
- Ms. Jasreen Singh v. Bharat Petroleum Corporation Ltd. Mumbai
- Shri Ashwini Kumar Gupta, Ms. Shweta Kaur Chhatwal v. State Bank of India, Mumbai, State Bank of India, Lucknow, State Bank of India, New Delhi, and Ministry of Finance, New and others
- Ms. Meenakshi Singh v. IDBI Bank Ltd
- The Chief Commissioner, Disabilities v. Medical Superintendent-cum-joint Director Health Services General Hospital Chandigarh 2000
- General Secretary, National Federation of the Blind v. Secretary to the Government of Maharashtra
- R.B. Singh v. Ordnance Factory Board
- Sonika v. LIC Housing Finance Limited
- Laxmikant Vijayvargiya v. Bharat Heavy Electrical Limited and ors
- Ved Prakash v. Kendriya Vidyalaya Sangathan
- Dheeraj Kumar v. Director, Intelligence Bureau
- Municipal Corporation of Greater Mumbai v. Srirang Anandrao Jadhav
- Belliyappa Gowda v. Karnataka state Road Transport Corporation, Bangalore & Anr
- Kunal Singh V. Union of India and ors
- Jaikumar Jagannath Kulkarni v. State of Maharashtra & orsr
- Maharashtra Road Transport Corporation & Anr. V. Deepak Shrikrishna Pandit
- Delhi Transport Corporation v. Harpal Singh, Ex. Security Guard
- Rupender Singh vs. State of Haryana and Ors
- Kunal Singh v. Union of India
- O.P. Sharma v. Delhi Transport Corporation and othrs
- Bhagwan Dass & Anr. V. Punjab State Electricity Board
- Dilbag Singh v. DTC

- Union of India Vs. Devender Kumar Pant
- P. Rathinavelu v. Steel Authority of India Limited
- Nandkumar J. Dalvi v. Employees State Insurance Corporation
- Bedanga Talukdar v. Saifudaullah Khan and Ors
- B. Meenakshi v. State of Tamil Nadu
- Javed Abidi v. Union of India and Ors
- Disabled Rights Group vs. Chief Election Commissioner
- P. Sudhakara Reddy v. Railway Board and ors
- Dinesk Gupta vs. Ministry of Transport & Ors
- Saira Parveen and Anr. V. head Master, Jawahar Lal Pratmicvidalaya.
- Suchita Srivastava v. Chandigarh Administration
- Dr. Upendra Baxi vs. State of Uttar Pradesh & Anr
- Rakesh Chandra Narayan vs. State of Bihar
- Anand Bihari & Ors. vs. Rajasthan State Road Transport Corporation & Anr
- R.D. Haitangadi vs. M/s. Pest Control (India) Pvt. Ltd
- K. Nandakumar vs. Thanthal Periyar Transport Corporation
- Swatantra Kumar vs. Qamar AH & Ors
- Ashwani Kumar Mishra vs. P. Muniam Babu & Ors
- Lance Dafadar Joginder Singh V. Union of India and Others
- Abdul Majid Shah v. Union of India
- J. B. Kumar vs. Secretary Labour and Anr
- Anubha Bhargava vs. Union of India and Ors
- Dilip Baruah V. State of Assam and Ors
- Prajwala v. Union of India & Ors
- Bihari Lai Thaw ait v. State of Chhattisgarh and othrs
- Gurnam Singh v. Union of India and ors
- Bhagwant Singh S/o Nanak Singh v. Union of India, Ministry of Defence, New Delhi

# Annexure—I

**PWD ACT, 1995 THE PERSONS WITH DISABILITIES**

(Equal Opportunities, Protection of Rights and Full Participation) Act, 1995

**PUBLISHED IN PART II, SECTION 1 OF THE EXTRAORDINARY GAZETTE OF INDIA**

**MINISTRY OF LAW, JUSTICE AND COMPANY AFFAIRS**

**(Legislative Department)**

New Delhi, the 1 st January, 1996/Pausa 11, 1917 (Saka)

The following Act of Parliament received the assent of the President on the 1st January, 1996, and is hereby published for general information:- No.1 OF 1996

[1st January 1996]

An Act to give effect to the Proclamation on the Full Participation and Equality of the People with Disabilities in the Asian and Pacific Region.

WHEREAS the Meeting to Launch the Asian and Pacific Decade of Disabled Persons 1993-2002 convened by the Economic and Social Commission for Asia and Pacific held at Beijing on 1st to 5 th December,1992, adopted the Proclamation on the Full Participation and Equality of People with Disabilities in the Asian and Pacific Region;

AND WHEREAS India is a signatory to the said Proclamation; AND WHEREAS it is considered necessary to implement the Proclamation aforesaid.

Be it enacted by Parliament in the Forty-sixth Year of the Republic of India as follows:-

Chapter XIII Social Security
Chapter XIV Miscellaneous

## CHAPTER I : PRELIMINARY

**1.** (1) This Act may be called the Persons With Disabilities (Equal Opportunities, Protection of Rights and Full Participation) Act, 1995.

(2) It extends to the whole of India except the State of Jammu and Kashmir.

(3) It shall come into force on such date as the Central Government may. by notification, appoint.

2. In this Act, unless the context otherwise requires,-

(a) "Appropriate Government" means,-

(i) In relation to the Central Government or any establishment wholly or substantially financed by that Government, or a Cantonment Board constituted under the Cantonment Act, 1924, the Central Government;

(ii) In relation to a State Government or any establishmet wholly or substantially financed by that Government, or any local authority., other than a Cantonment Board, the State Government;

(iii) In respect of the Central Co-ordination Committee and the Central Executive Committee, the Central Government;

(iv) In respect of the State Co-ordination Committee and the State Executive Committee, the State Government;

(b) "Blindness" refers to a condition where a person suffers from any of the following conditions, namely:-

(i) Total absence of sight. or

(ii) Visual acuity not exceeding 6160 or 201200 (snellen) in the better eye with correcting lenses; or

(iii) Limitation of the field of vision subtending an angle of 20 degree or worse;

(c) "Central Co-ordination Committee" means the Central Co-ordination Committee constituted under sub-section (1) of section 3;

(d) "Central Executive Committee" means the Central Executive Committee constituted under sub-section (1) of section 9;

(e) "Cerebral palsy" means a group of non-progressive conditions of a person characterized by abnormal motor control posture resulting from brain insult or injuries occurring in the pre-natal, peri-natal or infant period of development;

(f) "Chief Commissioner" means the Chief Commissioner appointed under subsection (1) of section 57;

(g) "Commissioner" means the Commissioner appointed under sub-section (1) of section 60;

(h) "Competent authority" means the authority appointed under section 50;

(i) "Disability" means- (I) Blindness;

(ii) Low vision;

(iii) Leprosy-cured;

(iv) Hearing impairment;

(v) Loco motor disability;

(vi) Mental retardation;

(vii) Mental illness;

(j) "Employer" means,-

(i) In relation to a Government, the authority notified by the Head of the Department in this behalf or where no such authority is notified, the Head of the Department; and

(ii) In relation to an establishment, the chief executive officer of that the establishment;

(k) "Establishment" means a corporation established by or under a Central, Provincial or State Act, or an authority or a body owned or controlled or aided by the Government or a local authority or a Government company as defined in section 617 of 'the Companies Act, 1956 and includes Departments of a Government;

(l) "Hearing impairment" means loss of sixty decibels or more in the better year in the conversational range of[1] frequencies;

(m) "Institution for persons with disabilities" means an institution for the reception. Care, protection, education, training, rehabilitation or any other service of persons with disabilities;

(n) "Leprosy cured person" means any person who has been cured of leprosy but is suffering from-

(i) Loss of sensation in hands or feet as well as loss of sensation and paresis in the eye and eye-lid but with no manifest deformity;

(ii) Manifest deformity and paresis; but having sufficient mobility in their hands and feet to enable them to engage in normal economic activity;

(iii) Extreme physical deformity as well as advanced age which prevents him from undertaking any gainful occupation, and the expression "leprosy cured" shall be construed accordingly;

(o) "Loco motor disability" means disability of the bones, joints muscles leading to substantial restriction of the movement of the limbs or any form of cerebral palsy,

(p) "Medical authority" means any hospital or institution specified for the purposes of this Act by notification by the appropriate Government;

(q) "Mental illness" means any mental disorder other than mental retardation;

(r) "Mental retardation" means a condition of arrested or incomplete development of mind of a person which is specially characterized by sub normality of intelligence;

(s) "Notification" means a notification published in the, Official Gazette;

(t) "Person with disability" means a person suffering from not less than forty per cent. of any disability as certified by a medical authority;

(u) "Person with low vision" means a person with impairment of visual functioning even after treatment or standard refractive correction but who uses or is potentially capable of using vision for the planning or execution of a task with appropriate assistive device;

(v) "Prescribed" means prescribed by rules made under this Act;

(w) "Rehabilitation" refers to a process aimed at enabling persons with disabilities to reach and maintain their optimal physical, sensory, intellectual, psychiatric or social functional levels;

(x) "Special Employment Exchange" means any office or place established and maintained by the Government for the collection and furnishing of information, either by keeping of registers or otherwise, respecting-

(i) Persons who seek to engage employees from amongst the persons suffering from disabilities;

(ii) Persons with disability who seek employment;

(iii) Vacancies to which person with disability seeking employment may be appointed;

(y) "State Co-ordination Committee" means the State Co-ordination Committee constituted under sub-section (1) of section 19;

(z) "State Executive Committee" means the State Executive Committee constituted under sub-section (1) of section 19

## CHAPTER II: THE COORDINATION COMMITTEE

**3. (1)** The Central Government shall by notification constitute a body to be known as the Central Co-ordination Committee to exercise the powers conferred on, and to perform the functions assigned to it, under this Act.

**(2)** The Central Co-ordination Committee shall consist of-

(a) The Minister in charge of the Department of Welfare in the Central Government, Chairperson, ex officio;

(b) The Minister of State in-charge of the Department of Welfare in the Central Government, Vice- Chairperson, ex officio;

(c) Secretaries to the Government of India in-charge of the Departments of Welfare, Education, Woman and Child Development, Expenditure, Personnel, Training and Public Grievances, Health, Rural Development, Industrial Development, Urban Affairs and Employment, Science and Technology. Legal Affairs, Public Enterprises, Members, ex officio;

(d) Chief Commissioner, Member, ex officio;

(e) Chairman Railway Board, Member, ex officio;

(f) Director-General of Lab our, Employment and Training, Member, ex officio;

(g) Director, National Council for Educational Research and Training, Member, ex officio;

(h) Three Members of Parliament. of whom two shall be elected by the House of the People and one by the Council of States, Members;

(i) Three persons to be nominated by the Central Government to represent the interests, which in the opinion of that Government ought to be represented, Members;

(j) Directors of the-

(i) National Institute for the Visually Handicapped, Dehradun;

(ii) National Institute for the Mentally Handicapped, Secundrabad;

(iii) National Institute for the Orthopaedically Handicapped, Calcutta;

(iv) Ali Yavar Jung National Institute for the Hearing Handicapped, Bombay, Members, ex officio;

(k) Four Members to be nominated by the Central Government by rotation to represent the States and the Union territories in such manner as may be prescribed by the Central Government:

Provided that no appointment under this clause shall be made except on the recommendation of the State Government or, as the case may be, the Union territory;

(1) Five persons as far as practicable, being persons with disabilities. to represent non-governmental Organizations or associations which are concerned with disabilities, to he nominated by the Central Government, one from each area of disability, Members:

Provided that while nominating persons under this clause, the Central Government shall nominate at least one woman and one person belonging to Scheduled Castes or Scheduled Tribes;

(m) Joint Secretary to the Government of India in the Ministry of Welfare dealing with the welfare of the handicapped, Member-Secretary, ex officio.

(3) The office of the Member of the Central Co-ordination Committee shall not disqualify its holder for being chosen as or for being a Member of either House of Parliament.

4. (1) Save as otherwise provided by or under this Act a Member of Central Co-ordination Committee nominated under clause (i) or clause (l) of sub-section (2) of section 3 shall hold office for a term of three years from the date of his nomination:

Provided that such a Member shall, notwithstanding the expiration of his term, continue to hold office until his successor enters upon his office.

(2) The term of office of an ex officio Member shall come to an end as soon as he ceases to hold the office by virtue of which he was so nominated.

(3) The Central Government may if it thinks fit remove any Member nominated under clause (i) or clause (1) of subsection (2) of section 3, before the expiry of his term of office after giving him a reasonable opportunity of showing cause against the same.

(4) A Member nominated under clause (i) or clause (1) of subsection (2) of section 3 may at any time resign his office by writing under his hand addressed to the Central Government and the seat of the said Member shall thereupon become vacant.

(5) A casual vacancy in the Central Co-ordination Committee shall be filled by a fresh nomination and the person nominated to fill the vacancy shall hold office only for the remainder of the term for which the Member in whose place he was so Dominated.

(6) A Member nominated under clause (i) or clause (l) of subsection (2) of section 3 shall be eligible for (7) Members nominated under clause (i) and

clause (1) of sub-section (2) of section 3 shall receive such allowances as may, be prescribed by the Central Government.

**(1)** No person shall be a Member of the Central Coordination Committee, who-

(a) Is, or at any time has been, adjudged insolvent or has suspended payment of his debts or has compounded with his creditors, or

(b) Is of unsound mind and stands so declared by a competent court, or

(c) Is or has been convicted of an offence which, in the opinion of the Central Government, involves moral turpitude, or

(d) Is or at any time has been convicted of an offence under this Act. or

(e) Has so abused in the opinion of the Central Government his position as a Member as to render his continuance in the Central Coordination Committee detrimental to the interests of the general public.

**(2)** No order of removal shall be made by the Central Government under this section unless the Member concerned has been given a reasonable opportunity of showing cause against the same.

**(3)** Notwithstanding anything contained in sub-section (1) or sub-section (6) of section 4, a Member who has been removed under this section shall not be eligible for renomination as a Member.

**6.** If a Member of the Central Coordination Committee becomes subject to any of the disqualifications specified in section 5, his scat shall become vacant.

**7.** Lie Central Coordination Committee shall meet at least once in every six months and shall observe such rules of procedure in regard to the transaction of business at its meetings as may be prescribed by the Central Government.

**8. (1)** Subject to the provisions of this Act, the function of the Central Coordination Committee shall be to serve as the national focal point on disability matters and facilitate the continuous evolution of a comprehensive policy towards solving the problems faced by persons with disabilities.

**(2)** In particular and without prejudice to the generality of the foregoing, the Central Coordination Committee may perform all or any, of the following functions, namely:-

(a) Review and coordinate the activities of all the Departments of Government and other Governmental and non-Govemmental Organizations which are dealing with matters relating to persons with disabilities;

(b) Develop a national policy to address issues faced by, persons with disabilities;

(c) Advise the Central Government on the formulation oil policies, programmes, legislation and projects with respect to disability,

(d) Take up the cause of persons with disabilities with the concerned authorities and the international organizations with a view, to provide for schemes and projects for the disabled in the national plans and other programmes and policies evolved by the international agencies;

(e) Review in consultation with the donor agencies their funding policies from the perspective of their impact on persons with disabilities;

(f) Take such other steps to ensure barrier free environment in public places, work places, public utilities, schools and other institutions;

(g) Monitor and evaluate the impact of policies and programmes designed for achieving equality and full participation of persons with disabilities;

(h) To perform such other functions as may be prescribed by the Central Government.

**9. (1)** The Central Government shall constitute a Committee to be known as the Central Executive Committee to perform the functions assigned to it under this Act.

**(2)** The Central Executive Committee shall consist of-

(a) The Secretary to the Government of India in the Ministry of Welfare, Chairperson, ex officio;

(b) The Chief Commissioner, Member, ex officio;

(c) The Director-General for Health Services, Member, ex officio;

(d) The Director-General, Employment and Training, Member, ex officio;

(e) Six persons not below the rank of a Joint Secretary to the Government of India, to represent the Ministries or Departments of Rural Development, Education. Welfare, Personnel Public Grievances and Pension and Urban Affairs and Employment, Science and Technology, Members, ex officio;

(f) The Financial Advisor, Ministry of Welfare in the Central Government, Member, ex officio;

(g) Advisor (Tariff) Railway Board, Member, ex officio;

(h) Four members to be nominated by the Central Government, by rotation, to represent the State Governments and the Union territories in such manner as may be prescribed by the Central Government;

(i) One person to be nominated by the Central Government to represent the interest, which in the opinion of the Central Government ought to be represented, Member;

(j) Five persons, as far as practicable, being persons with disabilities, to represent non-governmental organizations or associations which are concerned with disabilities, to he nominated by the Central Government, one from each area of disability, Members:

Provided that while nominating persons under this clause, the Central Government shall nominate at least one woman and one person belonging to Scheduled Castes or Scheduled Tribes;

(k) Joint Secretary to the Government of India in the Ministry of Welfare dealing with the welfare of the handicapped, Member-Secretary, ex officio.

**(3)** Members nominated under clause (i) and clause (j) of sub-section (2) shall receive such allowances as may be prescribed by the Central Government.

**(4)** A Member nominated under clause (i) or clause (i) of sub-section (2) may at any time resign his office by writing under his hand addressed to the Central Government and the scat of the said Member shall thereupon become vacant.

**10.** **(1)** The Central Executive Committee shall be the executive body of the Central Coordination Committee and shall be responsible for carrying out the decisions of the Central Coordination Committee.

**(2)** Without prejudice to the provisions of sub-section (1), the Central Executive Committee shall also perform such other functions as may be delegated to it by the Central Coordination Committee.

**11.** The Central Executive Committee shall meet at least once in three months and shall observe such rules of procedure in regard to the transaction of business at its meetings as may be prescribed by the Central Government.

**12.** **(1)** The Central Executive Committee may associate with itself in such manner and for such purposes as may be prescribed by the Central Government any person whose assistance or advice it may desire to obtain in performing any of its functions under this Act.

**(2)** A person associated with the Central Executive Committee under sub-section (1) for any purpose shall have the right to take part in the discussions of the Central Executive Committee relevant to that purpose, but shall not have a right to vote at a meeting of the said Committee, and shall not be a member for any other purpose.

**(3)** A person associated with the said Committee under sub-section (1) for any purpose shall be paid such fees and allowances, for attending its meetings and for attending to any other work of the said Committee, as may be prescribed by the Central Government.

## CHAPTER III: THE STATE COORDINATION COMMITTEE

**13.** **(1)** Every State Government shall, by notification, constitute a body to be known as the State Coordination Committee to exercise the powers conferred on, and to perform the function assigned to it, under this Act.

**(2)** the State Coordination Committee shall consist of-

(a) The Minister in-charge of the Department of Social Welfare in the State Government, Chairperson, ex officio;

(b) the Minister of State in-charge of the Department of Social Welfare, if any, Vice-Chairperson, ex officio;

(c) Secretaries to the State Government in-charge of the Departments of Welfare, Education, Woman and Child Development, Expenditure, Personnel Training and Public Grievances, Health, Rural Development, Industrial Development, Urban Affairs and Employment, Science and Technology. Public Enterprises, by whatever name called, Members, ex officio;

(d) Secretary of any other Department, which the State Government considers necessary, Member, ex officio;

(e) Chairman Bureau of Public Enterprises (by whatever name called) Member, ex officio;

(f) Five persons, as far as practicable, being persons with disabilities, to represent non-governmental organizations or associations which are concerned with disabilities, to be nominated by the State Government, one from each area of disability, Members:

Provided that while nominating persons under this clause, the State Government shall nominate at least one woman and one person belonging to Scheduled Castes or Scheduled Tribes;

(g) Three Members of State Legislature, of whom two shall be elected by the Legislative Assembly and one by the Legislative Council, if any;

(h) Three persons to be nominated by that State Government to represent agriculture, industry or trade or any other interest, which in the opinion of State Government ought to be represented, Members, ex officio;

(i) The Commissioner, Member, ex officio;

(j) Secretary to the State Government dealing with the welfare of the handicapped, Member-Secretary, ex officio.

(3) Notwithstanding anything contained in this section, no State Coordination Committee shall be constituted for a Union territory and in relation to a Union territory; the Central Coordination Committee shall exercise the functions and perform the functions of a State Coordination Committee for the Union territory:

Provided that in relation to a Union territory. The Central Coordination Committee may delegate all or any of its powers and functions under this sub-section to such person or body of persons as the Central Government may specify.

**14. (1)** Save as otherwise provided by or under this Act, a Member of a State Coordination Committee nominated under clause (f) or clause (h) of subsection (2) of section 13 shall hold office for a term of three years from the date of his nomination:

Provided that such a Member shall, notwithstanding the expiration of his term, continue to hold office until his successor enters upon his office.

(2) The term of office of an ex officio Member shall come to an end as soon as he ceases to hold the office by virtue of which he was so nominated.

(3) The State Government may, if it thinks fit, remove any7 Member nominated under clause (f) or clause (h) of sub-section (2) of section 13, before the expiry of his term of office after giving him a reasonable opportunity of showing cause against the same.

(4) A Member nominated under clause (f) or clause (h) of sub-section (2) of section 13 may. At any time, resign his office by writing under his hand addressed to the State Government and the seat of the said Member shall thereupon become vacant.

(5) A casual vacancy in the State Coordination Committee shall be filled by a fresh nomination and the person nominated to fill the vacancy shall hold office only for the remainder of the term for which the Member in whose place he was so nominated.

(6) A Member nominated under clause (f) and clause (h) of sub-section (2) of section 13 shall be eligible for renomination.

(7) Members nominated under clause (f) and clause (h) of sub-section (2) of section13 shall receive such allowances as may he prescribed by the State Government.

**15. (1)** No pet-son shall he a Member of the State Coordination Committee, who—

(a) Is, or at any time, has been adjudged insolvent or has suspended payment of his debts or has compounded with his creditors, or

(b) Is of unsound mind and stands so declared by a competent court, or

(c) Is or has been convicted of an offence which in the opinion of the State Government involves moral turpitude, or

(d) Is or at any time has been convicted of an offence under this Act or

(e) Has so abused, in the opinion of the State Government, his position as a member as to render his continuance in the State Coordination Committee detrimental to the interests of the general public.

**(2)** No order of removal shall be made by the State Government under this section unless the Member concerned has been given a reasonable opportunity of showing cause against the same.

**(3)** Notwithstanding anything contained in sub-section (1) or sub-section (6) of section 14, a Member who has been removed under this section shall net be eligible for renomination as a Member.

**16.** If a Member of the State Coordination Committee becomes subject to any of the disqualifications specified in section 15, his seat shall become vacant.

**17.** The State Coordination Committee shall meet at least once in every six months and shall observe such rules of procedure in regard to the transaction of business at its meetings as may be prescribed.

**18. (1)** Subject to the provisions of this Act, the function of the State Coordination Committee shall be to serve as the state focal point on disability matters and facilitate the continuous evolution of a comprehensive policy towards solving the problems faced by persons with disabilities.

**(2)** In particular and without prejudice to the generality of the foregoing function the State Coordination Committee may, within the State perform all or any of the following functions, namely.-

(a) Review and coordinate the activities of all the Departments of Government and other Governmental and non-Govemmental Organizations which are dealing with matters relating to persons with disabilities.,

(b) Develop a State policy to address issues faced by persons with disabilities;

(c) Advise the State Government on the formulation of policies. Programmes, legislation and projects with respect to disability;

(d) Review, in consultation with the donor agencies, their funding from the perspective of their impact on persons with disabilities;

(e) Take such other steps to ensure barrier free environment in pupil's places. Work places, public utilities, schools and other institutions;

(f) Monitor and evaluate the impact of policies and programmes designed for achieving equality and full participation of persons with disabilities;

(g) To perform such other functions as may be prescribed by the State Government

**19. (1)** The State Government shall constitute a committee to be known as the State Executive Committee to perform the functions assigned to it under this Act.

(2) The State Executive Committee shall consist of-

(a) The Secretary, Department of Social Welfare, Chairperson, ex officio;

(b) The Commissioner, Member, ex officio;

(c) Nine persons not below the rank of a Joint Secretary to the State Government, to represent the Departments of Health, Finance, Rural Development, Education, Welfare, Personnel Public Grievances, Urban Affairs Labor and Employment, Science and Technology, Members, ex officio;

(d) One person to be nominated by the State Government to represent the interest, which in the opinion of the State Government ought to be represented. Member;

(e) Five persons, as far as practicable being persons with disabilities. to represent non-governmental organizations or associations which arc concerned with disabilities, to be nominated by the State Government, one from each area of disability, Members:

Provided that while nominating persons under this clause, the State Government shall nominate at least one woman and one person belonging to Scheduled Castes or Scheduled Tribes;

(f) Joint Secretary dealing with the disability division in the Department of Welfare, Member- Secretary, ex officio.

(3) Members nominated under clause (d) and clause (e) of sub-section (2) shall receive such allowances as may be prescribed by the State Government.

(4) A Member nominated under clause (d) or clause (e) may at any time resign his office by writing under his hand addressed to the State Government and the scat of the said Member shall thereupon become vacant.

**20. (1)** The State Executive Committee shall be the executive body of the State Coordination Committee and shall be responsible for carrying out the decisions of the State Coordination Committee.

(2) Without prejudice to the provisions of sub-section (1), the State Executive Committee shall also perform such other functions as may be delegated to it by the State Coordination Committee.

**21.** The State Executive Committee shall meet at least once in three months and shall observe such rules of procedure in regard to the transaction of business at its meetings as may be prescribed by, the State Government.

**22. (1)** The State Executive Committee may associate with itself in such manner and for such purposes as may he prescribed by the State Government any person whose assistance or advice it may desire to obtain in performing any of its functions under this Act.

(2) A person associated with the State Executive Committee under sub-section (1) for any purpose shall have the right to take part in the discussions of the State Executive Committee relevant to that purpose, but shall not

have a right to vote at a meeting of the said Committee, and shall not he a member for any other purpose.

**(3)** A person associated wills the said Committee under sub-section (1) for any purpose shall be paid such fees and allowances, for attending its meetings and for attending to any other work of the said Committee, as may be prescribed by the State Government.

**23.** In the performance of its functions under this Act,-

(a) The Central Coordination Committee shall be bound by such directions in writing, as the Central Government may give to it; and

(b) The State Coordination Committee shall be bound by such directions in writing, as the Central Coordination Committee or the State, Government may give to it:

Provided that where a direction given by the State Government is inconsistent with any direction given by the Central Coordination Committee, the matter shall be referred to the Central Government for its decision.

**24.** No act or proceeding of the Central Coordination Committee, the Central Executive Committee, a State Coordination Committee or a State Executive Committee shall be called in question on the ground merely on the existence of any vacancy in or any defect in the constitution of such Committees.

## CHAPTER IV: PREVENTATION AND EARLY DETECTION OF DISABILITIES

**25.** Within the limits of their economic capacity and development, the appropriate Governments and the local authorities, with a view to preventing the occurrence of disabilities, shall-

(a) Undertake or cause to be undertaken surveys, investigations and research concerning the cause of occurrence of disabilities;

(b) Promote various methods of preventing disabilities;

(c) Screen all the children at least once in a year for the purpose of identifying "at-risk" cases;

(d) Provide facilities for training to the staff at the primary health centers;

(e) Sponsor or cause to be sponsored awareness campaigns and is disseminated or cause to be disseminated information for general hygiene. Health and sanitation,

(f) Take measures for pre-natal, parental and post-natal care of mother and child;

(g) Educate the public through the pre-schools, schools, primary health Centers, village level workers and anganwadi workers;

(h) Create awareness amongst the masses through television, radio and other mass media on the causes of disabilities and the preventive measures to be adopted;

## CHAPTER V: EDUCATION

**26.** The appropriate Governments and the local authorities shall-

(a) Ensure that every child with a disability has access to free education in an appropriate environment till he attains the age of eighteen years;

(b) Endeavor to promote the integration of students with disabilities in the normal schools;

(c) Promote setting up of special schools in Government and private sector for those in need of special education, in such a manner that children with disabilities living in any part of the country have access to such schools;

(d) Endeavor to equip the special schools for children with disabilities with vocational training facilities.

**27.** The appropriate Governments and the local authorities shall by notification make schemes for-

(a) Conducting part-time classes in respect of children with disabilities who having completed education up to class fifth and could not continue their studies on a whole-time basis;

(b) Conducting special part-time classes for providing functional literacy for children in the age group of sixteen and above;

(c) Imparting non-formal education by utilizing the available manpower in rural areas after giving them appropriate orientation;

(d) Imparting education through open schools or open universities;

(e) Conducting class and discussions through interactive electronic or other media;

(f) Providing every child with disability free of cost special books and equipments needed for his education.

**28.** The appropriate Governments shall initiate or cause to be initiated research by official and non-governmental agencies for the purpose of designing and developing new assistive devices, teaching aids, special teaching materials or such other items as are necessary to give a child with disability equal opportunities in education.

**29.** The appropriate Governments shall set up adequate number of teachers' training institutions and assist the national institutes and other voluntary organizations to develop teachers' training programmes specializing in disabilities so that requisite trained manpower is available for special schools and integrated schools for children with disabilities.

**30.** Without prejudice to the foregoing provisions, (be appropriate Governments shall by notification prepare a comprehensive education scheme which shall make Provision for-

(a) Transport facilities to the children with disabilities or in the alternative financial incentives to parents or guardians to enable their children with disabilities to attend schools.

(b) The removal of architectural barriers from schools. colleges or other institution, imparting vocational and professional training;

(c) The supply of books, uniforms and other materials to children with disabilities attending school.

(d) The grant of scholarship to students with disabilities..

(e) Setting up of appropriate fora for the redressal of grievances of parent, regarding the placement of their children with disabilities;

(f) Suitable modification in the examination system to eliminate purely mathematical questions for the benefit of blind students and students with low vision;

(g) Restructuring of curriculum for the benefit of children with disabilities;

(h) restructuring the curriculum for benefit of students with hearing impairment to facilitate them to take only one language as part of their curriculum.

**31.** All educational institutions shall provide or cause to be provided amanuensis to blind students and students with or low vision.

## CHAPTER VI: EMPLOYMENT

**32.** Appropriate Governments shall—

(a) Identify posts, in the establishments, which can be reserved for the persons with disability;

(b) At poriodical intervals not exceeding three years, review the list of posts identified and up-date the list taking into consideration the developments in technology.

**33.** Every appropriate Government shall appoint in every establishment such percentage of vacancies not less than three per cent. for persons or class of persons with disability of which one per cent. each shall be reserved for persons suffering from-

(i) Blindness or low vision;

(ii) Bearing impairment;

(iii) Loco motor disability or cerebral palsy, in the posts identified for each disability:

Provided that the appropriate Government may, having regard to the type of work carried on in any department or establishment, by notification subject to such conditions, if any, as may be specified in such notification, exempt any establishment from the provisions of this section.

**34. (1)** The appropriate Government may, by notification. Require that from such date as May he specified. By notification. The employer in every establishment shall furnish such information or return as may be prescribed in relation to vacancies appointed for person, with disability that have occurred or are about to occur in that establishment to such Special Employment Exchange as may be prescribed and the establishment shall thereupon comply with such requisition.

**(2)** The form in which and the intervals of time for which information or returns shall be furnished and the particulars, they shall contain shall be such as may be prescribed.

**35.** Any person authorized by the Special Employment Exchange in writing, shall have access to any relevant record or document in the possession of any establishment, and may enter at any reasonable time and premises where he believes such record or document to be, and inspect or take copies of relevant records or documents or ask any question necessary for obtaining any information.

**36.** Where in any recruitment year any vacancy under section 33, cannot be filled up due to non-availability of a suitable person with disability or, for any other sufficient reason, such vacancy shall be carried forward in the succeeding recruitment year and if ;r the succeeding recruitment year also suitable person with disability is not available, it may first be filled by interchange among the three categories and only when there is no parson with disability available for the post in that Year, the employer shall fill up the vacancy by appointment of a person, other than a person with disability:

Provided that if the nature of vacancies in an establishment is such that a given category of person can not be employed, the vacancies may be interchanged among the three categories with the prior approval of the appropriate Government.

**37. (1)** Every employer shall maintain such record in relation to the person. With disability employed in his establishment in such form and in such manner as may be prescribed by the appropriate Government.

**(2)** The records maintained under sub-section (1) shall be open to inspection at all reasonable hours by such persons as may be authorized in this behalf by general or special order by the appropriate Government.

**38. (1)** The appropriate Governments and local authorities shall by notification formulate schemes for ensuring employment of persons with disabilities, and such schemes may provide for-

(a) The training and welfare of persons with disabilities;

(b) The relaxation of upper age limit;

(c) Regulating the employment;

(d) Health and safety measures and creation of a non-handicapping environment in places where persons with disabilities are employed;

(e) The manner in which and the person by whom the cost of operating the schemes is to be defrayed; and

(f) Constituting the authority responsible for the administration of the scheme.

**39.** All Government educational institutions and other educational institutions receiving aid from the Government, shall reserve not less than three per cent seat for persons with disabilities.

**40.** The appropriate Governments and local authorities shall reserve not less than three per cent. in all poverty alleviation schemes for the benefit of persons with disabilities.

**41.** The appropriate Governments and the local authorities shall, within the limits of their economic capacity and development, provide incentives to employers both in public and private sectors to ensure that at least five per cent. of their work force is composed of persons with disabilities.

## CHAPTER VII: AFFIRMATIVE ACTION

**42.** The appropriate Governments shall by notification make schemes to provide aids and appliances to persons with disabilities.

**43.** The appropriate Governments and local authorities shall by notification frame schemes in favor of persons with disabilities, for the preferential allotment of land at concession] rates for-

(a) House;

(b) Setting up business;

(c) Setting up of special recreation centers;

(d) Establishment of special schools;

(e) Establishment of research centers;

(f) Establishment of factories by entrepreneurs with disabilities

## CHAPTER VIII: NON-DISCRIMINATION

**44.** Establishments in the transport sector shall, within the limits of their economic capacity and development for the benefit of persons with disabilities, take special measures to-

(a) Adapt rail compartments, buses. Vessels and aircrafts in such a way as to permit easy access to such persons;

(b) Adapt toilets in rail compartments, vessels, aircrafts and waiting rooms in such a way as to permit the wheel chair users to use them conveniently.

**45.** The appropriate Governments and the local authorities shall, within the limits of their economic capacity and development. Provide for-

(a) Installation of auditory signals at red lights in the public roads for the benefit of persons with visually handicap;

(b) Causing curb cuts and slopes to be made in pavements for the easy access of wheel chair users;

(c) Engraving on the surface of the zebra crossing for the blind or for persons with low vision;

(d) Engraving on the edges of railway platforms for the blind or for persons with low vision;

(e) Devising appropriate symbols of disability;

(f) Warning signals at appropriate places.

**46.** The appropriate Governments and the local authorities shall, within the limits of their economic capacity and development, provide for-

(a) Ramps in public buildings;

(b) Braille symbols and auditory signals in elevators or lifts;

(c) Braille symbols and auditory signals in elevators or lifts;

(d) Ramps in hospitals, primary health centers and other medical care and rehabilitation institutions.

**47. (1)** No establishment shall dispense with or reduce in rank, an employee who acquires a disability during his service.

Provided that, if an employee, after acquiring disability is not suitable for the post he was holding, could be shifted to some other post with the same pay scale and service benefits.

Provided further that if it is not possible to adjust the employee against any post, he may be kept on a supernumerary post until a suitable post is available or he attains the age of superannuation, whichever is earlier.

(2) No promotion shall be denied to a person merely on the ground of his disability:

Provided that the appropriate Government may, having regard to the type of work carried on in any establishment, by notification and subject to such conditions, if any, as may be specified in such notification, exempt any establishment from the provisions of this section.

## CHAPTER IX: RESEARCH AND MANPOWER DEVELOPMENT

**48.** The appropriate Governments and local authorities shall promote and sponsor research, inter alia,, in the following areas-

(a) Prevention of disability;

(b) Rehabilitation including community based rehabilitation;

(c) Development of assistive devices including their psychosocial aspects;

(d) Job identification;

(e) On site modifications in offices and factories.

**49.** The appropriate Governments shall provide financial assistance to universities, other institutions of higher learning, professional bodies and non-governmental research-. units or institutions, for undertaking research for special education. rehabilitation and manpower development.

## CHAPTER X: RECOGNITION OF INSTITUTIONS FOR PERSONS WITH DISABILITIES

**50.** The State Government shall appoint any authority, as it deems fit to be a competent authority for the purposes of this Act.

**51.** Save as otherwise provided under this Act, no person shall establish or maintain any institution for persons with disabilities except under and in accordance with a certificate of registration issued in this behalf by the competent authority:

Provided that a person maintaining an institution for persons with disabilities immediately before the commencement of this Act may continue to maintain such institution for a period of six months from such commencement and if he has made an application for such certificate under this section within the said period of six months, till the disposal of such application.

**52. (1)** Every application for a certificate of registration shall be made to the competent authority in such form and in such manner as may be prescribed by the State Government.

**(2)** On receipt of an application under sub-section (1), the competent authority shall make such enquiries as it may deem fit and where it is satisfied that the applicant has complied with the requirements of this Act and the rules made thereunder it shall grant a certificate of registration to the applicant and where it is not so satisfied the competent authority shall. by order. refuse to grant the certificate applied for:

Provided that before making any order refusing to grant a certificate the competent authority shall give to the applicant a reasonable opportunity of being heard and every order of refusal to grant a certificate shall he communicated to the applicant in such manner as may be prescribed by the State Government.

**(3)** No certificate of registration shall be granted under sub-section (2) unless the institution with respect to which an application has been made is in a position to provide such facilities and maintain such standards as may be prescribed by the State Government.

**(4)** A certificate of registration granted under this section,-

(a) Shall, unless revoked under section 53, remain in force for such period as may, be prescribed by, the State Government.

(b) May be renewed from time to time for a like period; and

(c) Shall be in such form and shall be subject to such conditions as may be Prescribed by the State Government

**(5)** An application for renewal of a certificate of registration shall be made not less than sixty days before the period of validity.

**(6)** The certificate of registration shall he displayed by the institution in a conspicuous place.

**53. (1)** the competent authority may, if it has reasonable cause to believe that the Holder of the certificate of registration granted under sub-section (2) of section 52 has -

(a) Made a statement in relation to any application for the issue of renewal of the certificate which is incorrect or false in material particulars; or

(b) Committed or has caused to be committed any breach of rules or any conditions subject to which the certificate was granted, it may after making such inquiry, as it deems fit, by order, revoke the certificate:

Provided that no such order shall he made until an opportunity is given to the holder of the certificate to show cause as to why the certificate should not be revoked.

**(2)** Where a certificate in respect of an institution has been revoked under sub-section (1), such institution shall cease to function from the date of such revocation.

Provided that where an appeal lies under section 54 against the order of revocation, such institution shall cease to function—

(a) Where no appeal has been preferred immediately on the expiry of the period prescribed for the filing of such appeal, or

(b) Where such appeal has been preferred, but the order of revocation has been upheld, from the date of the order of appeal.

**(3)** On the revocation of a certificate in respect of an institution, the competent authority may direct that any person with disability who is an inmate of such institution on the date of such revocation, shall be-

(a) Restored to the custody of her or his parent, spouse or lawful guardian, as the case may be, or

(b) Transferred to any other institution specified by the competent authority.

(4) Every institution, which holds a certificate of registration, which is revoked, under this section shall, immediately after such revocation. Surrender such certificate to the Competent authority.

54. (1) Any person aggrieved by the order of the competent authority, refusing to grant a certificate or revoking a certificate may, within such period as may he prescribed by the State Government, prefer an appeal to that Government against such refusal or revocation.

(2) The order of the State Government on such appeal shall he final.

55. Nothing contained in this Chapter shall apply, to an institution for persons with disabilities established or maintained by the Central Government or State Government.

## CHAPTER XI: INSTITUTION FOR PERSONS WITH SEVERE DISABILITIES

56. The appropriate Government may establish and maintain institutions for persons with severe disabilities at such places as it thinks fit.

(2) Where, the appropriate Government is of opinion that any institution other than an institution. Established under sub-section (1), is fit for the rehabilitation of the persons with severe disabilities, the Government may recognize such institution as an institution for persons with severe disabilities for the purposes of this Act:

Provided that no institution shall be recognized under this section unless such institution has complied with the requirements of this Act and the rules made there under.

(3) Every institution established under sub-section (1) shall be maintained in such manner and satisfy such conditions as may be prescribed b), the appropriate Government.

(4) For the purposes of this section "person with severe disability" means a person with eighty per cent. or more of one or more disabilities.

## CHAPTER XII : THE CHIEF COMMISSIONER AND COMMISSIONERS FOR PERSONS WITH DISABILITIES

57. (1) The Central Government may, by notification appoint a Chief Commissioner for persons with disabilities for the purposes of this Act.

(2) A person shall not be qualified for appointment as the Chief Commissioner unless he has special knowledge or practical experience in respect of matters relating to rehabilitation.

(3) The salary and allowances payable to and other terms and conditions of service (including pension, gratuity and other retirement benefits of the Chief Commissioner shall be such as may be prescribed by the Central Government.

(4) The Central Government shall determine the nature and categories of officers and other employees required to assist the Chief Commissioner in the discharge of his functions and provide the Chief Commissioner with such officers and other employees as it thinks fit.

**(5)** The officers and employees provided to the Chief Commissioner shall discharge their functions under the general superintendence of the Chief Commissioner.

**(6)** The salaries and allowances and other conditions of service of officers and employees provided to the Chief Commissioner shall be such as may be prescribed by the Central Government.

**58.** The Chief commissioner shall —-

(a) Coordinate the work of the Commissioners;

(b) Monitor the utilization of funds disbursed by the Central Government;

(c) Take steps to safeguard the rights and facilities made available to Persons with disabilities;

(d) Submit reports to the Central Government on the implementation of the Act at such intervals as that Government may prescribe.

**59.** Without prejudice to the provisions of section 58 the Chief Commissioner may of his own motion or on the application of any aggrieved person or otherwise look into complaints with respect to matters relating to --

(a) Deprivation of rights of persons with Disabilities.

(b) Non-implementation of laws, rules, byelaws, regulations. Executive orders, guidelines or instructions made or issued by the appropriate Governments and the local authorities for the welfare and protection of rights or persons with disabilities. And take up the matter with the appropriate authorities.

**60. (1)** Every State Government may, by notification appoint a Commissioner for persons with disabilities for the purpose of this Act.

**(2)** A person shall not be qualified for appointment as a Commissioner unless he has special knowledge or practical experience in respect of matters relating to rehabilitation.

**(3)** The salary and allowances payable to and other terms and conditions of service (including pension gratuity and other retirement benefits) of the Commissioner shall be such as may he prescribed by the State Government.

**(4)** The State Government shall determine the nature and categories of officers and other employees required to assist the Commissioner in the discharge of his functions and provide the Commissioner with such officers and other employees as it thinks fit.

**(5)** The officers and employees provided to the Commissioner shall discharge their functions under the general superintendence of the Commissioner.

**(6)** The salaries and allowances and other conditions of service of officers and employees provided to the Commissioner shall be such as may he prescribed by the State Government.

**61.** The Commissioner within the State shall-

(a) Coordinate with the departments of the State Government for the programmes and schemes, for the benefit of persons with disabilities;

(b) Monitor the utilization of funds disbursed by the State Government;

(c) Take steps to safeguard the rights and facilities made available to persons with disabilities.

(d) Submit reports to the State Government on the implementation of the Act at such intervals as that Government may prescribe and forward a copy thereof to the Chief Commissioner.

62. Without prejudice to the provisions of section 61 the Commissioner may of his own motion or on the application of any aggrieved person or otherwise look into complaints with respect to matters relating to—

(a) Deprivation of rights of persons with disabilities;

(b) Non-implementation of laws, rules, bye-laws, regulations, executive orders, guidelines or instructions made or issued by the appropriate Governments and the local authorities for the welfare and protection of rights of persons with disabilities, And take up the matter with the appropriate authorities.

63. The Chief Commissioner and the Commissioners shall, for the purpose of discharging their functions under this Act, have the same powers as are vested in a court under the Code of Civil Procedure, 1908 while trying a suit, in respect of the following matters, namely:-

(a) Summoning and enforcing the attendance of witnesses;

(b) Requiring the discovery and production of any documents;

(c) Requisitioning any public record or copy thereof from any court or office;

(d) Receiving evidence on affidavits; and

(e) Issuing commissions for the examination of witnesses or documents.

(2) Every proceeding before the Chief Commissioner and Commissioners shall be a judicial proceeding within the meaning directions 193 and 228 of the Indian Penal Code and the Chief Commissioner, the Commissioner, the competent authority, shall be deemed to he a civil court for the purposes of section 195 and Chapter XXVI of the Code of Criminal Procedure, 1973.

64. (1) The Chief Commissioner shall prepare in such form and at such time for each financial year as may be prescribed by the Central Government an annual report giving a full account of his activities during the previous financial year and forward a copy thereof to the Central Government.

(2) The Central Government shall cause the annual report to be laid before each House of Parliament along with the recommendations explaining the action taken or proposed to be taken on the recommendation made therein in so far as they relate to the Central Government and the reasons for non-acceptance, if any, of any such recommendation or part.

65. (1) The Commissioner shall prepare in such form and at such time for each financial year as may be prescribed by the State Government an annual report giving a full account of his activities during the previous financial year and forward a copy thereof to the State Government.

The State Government shall cause the annual report to be laid before each State Legislature along with the recommendations explaining the action taken or proposed to be taken on the recommendation made therein in so far as they relate to the State Government and the reasons for non-acceptance, if any, of any such recommendation or part.

## CHAPTER XIII: SOCIAL SECURITY

66. (1) The appropriate Governments and the local authorities shall within the limits of their economic capacity and development undertake or cause

to be undertaken rehabilitation of all persons with disabilities.

**(2)** For purposes of sub-section (1), the appropriate Governments and local authorities shall grant financial assistance to non-governmental organizations.

**(3)** The appropriate Governments and local authorities while formulating rehabilitation policies shall consult the non-governmental organizations working for the cause of persons with disabilities.

**67. (1)** The appropriate Government shall by notification frame an insurance scheme for the benefit of its employees with disabilities.

**(2)** Notwithstanding anything contained in this section, the appropriate Government may instead of framing an insurance scheme frame an alternative security scheme for its employees with disabilities.

**68.** The appropriate Governments shall within the limits of their economic capacity and development shall by notification frame a scheme for payment of an unemployment allowance to persons with disabilities registered with the Special Employment Exchange for more than two years and who could not he placed in any gainful occupation.

## CHAPTER XIV: MISCELLANEOUS

**69.** Whoever fraudulently avails or attempts to avail, any benefit meant for persons with disabilities, shall be punishable with imprisonment for a term which may extend to two years or with fine which may extend to twenty thousand rupees or with both.

**70.** The Chief Commissioner, the Commissioners and other officers and staff provided to them shall be deemed to be public servants within the meaning of section 21 of the Indian Penal Code.

**71.** No suit, prosecution or other legal proceeding shall lie against the Central Government, the State Governments or the local authority or any officer of the Government in respect of anything which is done in good faith or intended to be done in pursuance of this Act and any rules or orders made there under.

**72.** The provisions of this Act, or the rules made there under shall be in addition to, and not in derogation of any other law for the time being in force or any rules, order or any instructions issued there under, enacted or issued for the benefit of persons with disabilities.

**73. (1)** The appropriate Government may, by notification, make rules for carrying out the provisions of this Act.

**(2)** In particular, and without prejudice to the generality of the foregoing powers, such rules may provide for all or any of the following matters, namely:-

(a) The manner in which a State Government or a Union territory shall be chosen under clause (k) of sub-section (2) of section 3;

(b) Allowances, which members shall receive under subsection (7) of section 4;

(c) Rules of procedure, which the Central Coordination Committee shall observe in regard to the transaction of business in its meetings under section 7;

(d) Such other functions, which the Central Coordination Committee may perform under clause (h) of sub-section (2) of section 8;

(e) The manner in which a State Government or a Union Territory shall be chosen under clause (h) of sub-section (2) of section 9;

(f) The allowances, which the Members shall receive under sub-section (3) of section 9;

(g) Rules of procedure, which the Central Executive Committee shall observe in regard to transaction of business at its meetings under section 11;

(h) The manner and purposes for which a person may be associated under sub-section (I) of section 12;

(i) Fees and allowances which a person associated with the Central Executive Committee shall received under sub-section (3) of section 12;

(j) Allowances which members shall received under sub-section (7) of section 14;

(k) Rules of procedure, which a State Coordination Committee shall observe in regard to transaction of business in its meetings under section 17;

(l) Such other functions, which a State Coordination Committee may perform under clause (g) of sub-section (2) of section 18;

(m) The allowances, which Members shall receive under sub-section (3) of section 19;

(n) Rules of procedure, which a State Executive Committee shall observe in regard to transaction of business at its meetings under section 21;

(o) The manner and purposes for which a person may be associated under sub-section (1) of section 22;

(p) Fees and allowances which a person associated with the State Executive Committee may receive under sub-section (3) of Section 22;

(q) Information or return which the employer in every establishment should furnish and the Special Employment Exchange to which such information or return shall be furnished under sub-section (1) of section 34;

(r) The form and the manner in which record shall be maintained by an employer under sub-section (1) of section 37;

(s) The form and manner in which an application shall be made under sub-section (1) of section 52;

(t) The manner in which an order of refusal shall be communicated under sub-section (2) of section 52;

(u) Facilities or standards required to be provided or maintained under sub-section (3) of section 52;

(v) The period for which a certificate of registration shall be valid under clause (a) of sub-section (4) of section 52;

(w) The form in which and conditions subject to which a certificate of registration shall be granted under clause (c) of sub-section (4) of section 52;

(x) Period within which an appeal shall lie under sub-section (1) of section 54;

(y) The manner in which an institution for persons with severe disabilities shall be maintained and conditions which have to be satisfied under sub-section (3) of section 56;

(z) The salary, allowances and other terms and conditions of service of the Chief Commissioner under sub-section (6) of section 57;

(za) the salary, allowances and other conditions of service of officers and employees under sub-section (6) of section 57;

(zb) intervals at which the Chief Commissioner shall report to the Central Government under clause (d) of section 58;

(zc) the salary, allowances and other terms and conditions of service of the Commissioner under sub-section (3) of section 60;

(zd) the salary, allowances and other conditions of service of officers and employees under sub-section (6) of section 60;

(ze) intervals within which the Commissioner shall report to the State Government under clause (d) of section 61;

(zf) the form and time in which annual report shall be prepared under sub-section (1) of section 64; **(zg)** the form and time in which annual report shall be prepared under sub-section (1) of section 65;

(zh) any other matter which is required to be or may be prescribed.

**(3)** Every notification made by the Central Government under die proviso to section 33, proviso to sub-section (2) of section 47, every scheme framed by it under section 27, section 30, sub-section (1) of section 38. section 42, section 43, section 67, section 68 and every rule made by it under sub-section (1). shall be laid. as soon as may be after it is made, before each House of Parliament, while it is in session for a tow period of thirty days which may be comprised in one session or in two or more successive sessions, and if. before the expiry of the session immediately following the session or the successive sessions aforesaid, berth Houses agree in making any modification in the rule, notification or scheme, both Houses agree that the rule, notification or scheme should not be Made, the rule, notification or scheme shall thereafter have effect only in such modified form or be of no effect, as the case may be; so, however, that any such modification or annulment shall be without prejudice to the validity of anything previously done under that rule. Notification or scheme, as the case may be.

(4) Every notification made by the State Government under the provison to section 33 proviso to sub-section (2) of section 47, every scheme made by it under section 27, section 30, sub-section (1) of section 38, section 42. section 43, section 67. section 68 and every rule made by it under sub-section (1), shall be laid. as soon as may be after it is made, before each House of State Legislature, where it consists of two Houses or where such legislature consists of one House before that House.

74. In section 12 of the Legal Services Authorities Act. 1987, for clause (d), the following clause shall he substituted, namely:-

"(d) a person with disability as defined in clause (i) of section 2 of the Persons With Disabilities (Equal Opportunities, Protection of Rights and Full Participation) Act. 1995."

# Annexure—II

## CONVENTION ON THE RIGHTS OF PERSONS WITH DISABILITIES

**Preamble**

The States Parties to the present Convention,

(a) *Recalling* the principles proclaimed in the Charter of the United Nations which recognize the inherent dignity and worth and the equal and inalienable rights of all members of the human family as the foundation of freedom, justice and peace in the world,

(b) *Recognizing* that the United Nations, in the Universal Declaration of Human Rights and in the International Covenants on Human Rights, has proclaimed and agreed that everyone is entitled to all the rights and freedoms set forth therein, without distinction of any kind,

(c) *Reaffirming* the universality, indivisibility, interdependence and interrelatedness of all human rights and fundamental freedoms and the need for persons with disabilities to be guaranteed their full enjoyment without discrimination,

(d) *Recalling* the International Covenant on Economic, Social and Cultural Rights, the International Covenant on Civil and Political Rights, the International Convention on the Elimination of All Forms of Racial Discrimination, the Convention on the Elimination of All Forms of Discrimination against Women, the Convention against Torture and Other Cruel, Inhuman or Degrading Treatment or Punishment, the Convention on the Rights of the Child, and the International Convention on the Protection of the Rights of All Migrant Workers and Members of Their Families,

(e) *Recognizing* that disability is an evolving concept and that disability results from the interaction between persons with impairments and attitudinal and environmental barriers that hinders their full and effective participation in society on an equal basis with others,

(f) *Recognizing* the importance of the principles and policy guidelines contained in the World Programme of Action concerning Disabled Persons and in the Standard Rules on the Equalization of Opportunities for Persons with Disabilities in influencing the promotion, formulation and evaluation of the policies, plans, programmes and actions at the national, regional and international levels to further equalize opportunities for persons with disabilities,

(g) *Emphasizing* the importance of mainstreaming disability issues as an integral part of relevant strategies of sustainable development,*(h) Recognizing also* that discrimination against any person on the basis of disability is a violation of the inherent dignity and worth of the human person,

(i) *Recognizing further* the diversity of persons with disabilities,

(j) *Recognizing* the need to promote and protect the human rights of all persons with disabilities, including those who require more intensive support,

(k) *Concerned* that, despite these various instruments and undertakings, persons with disabilities continue to face barriers in their participation as equal members of society and violations of their human rights in all parts of the world,

(l) *Recognizing* the importance of international cooperation for improving the living conditions of persons with disabilities in every country, particularly in developing countries,

(m) *Recognizing* the valued existing and potential contributions made by persons with disabilities to the overall well-being and diversity of their communities, and that the promotion of the full enjoyment by persons with disabilities of their human rights and fundamental freedoms and of full participation by persons with disabilities will result in their enhanced sense of belonging and in significant advances in the human, social and economic development of society and the eradication of poverty,

(n) *Recognizing* the importance for persons with disabilities of their individual autonomy and independence, including the freedom to make their own choices,

(o) *Considering* that persons with disabilities should have the opportunity to be actively involved in decision-making processes about policies and programmes, including those directly concerning them,

(p) *Concerned* about the difficult conditions faced by persons with disabilities who are subject to multiple or aggravated forms of discrimination on the basis of race, colour, sex, language, religion, political or other opinion, national, ethnic, indigenous or social origin, property, birth, age or other status,

(q) *Recognizing* that women and girls with disabilities are often at greater risk, both within and outside the home, of violence, injury or abuse, neglect or negligent treatment, maltreatment or exploitation,

(r) *Recognizing* that children with disabilities should have full enjoyment of all human rights and fundamental freedoms on an equal basiswith other children, and recalling obligations to that end undertaken by States Parties to the Convention on the Rights of the Child,

(s) *Emphasizing* the need to incorporate a gender perspective in all efforts to promote the full enjoyment of human rights and fundamental freedoms by persons with disabilities,

(t) *Highlighting* the fact that the majority of persons with disabilities live in conditions of poverty, and in this regard recognizing the critical need to address the negative impact of poverty on persons with disabilities,

(u) *Bearing in mind* that conditions of peace and security based on full respect for the purposes and principles contained in the Charter of the United Nations and observance of applicable human rights instruments are indispensable for the full protection of persons with disabilities, in particular during armed conflicts and foreign occupation,

(v) *Recognizing* the importance of accessibility to the physical, social, economic and cultural environment, to health and education and to information and communication, in enabling persons with disabilities to fully enjoy all human rights and fundamental freedoms,

(w) *Realizing* that the individual, having duties to other individuals and to the community to which he or she belongs, is under a responsibility to strive for the promotion and observance of the rights recognized in the International Bill of Human Rights,

(x) *Convinced* that the family is the natural and fundamental group unit of society and is entitled to protection by society and the State, and that persons with disabilities and their family members should receive the necessary protection and assistance to enable families to contribute towards the full and equal enjoyment of the rights of persons with disabilities,

(y) *Convinced* that a comprehensive and integral international convention to promote and protect the rights and dignity of persons with disabilities will make a significant contribution to redressing the profound social disadvantage of persons with disabilities and promote their participation in the civil, political, economic, social and cultural spheres with equal opportunities, in both developing and developed countries,

*Have agreed* as follows:

### Article 1

### *Purpose*

The purpose of the present Convention is to promote, protect and ensure the full and equal enjoyment of all human rights and fundamental freedoms by all persons with disabilities, and to promote respect for their inherent dignity.

Persons with disabilities include those who have long-term physical, mental, intellectual or sensory impairments which in interaction with various barriers may hinder their full and effective participation in society on an equal basis with others.

### Article 2

### Definitions

For the purposes of the present Convention:

"Communication" includes languages, display of text, Braille, tactile communication, large print, accessible multimedia as well as written, audio, plain-language, human-reader and augmentative and alternative modes, means and formats of communication, including accessible information and communication technology;

"Language" includes spoken and signed languages and other forms of non spoken languages;

"Discrimination on the basis of disability" means any distinction, exclusion or restriction on the basis of disability which has the purpose or effect of impairing or nullifying the recognition, enjoyment or exercise, on an equal basis with others, of all human rights and fundamental freedoms in the political, economic, social, cultural, civil or any other field. It includes all forms of discrimination, including denial of reasonable accommodation;

"Reasonable accommodation" means necessary and appropriate modification and adjustments not imposing a disproportionate or undue burden, where needed in a particular case, to ensure to persons with disabilities the enjoyment or exercise on an equal basis with others of all human rights and fundamental freedoms;

"Universal design" means the design of products, environments, programmes and services to be usable by all people, to the greatest extent possible, without the need for adaptation or specialized design. "Universal design" shall not exclude assistive devices for particular groups of persons with disabilities where this is needed.

## Article 3
## General principles

The principles of the present Convention shall be:

(*a*) Respect for inherent dignity, individual autonomy including the freedom to make one's own choices, and independence of persons;

(*b*) Non-discrimination;

(*c*) Full and effective participation and inclusion in society;

(*d*) Respect for difference and acceptance of persons with disabilities as part of human diversity and humanity;

(e) *Equality of opportunity;*

(f) Accessibility;

(g) Equality between men and women;

(h) Respect for the evolving capacities of children with disabilities and respect for the right of children with disabilities to preserve their identities.

## Article 4
## General obligations

1. States Parties undertake to ensure and promote the full realization of all human rights and fundamental freedoms for all persons with disabilities without discrimination of any kind on the basis of disability. To this end, States Parties undertake:

(a) To adopt all appropriate legislative, administrative and other measures for the implementation of the rights recognized in the present Convention;

(b) To take all appropriate measures, including legislation, to modify or abolish existing laws, regulations, customs and practices that constitute discrimination against persons with disabilities;

(c) To take into account the protection and promotion of the human rights of persons with disabilities in all policies and programmes;

(d) To refrain from engaging in any act or practice that is inconsistent with the present Convention and to ensure that public authorities and institutions act in conformity with the present Convention;

(e) To take all appropriate measures to eliminate discrimination on the basis of disability by any person, organization or private enterprise;

(f) To undertake or promote research and development of universally designed goods, services, equipment and facilities, as defined in article 2 of the present Convention, which should require the minimum possible adaptation and the least cost to meet the specific needs of a person with disabilities, to promote their availability and use, and to promote universal design in the development of standards and guidelines;

(g) To undertake or promote research and development of, and to promote the availability and use of new technologies, including information and communications technologies, mobility aids, devices and assistive technologies, suitable for persons with disabilities, giving priority to technologies at an affordable cost;

(h) To provide accessible information to persons with disabilities about mobility aids, devices and assistive technologies, including new technologies, as well as other forms of assistance, support services and facilities;

(i) To promote the training of professionals and staff working with persons with disabilities in the rights recognized in the present Convention so as to better provide the assistance and services guaranteed by those rights.

2. With regard to economic, social and cultural rights, each State Party undertakes to take measures to the maximum of its available resources and, where needed, within the framework of international cooperation, with a view to achieving progressively the full realization of these rights, without prejudice to those obligations contained in the present Convention that are immediately applicable according to international law.

3. In the development and implementation of legislation and policies to implement the present Convention, and in other decision-making processes concerning issues relating to persons with disabilities, States Parties shall closely consult with and actively involve persons with disabilities, including children with disabilities, through their representative organizations.

4. Nothing in the present Convention shall affect any provisions which are more conducive to the realization of the rights of persons with disabilities and which may be contained in the law of a State Party or international law in force for that State. There shall be no restriction upon or derogation from any of thehuman rights and fundamental freedoms recognized or existing in any State Party to the present Convention pursuant to law, conventions, regulation or custom on the pretext that the present Convention does not recognize such rights or freedoms or that it recognizes them to a lesser extent.

5. The provisions of the present Convention shall extend to all parts of federal States without any limitations or exceptions.

### Article 5
### Equality and non-discrimination

1. States Parties recognize that all persons are equal before and under the law and are entitled without any discrimination to the equal protection and equal benefit of the law.
2. States Parties shall prohibit all discrimination on the basis of disability and guarantee to persons with disabilities equal and effective legal protection against discrimination on all grounds.
3. In order to promote equality and eliminate discrimination, States Parties shall take all appropriate steps to ensure that reasonable accommodation is provided.
4. Specific measures which are necessary to accelerate or achieve de facto equality of persons with disabilities shall not be considered discrimination under the terms of the present Convention.

### Article 6
### Women with disabilities

1. States Parties recognize that women and girls with disabilities are subject to multiple discrimination, and in this regard shall take measures to ensure the full and equal enjoyment by them of all human rights and fundamental freedoms.
2. States Parties shall take all appropriate measures to ensure the full development, advancement and empowerment of women, for the purpose of guaranteeing them the exercise and enjoyment of the human rights and fundamental freedoms set out in the present Convention.

### Article 7
### Children with disabilities

1. States Parties shall take all necessary measures to ensure the full enjoyment by children with disabilities of all human rights and fundamental freedoms on an equal basis with other children.
2. In all actions concerning children with disabilities, the best interests of the child shall be a primary consideration.
3. States Parties shall ensure that children with disabilities have the right to express their views freely on all matters affecting them, their views being given due weight in accordance with their age and maturity, on an equal basis with other children, and to be provided with disability and age-appropriate assistance to realize that right.

### Article 8
### Awareness-raising

1. States Parties undertake to adopt immediate, effective and appropriate measures:

(a) To raise awareness throughout society, including at the family level, regarding persons with disabilities, and to foster respect for the rights and dignity of persons with disabilities;

(b) To combat stereotypes, prejudices and harmful practices relating to persons with disabilities, including those based on sex and age, in all areas of life;

(c) To promote awareness of the capabilities and contributions of persons with disabilities.

2. Measures to this end include:

(a) Initiating and maintaining effective public awareness campaigns designed:

To nurture receptiveness to the rights of persons with disabilities;

To promote positive perceptions and greater social awareness towards persons with disabilities;

To promote recognition of the skills, merits and abilities of persons with disabilities, and of their contributions to the workplace and the labour market;

(b) Fostering at all levels of the education system, including in all children from an early age, an attitude of respect for the rights of persons with disabilities;

(c) Encouraging all organs of the media to portray persons with disabilities in a manner consistent with the purpose of the present Convention;(d) Promoting awareness-training programmes regarding persons with disabilities and the rights of persons with disabilities.

**Article 9**

**Accessibility**

1. To enable persons with disabilities to live independently and participate fully in all aspects of life, States Parties shall take appropriate measures to ensure to persons with disabilities access, on an equal basis with others, to the physical environment, to transportation, to information and communications, including information and communications technologies and systems, and to other facilities and services open or provided to the public, both in urban and in rural areas. These measures, which shall include the identification and elimination of obstacles and barriers to accessibility, shall apply to, inter alia:

(a) Buildings, roads, transportation and other indoor and outdoor facilities, including schools, housing, medical facilities and workplaces;

(b) Information, communications and other services, including electronic services and emergency services.

2. States Parties shall also take appropriate measures:

(a) To develop, promulgate and monitor the implementation of minimum standards and guidelines for the accessibility of facilities and services open or provided to the public;

(b) To ensure that private entities that offer facilities and services which are open or provided to the public take into account all aspects of accessibility for persons with disabilities;

(c) To provide training for stakeholders on accessibility issues facing persons with disabilities;

(d) To provide in buildings and other facilities open to the public signage in Braille and in easy to read and understand forms;

(e) To provide forms of live assistance and intermediaries, including guides, readers and professional sign language interpreters, to facilitate accessibility to buildings and other facilities open to the public;

(f) To promote other appropriate forms of assistance and support to persons with disabilities to ensure their access to information;(g) To promote access for persons with disabilities to new information and communications technologies and systems, including the Internet;

(h) To promote the design, development, production and distribution of accessible information and communications technologies and systems at an early stage, so that these technologies and systems become accessible at minimum cost.

## Article 10
## Right to life

States Parties reaffirm that every human being has the inherent right to life and shall take all necessary measures to ensure its effective enjoyment by persons with disabilities on an equal basis with others.

## Article 11
## Situations of risk and humanitarian emergencies

States Parties shall take, in accordance with their obligations under international law, including international humanitarian law and international human rights law, all necessary measures to ensure the protection and safety of persons with disabilities in situations of risk, including situations of armed conflict, humanitarian emergencies and the occurrence of natural disasters.

## Article 12
## Equal recognition before the law

1. States Parties reaffirm that persons with disabilities have the right to recognition everywhere as persons before the law.
2. States Parties shall recognize that persons with disabilities enjoy legal capacity on an equal basis with others in all aspects of life.
3. States Parties shall take appropriate measures to provide access by persons with disabilities to the support they may require in exercising their legal capacity.
4. States Parties shall ensure that all measures that relate to the exercise of legal capacity provide for appropriate and effective safeguards to prevent abuse in accordance with international human rights law. Such safeguards shall ensure that measures relating to the exercise of legal capacity respect the rights, will and preferences of the person, are free of conflict of interest and undue influence, are proportional and tailored to the person's circumstances, apply for the shortest time possible and are subject to regular review by a competent, independent and impartial authority or judicial body. Thesafeguards shall be proportional to the degree to which such measures affect the person's rights and interests.
5. Subject to the provisions of this article, States Parties shall take all appropriate and effective measures to ensure the equal right of persons with disabilities to own or inherit property, to control their own financial affairs and to have equal access to bank loans, mortgages and other forms of financial credit, and shall ensure that persons with disabilities are not arbitrarily deprived of their property.

### Article 13
### Access to justice

1. States Parties shall ensure effective access to justice for persons with disabilities on an equal basis with others, including through the provision of procedural and age-appropriate accommodations, in order to facilitate their effective role as direct and indirect participants, including as witnesses, in all legal proceedings, including at investigative and other preliminary stages.
2. In order to help to ensure effective access to justice for persons with disabilities, States Parties shall promote appropriate training for those working in the field of administration of justice, including police and prison staff.

### Article 14
### Liberty and security of person

1. States Parties shall ensure that persons with disabilities, on an equal basis with others:

(a) Enjoy the right to liberty and security of person;

(b) Are not deprived of their liberty unlawfully or arbitrarily, and that any deprivation of liberty is in conformity with the law, and that the existence of a disability shall in no case justify a deprivation of liberty.

2. States Parties shall ensure that if persons with disabilities are deprived of their liberty through any process, they are, on an equal basis with others, entitled to guarantees in accordance with international human rights law and shall be treated in compliance with the objectives and principles of the present Convention, including by provision of reasonable accommodation.

### Article 15
### Freedom from torture or cruel, inhuman or degrading treatment or punishment

1. No one shall be subjected to torture or to cruel, inhuman or degrading treatment or punishment. In particular, no one shall be subjected without his or her free consent to medical or scientific experimentation.

2. States Parties shall take all effective legislative, administrative, judicial or other measures to prevent persons with disabilities, on an equal basis with others, from being subjected to torture or cruel, inhuman or degrading treatment or punishment.

### Article 16
### Freedom from exploitation, violence and abuse

1. States Parties shall take all appropriate legislative, administrative, social, educational and other measures to protect persons with disabilities, both within and outside the home, from all forms of exploitation, violence and abuse, including their gender-based aspects.
2. States Parties shall also take all appropriate measures to prevent all forms of exploitation, violence and abuse by ensuring, inter alia, appropriate forms of gender- and age-sensitive assistance and support for persons with disabilities and their families and caregivers, including through the provision of information and education on how to avoid, recognize and report instances of exploitation, violence and abuse.

States Parties shall ensure that protection services are age-, gender- and disability-sensitive.

3. In order to prevent the occurrence of all forms of exploitation, violence and abuse, States Parties shall ensure that all facilities and programmes designed to serve persons with disabilities are effectively monitored by independent authorities.
4. States Parties shall take all appropriate measures to promote the physical, cognitive and psychological recovery, rehabilitation and social reintegration of persons with disabilities who become victims of any form of exploitation, violence or abuse, including through the provision of protection services. Such recovery and reintegration shall take place in an environment that fosters the health, welfare, self-respect, dignity and autonomy of the person and takes into account gender- and age-specific needs.
5. States Parties shall put in place effective legislation and policies, including women- and child-focused legislation and policies, to ensure that instances of exploitation, violence and abuse against persons with disabilities are identified, investigated and, where appropriate, prosecuted.

### Article 17
### Protecting the integrity of the person

Every person with disabilities has a right to respect for his or her physical and mental integrity on an equal basis with others.

### Article 18
### Liberty of movement and nationality

1. States Parties shall recognize the rights of persons with disabilities to liberty of movement, to freedom to choose their residence and to a nationality, on an equal basis with others, including by ensuring that persons with disabilities:

- *(a)* Have the right to acquire and change a nationality and are not deprived of their nationality arbitrarily or on the basis of disability;
- *(b)* Are not deprived, on the basis of disability, of their ability to obtain, possess and utilize documentation of their nationality or other documentation of identification, or to utilize relevant processes such as immigration proceedings, that may be needed to facilitate exercise of the right to liberty of movement;
- *(c)* Are free to leave any country, including their own;
- *(d)* Are not deprived, arbitrarily or on the basis of disability, of the right to enter their own country.

2. Children with disabilities shall be registered immediately after birth and shall have the right from birth to a name, the right to acquire a nationality and, as far as possible, the right to know and be cared for by their parents.

### Article 19
### Living independently and being included in the community

States Parties to the present Convention recognize the equal right of all persons with disabilities to live in the community, with choices equal to others, and shall take effective and appropriate measures to facilitate full enjoyment by persons with disabilities of this right and their full inclusion and participation in the community, including by ensuring that:

(a) Persons with disabilities have the opportunity to choose their place of residence and where and with whom they live on an equal basis with others and are not obliged to live in a particular living arrangement;

(b) Persons with disabilities have access to a range of in-home, residential and other community support services, including personal assistance necessary to support living and inclusion in the community, and to prevent isolation or segregation from the community;

(c) Community services and facilities for the general population are available on an equal basis to persons with disabilities and are responsive to their needs.

**Article 20**
**Personal mobility**

States Parties shall take effective measures to ensure personal mobility with the greatest possible independence for persons with disabilities, including by:

*(a)* Facilitating the personal mobility of persons with disabilities in the manner and at the time of their choice, and at affordable cost;

*(b)* Facilitating access by persons with disabilities to quality mobility aids, devices, assistive technologies and forms of live assistance and intermediaries, including by making them available at affordable cost;

*(c)* Providing training in mobility skills to persons with disabilities and to specialist staff working with persons with disabilities;

*(d)* Encouraging entities that produce mobility aids, devices and assistive technologies to take into account all aspects of mobility for persons with disabilities.

**Article 21**
**Freedom of expression and opinion, and access to information**

States Parties shall take all appropriate measures to ensure that persons with disabilities can exercise the right to freedom of expression and opinion, including the freedom to seek, receive and impart information and ideas on an equal basis with others and through all forms of communication of their choice, as defined in article 2 of the present Convention, including by:

(a) Providing information intended for the general public to persons with disabilities in accessible formats and technologies appropriate to different kinds of disabilities in a timely manner and without additional cost;

(b) Accepting and facilitating the use of sign languages, Braille, augmentative and alternative communication, and all other accessible means,modes and formats of communication of their choice by persons with disabilities in official interactions;

(c) Urging private entities that provide services to the general public, including through the Internet, to provide information and services in accessible and usable formats for persons with disabilities;

(d) Encouraging the mass media, including providers of information through the Internet, to make their services accessible to persons with disabilities;

(e) Recognizing and promoting the use of sign languages.

## Article 22
## Respect for privacy

1. No person with disabilities, regardless of place of residence or living arrangements, shall be subjected to arbitrary or unlawful interference with his or her privacy, family, home or correspondence or other types of communication or to unlawful attacks on his or her honour and reputation. Persons with disabilities have the right to the protection of the law against such interference or attacks.

2. States Parties shall protect the privacy of personal, health and rehabilitation information of persons with disabilities on an equal basis with others.

## Article 23
## Respect for home and the family

1. States Parties shall take effective and appropriate measures to eliminate discrimination against persons with disabilities in all matters relating to marriage, family, parenthood and relationships, on an equal basis with others, so as to ensure that:

(a) The right of all persons with disabilities who are of marriageable age to marry and to found a family on the basis of free and full consent of the intending spouses is recognized;

(b) The rights of persons with disabilities to decide freely and responsibly on the number and spacing of their children and to have access to age-appropriate information, reproductive and family planning education are recognized, and the means necessary to enable them to exercise these rights are provided;(c) Persons with disabilities, including children, retain their fertility on an equal basis with others.

2. States Parties shall ensure the rights and responsibilities of persons with disabilities, with regard to guardianship, wardship, trusteeship, adoption of children or similar institutions, where these concepts exist in national legislation; in all cases the best interests of the child shall be paramount. States Parties shall render appropriate assistance to persons with disabilities in the performance of their child-rearing responsibilities.

3. States Parties shall ensure that children with disabilities have equal rights with respect to family life. With a view to realizing these rights, and to prevent concealment, abandonment, neglect and segregation of children with disabilities, States Parties shall undertake to provide early and comprehensive information, services and support to children with disabilities and their families.

4. States Parties shall ensure that a child shall not be separated from his or her parents against their will, except when competent authorities subject to judicial review determine, in accordance with applicable law and procedures, that such separation is necessary for the best interests of the child. In no case shall a child be separated from parents on the basis of a disability of either the child or one or both of the parents.

5. States Parties shall, where the immediate family is unable to care for a child with disabilities, undertake every effort to provide alternative care within the wider family, and failing that, within the community in a family setting.

## Article 24
## Education

1. States Parties recognize the right of persons with disabilities to education. With a view to realizing this right without discrimination and on the basis of equal opportunity, States Parties shall ensure an inclusive education system at all levels and lifelong learning directed to:
   (a) The full development of human potential and sense of dignity and self-worth, and the strengthening of respect for human rights, fundamental freedoms and human diversity;
   (b) The development by persons with disabilities of their personality, talents and creativity, as well as their mental and physical abilities, to their fullest potential;
   (c) Enabling persons with disabilities to participate effectively in a free society.
2. In realizing this right, States Parties shall ensure that:
   (a) Persons with disabilities are not excluded from the general education system on the basis of disability, and that children with disabilities are not excluded from free and compulsory primary education, or from secondary education, on the basis of disability;
   (b) Persons with disabilities can access an inclusive, quality and free primary education and secondary education on an equal basis with others in the communities in which they live;
   (c) Reasonable accommodation of the individual's requirements is provided;
   (d) Persons with disabilities receive the support required, within the general education system, to facilitate their effective education;
   (e) Effective individualized support measures are provided in environments that maximize academic and social development, consistent with the goal of full inclusion.
3. States Parties shall enable persons with disabilities to learn life and social development skills to facilitate their full and equal participation in education and as members of the community. To this end, States Parties shall take appropriate measures, including:
   (a) Facilitating the learning of Braille, alternative script, augmentative and alternative modes, means and formats of communication and orientation and mobility skills, and facilitating peer support and mentoring;
   (b) Facilitating the learning of sign language and the promotion of the linguistic identity of the deaf community;
   (c) Ensuring that the education of persons, and in particular children, who are blind, deaf or deafblind, is delivered in the most appropriate languages and modes and means of communication for the individual, and in environments which maximize academic and social development.

4. In order to help ensure the realization of this right, States Parties shall take appropriate measures to employ teachers, including teachers with disabilities, who are qualified in sign language and/or Braille, and to train professionals and staff who work at all levels of education. Such training shall incorporate disability awareness and the use of appropriate augmentative and alternative modes, means and formats of communication, educational techniques and materials to support persons with disabilities.

5. States Parties shall ensure that persons with disabilities are able to access general tertiary education, vocational training, adult education and lifelong learning without discrimination and on an equal basis with others. To this end, States Parties shall ensure that reasonable accommodation is provided to persons with disabilities.

**Article 25**
**Health**

States Parties recognize that persons with disabilities have the right to the enjoyment of the highest attainable standard of health without discrimination on the basis of disability. States Parties shall take all appropriate measures to ensure access for persons with disabilities to health services that are gender-sensitive, including health-related rehabilitation. In particular, States Parties shall:

(a) Provide persons with disabilities with the same range, quality and standard of free or affordable health care and programmes as provided to other persons, including in the area of sexual and reproductive health and population-based public health programmes;

(b) Provide those health services needed by persons with disabilities specifically because of their disabilities, including early identification and intervention as appropriate, and services designed to minimize and prevent further disabilities, including among children and older persons;

(c) Provide these health services as close as possible to people's own communities, including in rural areas;

(d) Require health professionals to provide care of the same quality to persons with disabilities as to others, including on the basis of free and informed consent by, inter alia, raising awareness of the human rights, dignity, autonomy and needs of persons with disabilities through training and the promulgation of ethical standards for public and private health care;

(e) Prohibit discrimination against persons with disabilities in the provision of health insurance, and life insurance where such insurance is permitted by national law, which shall be provided in a fair and reasonable manner;

(f) Prevent discriminatory denial of health care or health services or food and fluids on the basis of disability.

**Article 26**
**Habilitation and rehabilitation**

States Parties shall take effective and appropriate measures, including through peer support, to enable persons with disabilities to attain and maintain maximum independence, full physical, mental, social and vocational ability, and full inclusion and participation in all aspects of life. To that end, States Parties shall organize, strengthen and extend comprehensive habilitation and rehabilitation services and programmes, particularly in the areas of health, employment, education and social services, in such a way that these services and programmes:

(a) Begin at the earliest possible stage, and are based on the multidisciplinary assessment of individual needs and strengths;

(b) Support participation and inclusion in the community and all aspects of society, are voluntary, and are available to persons with disabilities as close as possible to their own communities, including in rural areas.

2. States Parties shall promote the development of initial and continuing training for professionals and staff working in habilitation and rehabilitation services.

3. States Parties shall promote the availability, knowledge and use of assistive devices and technologies, designed for persons with disabilities, as they relate to habilitation and rehabilitation.

### Article 27
### Work and employment

1. States Parties recognize the right of persons with disabilities to work, on an equal basis with others; this includes the right to the opportunity to gain a living by work freely chosen or accepted in a labour market and work environment that is open, inclusive and accessible to persons with disabilities. States Parties shall safeguard and promote the realization of the right to work, including for those who acquire a disability during the course of employment, by taking appropriate steps, including through legislation, to, inter alia:

(a) Prohibit discrimination on the basis of disability with regard to all matters concerning all forms of employment, including conditions of recruitment, hiring and employment, continuance of employment, career advancement and safe and healthy working conditions;

(b) Protect the rights of persons with disabilities, on an equal basis with others, to just and favourable conditions of work, including equal opportunities and equal remuneration for work of equal value, safe and healthy working conditions, including protection from harassment, and the redress of grievances;

(c) Ensure that persons with disabilities are able to exercise their labour and trade union rights on an equal basis with others;

(d) Enable persons with disabilities to have effective access to general technical and vocational guidance programmes, placement services and vocational and continuing training;

(e) Promote employment opportunities and career advancement for persons with disabilities in the labour market, as well as assistance in finding, obtaining, maintaining and returning to employment;

(f) Promote opportunities for self-employment, entrepreneurship, the development of cooperatives and starting one's own business;

(g) Employ persons with disabilities in the public sector;

(h) Promote the employment of persons with disabilities in the private sector through appropriate policies and measures, which may include affirmative action programmes, incentives and other measures;

(i) Ensure that reasonable accommodation is provided to persons with disabilities in the workplace;

(j) Promote the acquisition by persons with disabilities of work experience in the open labour market;

(k) Promote vocational and professional rehabilitation, job retention and return-to-work programmes for persons with disabilities.

2. States Parties shall ensure that persons with disabilities are not held in slavery or in servitude, and are protected, on an equal basis with others, from forced or compulsory labour.

**Article 28**

**Adequate standard of living and social protection**

1. States Parties recognize the right of persons with disabilities to an adequate standard of living for themselves and their families, including adequate food, clothing and housing, and to the continuous improvement of living conditions, and shall take appropriate steps to safeguard and promote the realization of this right without discrimination on the basis of disability.2. States Parties recognize the right of persons with disabilities to social protection and to the enjoyment of that right without discrimination on the basis of disability, and shall take appropriate steps to safeguard and promote the realization of this right, including measures:

(a) To ensure equal access by persons with disabilities to clean water services, and to ensure access to appropriate and affordable services, devices and other assistance for disability-related needs;

(b) To ensure access by persons with disabilities, in particular women and girls with disabilities and older persons with disabilities, to social protection programmes and poverty reduction programmes;

(c) To ensure access by persons with disabilities and their families living in situations of poverty to assistance from the State with disability- related expenses, including adequate training, counselling, financial assistance and respite care;

(d) To ensure access by persons with disabilities to public housing programmes;

(e) To ensure equal access by persons with disabilities to retirement benefits and programmes.

**Article 29**

**Participation in political and public life**

States Parties shall guarantee to persons with disabilities political rights and the opportunity to enjoy them on an equal basis with others, and shall undertake:

(a) To ensure that persons with disabilities can effectively and fully participate in political and public life on an equal basis with others, directly or through freely chosen representatives, including the right and opportunity for persons with disabilities to vote and be elected, inter alia, by:

(i) Ensuring that voting procedures, facilities and materials are appropriate, accessible and easy to understand and use;

(ii) Protecting the right of persons with disabilities to vote by secret ballot in elections and public referendums without intimidation, and to stand for elections, to effectively hold office and perform all public functions at all levels of government, facilitating the use of assistive and new technologies where appropriate;

(iii) Guaranteeing the free expression of the will of persons with disabilities as electors and to this end, where necessary, at their request, allowing assistance in voting by a person of their own choice;

(b) To promote actively an environment in which persons with disabilities can effectively and fully participate in the conduct of public affairs, without discrimination and on an equal basis with others, and encourage their participation in public affairs, including:

(i) Participation in non-governmental organizations and associations concerned with the public and political life of the country, and in the activities and administration of political parties;

(ii) Forming and joining organizations of persons with disabilities to represent persons with disabilities at international, national, regional and local levels.

## Article 30
## Participation in Cultural Life, Recreation, Leisure and Sport

1. States Parties recognize the right of persons with disabilities to take part on an equal basis with others in cultural life, and shall take all appropriate measures to ensure that persons with disabilities:

(a) Enjoy access to cultural materials in accessible formats;

(b) Enjoy access to television programmes, films, theatre and other cultural activities, in accessible formats;

(c) Enjoy access to places for cultural performances or services, such as theatres, museums, cinemas, libraries and tourism services, and, as far as possible, enjoy access to monuments and sites of national cultural importance.

2. States Parties shall take appropriate measures to enable persons with disabilities to have the opportunity to develop and utilize their creative, artistic and intellectual potential, not only for their own benefit, but also for the enrichment of society.

3. States Parties shall take all appropriate steps, in accordance with international law, to ensure that laws protecting intellectual property rights do not constitute an unreasonable or discriminatory barrier to access by persons with disabilities to cultural materials.

4. Persons with disabilities shall be entitled, on an equal basis with others, to recognition and support of their specific cultural and linguistic identity, including sign languages and deaf culture.

5. With a view to enabling persons with disabilities to participate on an equal basis with others in recreational, leisure and sporting activities, States Parties shall take appropriate measures:

(a) To encourage and promote the participation, to the fullest extent possible, of persons with disabilities in mainstream sporting activities at all levels;

(b) To ensure that persons with disabilities have an opportunity to organize, develop and participate in disability-specific sporting and recreational activities and, to this end, encourage the provision, on an equal basis with others, of appropriate instruction, training and resources;

(c) To ensure that persons with disabilities have access to sporting, recreational and tourism venues;

(d) To ensure that children with disabilities have equal access with other children to participation in play, recreation and leisure and sporting activities, including those activities in the school system;

(e) To ensure that persons with disabilities have access to services from those involved in the organization of recreational, tourism, leisure and sporting activities.

## Article 31
## Statistics and data collection

1. States Parties undertake to collect appropriate information, including statistical and research data, to enable them to formulate and implement policies to give effect to the present Convention. The process of collecting and maintaining this information shall:

(a) Comply with legally established safeguards, including legislation on data protection, to ensure confidentiality and respect for the privacy of persons with disabilities;

(b) Comply with internationally accepted norms to protect human rights and fundamental freedoms and ethical principles in the collection and use of statistics.

2. The information collected in accordance with this article shall be disaggregated, as appropriate, and used to help assess the implementation of States Parties' obligations under the present Convention and to identify and address the barriers faced by persons with disabilities in exercising their rights.

3. States Parties shall assume responsibility for the dissemination of these statistics and ensure their accessibility to persons with disabilities and others.

## Article 32
## International cooperation

1. States Parties recognize the importance of international cooperation and its promotion, in support of national efforts for the realization of the purpose and objectives of the present Convention, and will undertake appropriate and effective measures in this regard, between and among States and, as appropriate, in partnership with relevant international and regional organizations and civil society, in particular organizations of persons with disabilities. Such measures could include, inter alia:

(a) Ensuring that international cooperation, including international development programmes, is inclusive of and accessible to persons with disabilities;

(b) Facilitating and supporting capacity-building, including through the exchange and sharing of information, experiences, training programmes and best practices;

(c) Facilitating cooperation in research and access to scientific and technical knowledge;

(d) Providing, as appropriate, technical and economic assistance, including by facilitating access to and sharing of accessible and assistive technologies, and through the transfer of technologies.

2. The provisions of this article are without prejudice to the obligations of each State Party to fulfil its obligations under the present Convention.

## Article 33
## National implementation and monitoring

1. States Parties, in accordance with their system of organization, shall designate one or more focal points within government for matters relating to the implementation of the present Convention, and shall give due consideration to the establishment or designation of a coordination mechanism within government to facilitate related action in different sectors and at different levels. States Parties shall, in accordance with their legal and administrative systems, maintain, strengthen, designate or establish within the State Party, a framework, including one or more independent mechanisms, as appropriate, to promote, protect and monitor implementation of the present Convention. When designating or establishing such a mechanism, States Parties shall take into account the principles relating to the status and functioning of national institutions for protection and promotion of human rights.

Civil society, in particular persons with disabilities and their representative organizations, shall be involved and participate fully in the monitoring process.

## Article 34
## Committee on the Rights of Persons with Disabilities

1. There shall be established a Committee on the Rights of Persons with Disabilities (hereafter referred to as "the Committee"), which shall carry out the functions hereinafter provided.

2. The Committee shall consist, at the time of entry into force of the present Convention, of twelve experts. After an additional sixty ratifications or accessions to the Convention, the membership of the Committee shall increase by six members, attaining a maximum number of eighteen members.

3. The members of the Committee shall serve in their personal capacity and shall be of high moral standing and recognized competence and experience in the field covered by the present Convention. When nominating their candidates, States Parties are invited to give due consideration to the provision set out in article 4, paragraph 3, of the present Convention.

4. The members of the Committee shall be elected by States Parties, consideration being given to equitable geographical distribution, representation of the different forms of civilization and of the principal legal systems, balanced gender representation and participation of experts with disabilities.

5. The members of the Committee shall be elected by secret ballot from a list of persons nominated by the States Parties from among their nationals

at meetings of the Conference of States Parties. At those meetings, for which two thirds of States Parties shall constitute a quorum, the persons elected to the Committee shall be those who obtain the largest number of votes and an absolute majority of the votes of the representatives of States Parties present and voting.

6. The initial election shall be held no later than six months after the date of entry into force of the present Convention. At least four months before the date of each election, the Secretary-General of the United Nations shall address a letter to the States Parties inviting them to submit the nominations within two months. The Secretary-General shall subsequently prepare a list in alphabetical order of all persons thus nominated, indicating the State Parties which have nominated them, and shall submit it to the States Parties to the present Convention.

7. The members of the Committee shall be elected for a term of four years. They shall be eligible for re-election once. However, the term of six of the members elected at the first election shall expire at the end of two years; immediately after the first election, the names of these six members shall be chosen by lot by the chairperson of the meeting referred to in paragraph 5 of this article.

8. The election of the six additional members of the Committee shall be held on the occasion of regular elections, in accordance with the relevant provisions of this article.

9. If a member of the Committee dies or resigns or declares that for any other cause she or he can no longer perform her or his duties, the State Party which nominated the member shall appoint another expert possessing the qualifications and meeting the requirements set out in the relevant provisions of this article, to serve for the remainder of the term.

10. The Committee shall establish its own rules of procedure.

11. The Secretary-General of the United Nations shall provide the necessary staff and facilities for the effective performance of the functions of the Committee under the present Convention, and shall convene its initial meeting.

12. With the approval of the General Assembly of the United Nations, the members of the Committee established under the present Convention shall receive emoluments from United Nations resources on such terms and conditions as the Assembly may decide, having regard to the importance of the Committee's responsibilities.

13. The members of the Committee shall be entitled to the facilities, privileges and immunities of experts on mission for the United Nations as laid down in the relevant sections of the Convention on the Privileges and Immunities of the United Nations.

### Article 35
### Reports by States Parties

1. Each State Party shall submit to the Committee, through the Secretary-General of the United Nations, a comprehensive report on measures taken to give effect to its obligations under the present Convention and on the progressmade in that regard, within two years after the entry into force of the present Convention for the State Party concerned.

2. Thereafter, States Parties shall submit subsequent reports at least every four years and further whenever the Committee so requests.

3. The Committee shall decide any guidelines applicable to the content of the reports.

4. A State Party which has submitted a comprehensive initial report to the Committee need not, in its subsequent reports, repeat information previously provided. When preparing reports to the Committee, States Parties are invited to consider doing so in an open and transparent process and to give due consideration to the provision set out in article 4, paragraph 3, of the present Convention.

5. Reports may indicate factors and difficulties affecting the degree of fulfilment of obligations under the present Convention.

**Article 36**
**Consideration of reports**

1. Each report shall be considered by the Committee, which shall make such suggestions and general recommendations on the report as it may consider appropriate and shall forward these to the State Party concerned. The State Party may respond with any information it chooses to the Committee. The Committee may request further information from States Parties relevant to the implementation of the present Convention.

2. If a State Party is significantly overdue in the submission of a report, the Committee may notify the State Party concerned of the need to examine the implementation of the present Convention in that State Party, on the basis of reliable information available to the Committee, if the relevant report is not submitted within three months following the notification. The Committee shall invite the State Party concerned to participate in such examination. Should the State Party respond by submitting the relevant report, the provisions of paragraph 1 of this article will apply.

3. The Secretary-General of the United Nations shall make available the reports to all States Parties.

4. States Parties shall make their reports widely available to the public in their own countries and facilitate access to the suggestions and general recommendations relating to these reports.

5. The Committee shall transmit, as it may consider appropriate, to the specialized agencies, funds and programmes of the United Nations, and other competent bodies, reports from States Parties in order to address a request or indication of a need for technical advice or assistance contained therein, along with the Committee's observations and recommendations, if any, on these requests or indications.

**Article 37**
**Cooperation between States Parties and the Committee**

1. Each State Party shall cooperate with the Committee and assist its members in the fulfilment of their mandate.

2. In its relationship with States Parties, the Committee shall give due consideration to ways and means of enhancing national capacities for the implementation of the present Convention, including through international cooperation.

### Article 38
### Relationship of the Committee with other bodies

In order to foster the effective implementation of the present Convention and to encourage international cooperation in the field covered by the present Convention:

(a) The specialized agencies and other United Nations organs shall be entitled to be represented at the consideration of the implementation of such provisions of the present Convention as fall within the scope of their mandate. The Committee may invite the specialized agencies and other competent bodies as it may consider appropriate to provide expert advice on the implementation of the Convention in areas falling within the scope of their respective mandates. The Committee may invite specialized agencies and other United Nations organs to submit reports on the implementation of the Convention in areas falling within the scope of their activities;

(b) The Committee, as it discharges its mandate, shall consult, as appropriate, other relevant bodies instituted by international human rights treaties, with a view to ensuring the consistency of their respective reporting guidelines, suggestions and general recommendations, and avoiding duplication and overlap in the performance of their functions.

### Article 39
### Report of the Committee

The Committee shall report every two years to the General Assembly and to the Economic and Social Council on its activities, and may makesuggestions and general recommendations based on the examination of reports and information received from the States Parties. Such suggestions and general recommendations shall be included in the report of the Committee together with comments, if any, from States Parties.

### Article 40
### Conference of States Parties

1. The States Parties shall meet regularly in a Conference of States Parties in order to consider any matter with regard to the implementation of the present Convention.

2. No later than six months after the entry into force of the present Convention, the Conference of States Parties shall be convened by the Secretary-General of the United Nations. The subsequent meetings shall be convened by the Secretary-General biennially or upon the decision of the Conference of States Parties.

### Article 41
### Depositary

The Secretary-General of the United Nations shall be the depositary of the present Convention.

### Article 42
### Signature

The present Convention shall be open for signature by all States and by regional integration organizations at United Nations Headquarters in New York as of 30 March 2007.

## Article 43
### Consent to be bound

The present Convention shall be subject to ratification by signatory States and to formal confirmation by signatory regional integration organizations. It shall be open for accession by any State or regional integration organization which has not signed the Convention.

## Article 44
### Regional Integration Organizations

1. "Regional integration organization" shall mean an organization constituted by sovereign States of a given region, to which its member States have transferred competence in respect of matters governed by the present Convention. Such organizations shall declare, in their instruments of formal confirmation or accession, the extent of their competence with respect to matters governed by the present Convention. Subsequently, they shall inform the depositary of any substantial modification in the extent of their competence.

2. References to "States Parties" in the present Convention shall apply to such organizations within the limits of their competence.

3. For the purposes of article 45, paragraph 1, and article 47, paragraphs 2 and 3, of the present Convention, any instrument deposited by a regional integration organization shall not be counted.

4. Regional integration organizations, in matters within their competence, may exercise their right to vote in the Conference of States Parties, with a number of votes equal to the number of their member States that are Parties to the present Convention. Such an organization shall not exercise its right to vote if any of its member States exercises its right, and vice versa.

## Article 45
### Entry into force

1. The present Convention shall enter into force on the thirtieth day after the deposit of the twentieth instrument of ratification or accession.

2. For each State or regional integration organization ratifying, formally confirming or acceding to the present Convention after the deposit of the twentieth such instrument, the Convention shall enter into force on the thirtieth day after the deposit of its own such instrument.

## Article 46
### Reservations

1. Reservations incompatible with the object and purpose of the present Convention shall not be permitted.
2. Reservations may be withdrawn at any time.

## Article 47
### Amendments

1. Any State Party may propose an amendment to the present Convention and submit it to the Secretary-General of the United Nations. The Secretary-General shall communicate any proposed amendments to States Parties, with a request to be notified whether they favour a conference of States Parties for the purpose of considering and deciding upon the proposals. In the event that, within four months from the date of such communication,

at least one third ofthe States Parties favour such a conference, the Secretary-General shall convene the conference under the auspices of the United Nations. Any amendment adopted by a majority of two thirds of the States Parties present and voting shall be submitted by the Secretary-General to the General Assembly of the United Nations for approval and thereafter to all States Parties for acceptance.

An amendment adopted and approved in accordance with paragraph 1 of this article shall enter into force on the thirtieth day after the number of instruments of acceptance deposited reaches two thirds of the number of States Parties at the date of adoption of the amendment. Thereafter, the amendment shall enter into force for any State Party on the thirtieth day following the deposit of its own instrument of acceptance. An amendment shall be binding only on those States Parties which have accepted it.

If so decided by the Conference of States Parties by consensus, an amendment adopted and approved in accordance with paragraph 1 of this article which relates exclusively to articles 34, 38, 39 and 40 shall enter into force for all States Parties on the thirtieth day after the number of instruments of acceptance deposited reaches two thirds of the number of States Parties at the date of adoption of the amendment.

### Article 48
### Denunciation

A State Party may denounce the present Convention by written notification to the Secretary-General of the United Nations. The denunciation shall become effective one year after the date of receipt of the notification by the Secretary-General.

### Article 49
### Accessible format

The text of the present Convention shall be made available in accessible formats.

### Article 50
### Authentic texts

The Arabic, Chinese, English, French, Russian and Spanish texts of the present Convention shall be equally authentic.

IN WITNESS THEREOF the undersigned plenipotentiaries, being duly authorized thereto by their respective Governments, have signed the present Convention.

## OPTIONAL PROTOCOL TO THE CONVENTION ON THE RIGHTS OF PERSONS WITH DISABILITIES

The States Parties to the present Protocol have agreed as follows:

### Article 1

1. A State Party to the present Protocol ("State Party") recognizes the competence of the Committee on the Rights of Persons with Disabilities ("the Committee") to receive and consider communications from or on behalf of individuals or groups of individuals subject to its jurisdiction who claim to be victims of a violation by that State Party of the provisions of the Convention.

2. No communication shall be received by the Committee if it concerns a State Party to the Convention that is not a party to the present Protocol.

**Article 2**

The Committee shall consider a communication inadmissible when:

(a) The communication is anonymous;

(b) The communication constitutes an abuse of the right of submission of such communications or is incompatible with the provisions of the Convention;

(c) The same matter has already been examined by the Committee or has been or is being examined under another procedure of international investigation or settlement;

(d) All available domestic remedies have not been exhausted. This shall not be the rule where the application of the remedies is unreasonably prolonged or unlikely to bring effective relief;

(e) It is manifestly ill-founded or not sufficiently substantiated; or when

(f) The facts that are the subject of the communication occurred prior to the entry into force of the present Protocol for the State Party concerned unless those facts continued after that date.

**Article 3**

Subject to the provisions of article 2 of the present Protocol, the Committee shall bring any communications submitted to it confidentially to the attention of the State Party. Within six months, the receiving State shall submit to the Committee written explanations or statements clarifying the matter and the remedy, if any, that may have been taken by that State.1. A t any time after the receipt of a communication and before a determination on the merits has been reached, the Committee may transmit to the State Party concerned for its urgent consideration a request that the State Party take such interim measures as may be necessary to avoid possible irreparable damage to the victim or victims of the alleged violation.

2. Where the Committee exercises its discretion under paragraph 1 of this article, this does not imply a determination on admissibility or on the merits of the communication.

**Article 5**

The Committee shall hold closed meetings when examining communications under the present Protocol. After examining a communication, the Committee shall forward its suggestions and recommendations, if any, to the State Party concerned and to the petitioner.

**Article 6**

1. If the Committee receives reliable information indicating grave or systematic violations by a State Party of rights set forth in the Convention, the Committee shall invite that State Party to cooperate in the examination of the information and to this end submit observations with regard to the information concerned.

2. Taking into account any observations that may have been submitted by the State Party concerned as well as any other reliable information available to it, the Committee may designate one or more of its members to conduct an inquiry and to report urgently to the Committee. Where warranted and

with the consent of the State Party, the inquiry may include a visit to its territory.

3. After examining the findings of such an inquiry, the Committee shall transmit these findings to the State Party concerned together with any comments and recommendations.

4. The State Party concerned shall, within six months of receiving the findings, comments and recommendations transmitted by the Committee, submit its observations to the Committee.

5. Such an inquiry shall be conducted confidentially and the cooperation of the State Party shall be sought at all stages of the proceedings.

1. The Committee may invite the State Party concerned to include in its report under article 35 of the Convention details of any measures taken in response to an inquiry conducted under article 6 of the present Protocol.
2. The Committee may, if necessary, after the end of the period of six months referred to in article 6, paragraph 4, invite the State Party concerned to inform it of the measures taken in response to such an inquiry

**Article 8**

Each State Party may, at the time of signature or ratification of the present Protocol or accession thereto, declare that it does not recognize the competence of the Committee provided for in articles 6 and 7.

**Article 9**

The Secretary-General of the United Nations shall be the depositary of the present Protocol.

**Article 10**

The present Protocol shall be open for signature by signatory States and regional integration organizations of the Convention at United Nations Headquarters in New York as of 30 March 2007.

**Article 11**

The present Protocol shall be subject to ratification by signatory States of the present Protocol which have ratified or acceded to the Convention. It shall be subject to formal confirmation by signatory regional integration organizations of the present Protocol which have formally confirmed or acceded to the Convention. It shall be open for accession by any State or regional integration organization which has ratified, formally confirmed or acceded to the Convention and which has not signed the Protocol.

**Article 12**

1. "Regional integration organization" shall mean an organization constituted by sovereign States of a given region, to which its member States have transferred competence in respect of matters governed by the Convention and the present Protocol. Such organizations shall declare, in their instruments of formal confirmation or accession, the extent of their competence with respect to matters governed by the Convention and the present Protocol.Subsequently, they shall inform the depositary of any substantial modification in the extent of their competence.

2. References to "States Parties" in the present Protocol shall apply to such organizations within the limits of their competence.

3. For the purposes of article 13, paragraph 1, and article 15, paragraph 2, of the present Protocol, any instrument deposited by a regional integration organization shall not be counted.

4. Regional integration organizations, in matters within their competence, may exercise their right to vote in the meeting of States Parties, with a number of votes equal to the number of their member States that are Parties to the present Protocol. Such an organization shall not exercise its right to vote if any of its member States exercises its right, and vice versa.

**Article 13**

1. Subject to the entry into force of the Convention, the present Protocol shall enter into force on the thirtieth day after the deposit of the tenth instrument of ratification or accession.

2. For each State or regional integration organization ratifying, formally confirming or acceding to the present Protocol after the deposit of the tenth such instrument, the Protocol shall enter into force on the thirtieth day after the deposit of its own such instrument.

**Article 14**

1. Reservations incompatible with the object and purpose of the present Protocol shall not be permitted.

2. Reservations may be withdrawn at any time.

**Article 15**

1. Any State Party may propose an amendment to the present Protocol and submit it to the Secretary-General of the United Nations. The Secretary-General shall communicate any proposed amendments to States Parties, with a request to be notified whether they favour a meeting of States Parties for the purpose of considering and deciding upon the proposals. In the event that, within four months from the date of such communication, at least one third of the States Parties favour such a meeting, the Secretary-General shall convene the meeting under the auspices of the United Nations. Any amendment adopted by a majority of two thirds of the States Parties present and voting shall be submitted by the Secretary-General to the General Assembly of the United Nations for approval and thereafter to all States Parties for acceptance.

2. An amendment adopted and approved in accordance with paragraph 1 of this article shall enter into force on the thirtieth day after the number of instruments of acceptance deposited reaches two thirds of the number of States Parties at the date of adoption of the amendment. Thereafter, the amendment shall enter into force for any State Party on the thirtieth day following the deposit of its own instrument of acceptance. An amendment shall be binding only on those States Parties which have accepted it.

**Article 16**

A State Party may denounce the present Protocol by written notification to the Secretary-General of the United Nations. The denunciation shall become effective one year after the date of receipt of the notification by the Secretary-General.

### Article 17

The text of the present Protocol shall be made available in accessible formats.

### Article 18

The Arabic, Chinese, English, French, Russian and Spanish texts of the present Protocol shall be equally authentic.

IN WITNESS THEREOF the undersigned plenipotentiaries, being duly authorized thereto by their respective Governments, have signed the present Protocol.

# Bibliography

Adams, M., Blumenfeld, W., Castaneda, R., Hackman, H., Peters, M., and Zuniga, X. (eds.) (2000). *Readings for Diversity and Social justice*. Routledge.

Albert, B., Dube, A.K., & Riis-Hansen, T. C. (2005). *Has Disability been Mainstreamed into Development Cooperation?* Disability Knowledge and Research Programme, Norwich/London: Overseas Development Group, University of East Anglia/Healthlink Worldwide. Available at: http://www.disabilitykar.net/research/thematic_main.html.

Albrecht, G. *The Disability Business*, Sage Library of Social Research, Vol. 190. Sage Publications.

Albrecht, Seelman, and Bury (eds.). (2001). *Handbook of Disability Studies*. Sage Publications.

Asch, A., & Fine, M. (eds.), (1988). *Women with Disabilities: Essays in Psychology, Culture and Politics.* Chicago: University of Chicago Press.

Barnes, Oliver, & Barton (eds.). (2002). *Disability Studies Today*. Polity.

Barnes and Mercer. (2003). *Disability*, Polity.

Barton, L. (Ed.). (1996). *Disability and Society: Emerging Issues and Insights*. London: Longman.

Black, K. (1997). *In the shadow of polio*.

Brody, H. (1987). *Stories of sickness*. New Haven: Yale University Press.

Brown, C. (1998). *My left foot*. London: Vintage. (Original work published 1954)

Bynoe, I, Oliver, M, and Barnes C, 1991, *Equal Rights for Disabled people*, London, IPPR

Baquer, A., & Sharma (1997). *Disability: Challenges versus responses*.

Crewe, N.M. et. al. 1983, *Independent Living for Physically Disabled People*, San Fransicco: Jossey- bass

Croft, A. (2010). *Including Disabled Children in Learning: Challenges in Developing Countries.* CREATE, University of Sussex.

Devlinger, P, Rusch F, and Pfeiffer, D 2003(eds) *Rethinking Disability: Emergent Definitions Concepts and Communities*, Antwerp, Garant.

Ghai, A. (2002). "Disability in the Indian Context: Post-Colonial Perspectives". In Corker, M. and Shakespeare, T. (Eds.) *Disability/Postmodernity: Embodying Disability Theory*. London.

Halder, S (2009). "Prospects of Higher Education of the Challenged Women in India". *International Journal of Inclusive Education, 13*(6): 633-646.

Helander, E.(1993) *Prejudice and Dignity*, United Nations Development Project

Kayess, R., & French, P. (2008). *Out of Darkness into Light? Introducing the Convention on the Rights of Persons with Disabilities.* Oxford Journals, 1-34.

Kisanji, J. (1995), *'Growign up disabled'* Inken and H. Mcconachie (eds.), Disabled Children and Developing Countries, Cambridge, Mckieth Press, Cambridge

Lang, R. (2007). *The Development and Critique of the Social Model of Disability* Working Paper 3, London, Leonard Cheshire Disability and Inclusive Development Centre, University College London. Available at: http://www.ucl.ac.uk/lcccr/centrepublications/workingpapers/WP03_Development_ Critique.pdf

Oliver, M. 1990, *The Politics of Disablement*, London Mcmillan

Oliverm, M. And Barnes C. 1999, *Disabled People and Social Policy: From Exclusion to Inclusion*, London, Macmillan

Pelka, F.1997, The *Disability Rights Movement*, California, ABC-CLIO.

Quinn, G., & Degener, T. (2002). *Human Rights & Disability-The current use & future potential of United Nations human rights instruments.* New York, Geneva: United Nations.

Riser, R. And Mason M 1992, *Disability Rights in Class Room: A Human Rights Issue*, London, Disability and Equality in Education.

Rieser, R. (2008). *Implementing Inclusive Education: A Commonwealth Guide to Implementing Article 24 of the UN Convention on the Rights of People with Disabilities.* London, Commonwealth Secretariat.

Save the Children Fund 1994 *Children, Disability and Development: Achievements and Challenges*, London, Save the Children Fund

Shakespeare, T. (2006). "The Social Model of Disability". In Davis, L. J. (Ed.) *The Disability Studies Reader.* New York, Routledge,

Shakespeare, T. (2009). "Disability: A Complex Interaction". In Daniels, H., Lauder, H., & Porter, J. (Eds.) *Knowledge, Values and Education Policy: A Critical Perspective.* London, Routledge,

Stiker, H-J. (1999) *A History of Disability*, Ann Arbor, University of Michigan Press.

Thomas, C. (2002). "Disability Theory: Key Ideas, Issues and Thinkers". In Barnes, C., Oliver, M., & Barton, L. (Eds.) *Disability Studies Today*, Cambridge, Polity, pp. 38-57

Werner, D. 'Preface' in H. Finkenfuggel (ed.), *The Handicapped Community, Amsterdam*, Vrij University Press.

W. Myriam, N. Osamu, D. Patrik, B, Stuart and Addlakha Renu (eds), (2009) *Disability And Society : A Reader,* Orient Blackswan, Delhi.

UGC. (2012). University Grants Commission Guidelines for Persons with Disabilities Scheme in Universities. New Delhi, India.

United Nations Secretary General. (2007). "Implementation of the World Programme of Action Concerning Disabled Persons: the Millennium Development Goals and Synergies with other United Nations Disability Instruments. A/62/157". New York, UN General Assembly. Available at: http://www.acfid.asn.au/resolveUid/8a441495dfd6915ffccfdb 46a276edf6

**Law Journals**

- ALL India Reporter
- Supreme Court Cases